# GETTING BY: ILLUSTRATIONS OF MARGINAL LIVING

# GETTING BY: ILLUSTRATIONS OF MARGINAL LIVING

JERRY JACOBS
*University of California*
*Riverside*

LITTLE, BROWN AND COMPANY   *Boston*

Library of Congress Catalog Card No. 77-179139

First Printing

*Published simultaneously in Canada*
*by Little, Brown & Company (Canada) Limited*

Printed in the United States of America

TO SUSAN

# Contents

# GETTING BY: ILLUSTRATIONS OF MARGINAL LIVING

# Introduction

Through this reader, the student will become familiar with several key categories of deviant behavior—prostitution, white-collar crime, drug use and abuse, mental illness, and suicide—from an interactionist perspective. The "careers" of the marginally employed characters presented in the readings are considered with respect to their modes of adaptation, i.e., the ways in which they work at "getting by." The problems faced by the characters have many parallels to those faced by sociologists and lay persons. Key among these is the problem of establishing the reality of a social scene. Inability to fathom the social meanings of social actions would lead one to exist in a world of nonsense—a theatre of the absurd. The book considers the different ways in which deviant and normal persons confront and deal with this basic problem.

In the first part of the Introduction, the sociological importance of uncovering the social meanings of social actions is established. One's success in this undertaking is considered a basic prerequisite for acquiring an understanding of the social interaction that underlies the organization and perpetuation of group life.

To begin with, I would like to consider two main branches of thought in American sociology, positivism and the interactionist perspective. The former, and by far the most popular methodological-theoretical orientation, was initiated by Durkheim and brought to prominence in this country by Merton and Parsons.[1]

[1] Emile Durkheim, *Suicide: A Study in Sociology* (New York: Free Press, 1951) and *The Rules of Sociological Method* (New York: Free Press, 1964); Robert K. Merton, "Social Structure and Anomie," in his *Social Theory and Social Structure* (New York: Free Press, 1957), pp. 131–160; and Talcott Parsons, *The Social System* (New York: Free Press, 1951).

1

As it applied to the study of suicide, this approach recommended that, in order to be "sociological," the researcher should discount all psychological considerations, such as the individual's motives, intentions, or morals. One way to do so was to adhere strictly to the "etiological approach"—a methodology suggesting that, instead of attempting to establish the various types of suicide by describing and categorizing actual cases according to their "essential characteristics" (the morphological approach), we seek instead their "causes" (the etiological approach). Durkheim meant by this that we try to relate the consistencies found in the official rates of suicide (and other social phenomena) to some external social causal agent.

Those utilizing the etiological approach were led to formulate such questions as what is it in society that causes men to suicide more often than women, single persons more often than married, Protestants more often than Jews, or rich more often than poor? The answer to these questions—the relative degree of social integration among the members of these groups—was offered by Durkheim not as an explanation of suicide, but of suicide rates.[2] Durkheim further assumed that the essential characteristics of suicide and other social phenomena would emerge once the causes were known, that is, in the process of establishing the causes for the relationships found in the rates (an explanation of the suicide rates), we would also find an explanation of suicide.[3] This methodological approach, in conjunction with other key Durkheimian conceptualizations, such as anomie (social disorganization resulting from the lack of social constraints) and society *sui generis* (the notion that society is a real entity that exists—in time and importance—prior to, and independently of, the individuals that constitute it) led criminologists and other social pathologists to search for the causes of suicide, delinquency, alcoholism, prostitution, and, more recently, student and urban unrest within the above framework.

This tradition is in sharp contrast to the Weberian approach, which holds that in order to understand social behavior, one first needs to understand the social meanings that social actions hold for the actors. From this point of view, one would be unable to reconstruct the reality of a social scene or gain a real understanding of any social phenomenon without first considering the individual, his intentions, motives, and morals. This we are urged to do through *verstehen,* i.e., attempting to understand one's own intentions

[2] Durkheim, *Suicide,* p. 147.
[3] *Ibid.,* p. 146.

through introspection and the motives of others through their professed or ascribed intentions.[4]

These two perspectives serve as the key planks in the platforms of what have come to be referred to as the "hard" and "soft" data schools of sociology. These two positions are generally linked to quantitative versus qualitative forms of analysis and are frequently associated with the positivist and interactionist perspectives respectively. The theme of this book, "The Interactionist Perspective,"[5] will be based upon the Weberian tradition of verstehen, as opposed to the Durkheimian tradition of interpreting the "causes" of "social facts." The author believes, like Weber and Simmel, that sociological understanding will not emerge without some proviso for establishing the situated meanings of social actions and their effects on the interaction patterns of the participants. By the situated meanings of social action, I mean that the meanings of words and/or behaviors do not inhere in the words or behaviors themselves but rather result from the meanings others confer upon them. These conferred meanings are in turn a consequence of the social context in which they occur and the relationship of the participants to one another prior to and at the time of the interaction itself. It is further assumed that there is no society sui generis with an existence greater than, prior to, or independent of the individuals that comprise it. Society *is* the sum total of the interactions of its members and the reciprocal effects of these interactions upon them.

The acceptance of the above orientation in the study of deviant behavior obliges one to think problematically, i.e., problems are formulated in an *if-then* fashion, where the *if* of human behavior remains an unknown. By this I mean that, although positivists and nonpositivists may both formulate questions of an if-then nature, the former frequently overlook the distinction between acts and events and treat acts *as* events, i.e., people as "things." If the term *acts* is reserved for humans' *active* responses to external stimuli based on their interpretation of the *meaning* of these stimuli, and events are concerned with the passive reaction of natural objects to external forces, then treating acts as events in the pursuit of a social science is a serious oversight. The seriousness stems from the failure to recognize that individuals are not only acted upon (as in the

---

[4] H. H. Gerth and C. Wright Mills, trans. and ed., *From Max Weber: Essays in Sociology* (New York: Galaxy Book, 1958), p. 56.

[5] For further information see Earl Rubington and Martin S. Weinberg, *Deviance/The Interactionist Perspective* (New York: Macmillan Company, 1968).

case of natural objects) by external forces, but confer *meaning* upon these forces so as to react to them in an unpredictable way. This is not true for the operation of forces upon nonhuman objects. For example, a physicist can plot the trajectory of a bullet with uncanny accuracy after formulating an if-then proposition. *If* we know the force, the mass of the projectile, the angle at which it was fired, and the effects of gravity, *then* the bullet will be found at point X. Predictability based upon the explanatory power of Newtonian physics is possible in the above instance only because the bullet is incapable of changing its mind in midflight and, for instance, reversing its path and striking the hunter instead of the hunted. The above is an example of an if-then statement relating to the occurrence of an *event* and the possibility of predicting its outcome. Whereas physics is capable of *predictability* based upon *understanding,* sociology is at best only capable of understanding. To use a medical metaphor, sociology is in principle capable of diagnosis but not prognosis, whereas physics is capable of both. The reason for this is as follows: If a doctor tells a patient that he has a cold, and *if* the patient goes to bed, drinks lots of liquids, and takes an occasional aspirin, *then* he will be well in a few days. However, if the patient takes cold showers and goes jogging in the rain, he will probably catch pneumonia and die. The doctor has no way of knowing which alternative the patient will choose or why, and insofar as humans choose the path they will take, and projectiles do not, the prognosis for humans (the probability of a correct prediction of an outcome) must always be in serious doubt, whereas for projectiles, it may approach certainty. In other words, one may establish the "necessary and sufficient" conditions for predicting the path of a projectile but not the path of human behavior, because humans in interaction are constantly redefining what these conditions are even as they are taking place. The outcome of human interactions is contingent upon persons' constant reevaluation of the definition of the situation as the situation is in the process of becoming. One's definition of the situation rests in turn upon the social meanings that social actions hold for him. Because these meanings are in a constant state of flux, the behavioral outcome of any interaction (or set of interactions) that rests upon persons' understanding of the situation at some point in time cannot be accurately anticipated in advance. Notwithstanding the positivists' position, the methodology of the physical sciences is not directly applicable to social science's research. Neither Newtonian physics nor quantum mechanics has a place for the notion of verstehen.

Nor have sociologists of the interactionist persuasion found a way to deal meaningfully with human interactions by viewing individuals as "social atoms."

If one is aware of and accepts the above distinctions, one is led to abandon the search for an explanation of a particular category of deviance in terms of its inferred "cause" and to find that deviant behavior is better understood if one allows for such problematic expressions as "drift,"[6] "contingency circumstances,"[7] "labeling" and "neutralizing" processes,[8] public and private behavior,[9] and/or the operation of "reflexivity," "background expectancies," and "tacit understandings."[10] To understand deviant behavior from an interactionist perspective, the task is not to understand "society" or the attitudes or attitudinal changes of its members. There are good grounds on which to suppose that "society," as the term is commonly used and understood by lay persons and many professionals, is a reification of the total of interactions of the individuals comprising "society,"[11] and that the relationship between attitudes and behaviors, i.e., between "words and deeds," is, to be generous, only imperfectly understood.[12] Rather, it is suggested that we observe and record the patterns of interaction between members and the foundations of these interaction patterns, i.e., the reciprocal effects of the social meanings of social actions upon the members within different social contexts. In attempting to reconstruct the situated meanings of social actions, we must rely upon methodological procedures more in the tradition of Weber, Simmel, and Cooley than Durkheim, Merton, or Parsons. An example of an application of these procedures is presented in the introduction to Chapter Six.

The following readings were chosen because they lend them-

[6] David Matza, *Delinquency and Drift* (New York: John Wiley and Sons, 1964).

[7] See, for example, Edwin M. Lemert, "Paranoia and the Dynamics of Exclusion," *Sociometry* 25, no. 1 (March 1962): 1–20; and Erving Goffman, "The Moral Career of the Mental Patient," *Psychiatry* 22 (1959): 123–142.

[8] For labeling, see Howard S. Becker, "On Labeling Outsiders," in *Deviance*, ed. Rubington and Weinberg, pp. 13–17. For examples of "neutralization," see Matza, *Delinquency and Drift*.

[9] Norman K. Denzin, "Rules of Conduct and the Study of Deviant Behavior: Some Notes on the Social Relationship," in *Deviance and Respectability: The Social Construction of Moral Meanings*, ed. Jack D. Douglas (New York: Basic Books, 1970), pp. 120–159.

[10] Harold Garfinkel, *Studies in Ethnomethodology* (Englewood Cliffs, N.J.: Prentice-Hall, 1967).

[11] George Simmel, "The Field of Sociology," in *The Making of Society*, ed. Robert Bierstedt (New York: Modern Library, 1959), pp. 383–384.

[12] Irwin Deutsche, "Words and Deeds: Social Science and Social Policy," *Social Problems* 13 (Winter 1966): 235–254.

selves to interactionist analysis. Specifically, they meet the following criteria: 1) they deal with key categories of deviant behavior; 2) they do so within an interactionist perspective, i.e., they are concerned with the social-psychological states of mind of the actors and their consequences for the forms of interactions that result; 3) they are eminently readable; 4) the main characters are frequently faced with problems similar to those faced by the sociologist, that is, the task of establishing the reality of a social scene; and 5) the authors of these selections frequently showed greater sociological insight into the areas of deviance under consideration than have many sociologists. It can always be said, of course, of these selections (or any others I might have chosen) that others would have served as well or better. I have no quarrel with this position. My choice of the following readings was based primarily upon two considerations—the selections seem to fit the above criteria better than others, and I found them the most enjoyable to read.

I have attempted to ensure that the reader will avail himself of the insights that the readings provide by including introductory statements to each chapter, indicating what is sociologically relevant and important about each of these selections from an interactionist perspective and how they relate to a better understanding of both "deviant" and "normal" behavior. The kinds of sociology that are incorporated under the rubric "The Interactionist Perspective" include research dealing with "labeling theory"[13] and "dramaturgical models"[14] and phenomenological,[15] ethnomethodological,[16] ethnographic, observer, and participant observer studies.[17]

Notwithstanding the discipline's ideological commitments, not all sociologists share "a common discourse." Not only do positivists not always understand the interactionists' perspective (or vice versa), but there may be serious disagreements from within the same camp. Allowing for differences between or within schools of sociological thought, members of the same school may hold certain things in common. For example, interactionists usually concern themselves with the following:

---

[13] Becker, "On Labeling Outsiders."

[14] Erving Goffman, *The Presentation of Self in Everyday Life* (New York: Anchor Book, 1959).

[15] Alfred Schutz, *Collected Papers* (The Hague: Martinus Nijhoff, 1962).

[16] Garfinkel, *Studies in Ethnomethodology.*

[17] See, for example, Howard Becker, ed., *The Other Side* (New York: Free Press, 1964); William Foote Whyte, *Street Corner Society* (Chicago: University of Chicago Press, 1965); and Ned Polsky, *Hustlers, Beats, and Others* (New York: Doubleday and Company, 1967).

1. Firsthand observations (or primary data evaluations) of persons or accounts of persons in a variety of real-life settings. This is usually undertaken through the use of laboratory settings that are taken to be "natural settings" by the subjects, interviewing, observation, and participant observational techniques. The formal analysis of documents and accounts of persons and events such as suicide notes, diaries, court transcripts, etc., are also used.

2. The range of interactions that are possible in given settings or sets of settings, e.g., doctor-patient, police-shoplifter, probation officer-juvenile delinquent, or novice in a nudist camp.

3. The social meanings of these social actions to the participants involved.

4. The problematical outcome of any given encounter or sets of encounters.

5. The common denominators within and between these forms of interaction which are sought, not in some unique occurrence or characteristic, but in a *process.*

6. The *immediate consequences* for all parties of the situations under study, and why the interactions took one or another of many possible forms that may have occurred in that setting. For example, the outcome will probably be different in the case of a well-dressed, repentant juvenile versus an unkempt, belligerent juvenile and a probation officer, where both juveniles are being seen about a similar alleged offense.

7. The *long-term consequences* for either or both parties (or third parties) of partaking in a labeling process, i.e., the long-term repercussions resulting from the outcomes of the initial encounter for one's deviant or normal "career" (the role of "primary" and "secondary" deviance).

8. Providing a good descriptive account of real-life situations and their outcomes, as well as searching out the formal features of these encounters in order to determine their differences and similarities with other forms of deviant or "normal" behavior.

Many of these characteristics of the interactionist school will be incorporated into the explanatory notes introducing each of the chapters. The introduction to Chapter One, "Constructing the Reality of a Social Scene," will concern itself primarily with the features of "social typing," or "labeling." From this perspective, deviant behavior is not seen as something that inheres within the act or the actor but as a consequence of the reactions of others. A good summary of this position is given by Erikson, who states that:

> Deviance is not a property *inherent in* certain forms of behavior; it is a property *conferred upon* these forms by audiences which directly or indirectly witness them. The critical variable in the study of deviance, then, is the social audience rather than the individual actor, since it is the audience which eventually determines whether or not any episode of behavior or any class of episodes is labeled deviant.[18]

A concern with an explanation of deviant behavior from a labeling perspective leads to the formulation of certain sets of questions:

1. How does the labeler(s) establish for himself (themselves) whether or not the victim's (the person being labeled) behavior constituted "deviant behavior"?
2. Having decided that the behavior in question constituted deviant behavior, how does the labeler transform the victim's identity from a normal to a deviant one?
3. How does the victim present himself to the labeler in such a way as to provide the labeler with alternative interpretations of his behavior, i.e., how may the victim "neutralize" the labeler's suspicions that his behavior was "deviant behavior"?
4. What are the social consequences for the victim and others of a successful labeling process having taken place, i.e., how has it affected their respective "careers"?

The importance of the first chapter lies not only in the fact that it is the leitmotif of the entire work but also in the fact (noted above) that one's success in constructing the reality of a social scene is the basic prerequisite for acquiring any real understanding of social phenomena. This task, apart from its underlying sociological significance, is perhaps the most singly difficult sociological problem to overcome.

---

[18] Kai Erikson, "Notes on the Sociology of Deviance," in *The Other Side,* ed. Becker, p. 11.

# CHAPTER ONE

# Constructing
# the Reality of a Social Scene

*It* Is *So* (*If You Think So*) relates to the question of social typing (labeling), especially in reference to the more general problem of establishing the reality of a social scene. The reader is asked to note that the labeler and victim can be viewed interchangeably in a series of instances throughout the play. The problems for both, given the situations that develop in the play, are:

1. How does the labeler type the newcomer's behavior?
2. Having decided the behavior in question is deviant behavior, how does he transform the victim's identity in the public's eye and make that transformation "stick" in the light of the victim's attempt to neutralize the deviant label?
3. How may the victim shift the onus of the deviant label from himself by bestowing it upon another?

*The problem* for the reader (as well as for the characters in the play) is that just as one is almost convinced of who is really deviant (in this case insane), Signor Ponza or his mother-in-law, Signora Frola, a new piece of intelligence renders any final decision once again problematical. The inability of the players to resolve this dilemma and reconstruct "what is really going on," due to a lack of information (or from another perspective, a plethora of it), leads to an escalation of the level

9

of frustration and determination of all concerned, which in turn leads them to try harder. This, in conjunction with an extension of the above process (the introduction of new and equivocal evidence) leads to even greater frustration ad infinitum.

If we equate the fate of the characters in the play with the lot of the sociologist trying to reconstruct the reality of a social scene (as perceived by the members), we would almost certainly have discouraged the reader from pursuing his inquiry into the subject of sociology any further, at least from an interactionist perspective. Fortunately, this will not be necessary. Although the dilemma faced by the characters in the play is similar to that faced by the sociologist, the circumstances are not identical. For example, some sociologists (of the interactionist persuasion) have grounds for believing that an explanation of "causes" that relies upon a closed model of society is an unnecessary prerequisite for achieving a better understanding of social phenomena. As a result they are likely to be less concerned than the players that things are not resolved "once and for all." Then, too, sociologists have greater resources than the players for dealing with problems such as those presented in the play. For example, resolving the discrepancies between the stories of Signor Ponza and Signora Frola and establishing the credibility of one or the other hinges upon the acquisition of several key pieces of information, e.g., did Signora Frola's daughter die, did Signor Ponza remarry, and/or was Signora Frola's daughter ever in a sanatorium? Since the advent of the computer and its use as a virtually unlimited storehouse of official information, and the fast and easy retrieval of information that computers afford, it would now be unthinkable that such information as the players sought would not be readily available to the authorities. This is not to mention the ease with which others who have known the persons in question can also be retrieved (especially by police chiefs) in order to acquire such information firsthand.

The play exaggerates not only the problem of establishing the reality of the social scene (at least a reality that hinges upon retrieval of the information made crucial in the play), but also the resources of most lay persons, i.e., the cooperation of the prefect of police and all those under his command.

The average member of society may indeed be faced with such dilemmas as are noted in the play; however, the problems need not prove insurmountable to the sociologist. Whether the sociologist is better able than the players to deal with the problems and situations presented in the play depends in large part upon his access to official sources of data. Also at issue are the researcher's ethics in availing himself of these resources and his ethics in divulging his sources of information and/or his findings.

Granted that the problems given in the following reading need not present the sociologist with the dilemma that the players faced, the solutions to other problems may be more difficult. For example, at one point in his argument Durkheim asks how one would establish the motives or intentions of the suicide after the fact. The point is well taken. The problem that this question poses, although difficult to answer, is one that sociologists of the interactionist persuasion are obliged to deal with head on. The question of the imputation of motives and intentions has been effectively dealt with by interactionists from a variety of standpoints. The reader is referred to the author's discussion in the introduction to Chapter Six for one point of view, or for another treatment of motives from within the interactionist perspective to the works of Alan Blum and Peter McHugh.[1]

Notwithstanding the importance of the problem posed above, perhaps a prior question is whether the sociologist defines the situations in the play as having any sociological relevance. As previously noted, this will depend primarily upon one's general orientation to the discipline. Those who, in the Durkheimian tradition, seek to impute social "causes" to the relationships found in official statistical rates would not define the problem facing the characters in the play as having any "sociological" relevance. On the other hand, those pursuing the Weberian tradition of verstehen would. With this latter tradition in mind, I have chosen the play you are about to read as a literary example of what is probably *the* most important problem in sociology—the problem of how to reconstruct the situated meanings of social actions.

[1] Alan F. Blum and Peter McHugh, "The Social Ascription of Motives," *American Sociological Review* 36, no. 1 (February 1971): 98–109.

# LUIGI PIRANDELLO

## It Is So! (If You Think So)
### (Così è, se vi pare!)

A Parable in Three Acts

English version by Arthur Livingston

### CHARACTERS

LAMBERTO LAUDISI
SIGNORA FROLA
PONZA, son-in-law of Signora Frola
SIGNORA PONZA, Ponza's wife
COMMENDATORE AGAZZI, a provincial councillor
AMALIA, his wife
DINA, their daughter

SIRELLI
SIGNORA SIRELLI, his wife
THE PREFECT
CENTURI, a police commissioner
SIGNORA CINI
SIGNORA NENNI
A BUTLER
A NUMBER OF LADIES AND GENTLEMEN

*Our Own Times, in a Small Italian Town, the Capital of a Province*

### ACT I

*The parlor in the house of* COMMENDATORE AGAZZI.

*A door, the general entrance, at the back; doors leading to the wings, left and right.*

LAUDISI *is a man nearing the forties, quick and energetic in his movements. He is smartly dressed, in good taste. At this moment he is wearing a semi-formal street suit: a sack coat, of a violet cast, with black lapels, and with black braid around the edges; trousers of a light but different color.*

AMALIA, AGAZZI'S *wife, is* LAUDISI'S *sister. She is a woman of forty-five more or less. Her hair is already quite grey.* SIGNORA AGAZZI *is always showing a certain sense of her own importance from the positon occupied by her husband in the community; but she gives you to understand that if she had a free rein she would be quite capable of playing her own part in the world and, perhaps, do it somewhat better than* COMMENDATORE AGAZZI.

From the book *Naked Masks: Five Plays* by Luigi Pirandello. Edited by Eric Bentley. Copyright 1922, 1952 by E. P. Dutton and Co., Inc. Renewal 1950 in the names of Stefano, Fausto and Lietta Pirandello. Dutton Paperback Edition. Reprinted by permission of the publishers.

DINA *is the daughter of* AMALIA *and* AGAZZI. *She is nineteen. Her general manner is that of a young person conscious of understanding everything better than papa and mamma; but this defect must not be exaggerated to the extent of concealing her attractiveness and charm as a good-looking winsome girl.*

*As the curtain rises* LAUDISI *is walking briskly up and down the parlor to give vent to his irritation.*

LAUDISI. I see, I see! So he did take the matter up with the prefect!

AMALIA. But Lamberto *dear*, please remember that the man is a subordinate of his.

LAUDISI. A subordinate of his . . . very well! But a subordinate in the office, not at home nor in society!

DINA. And he hired an apartment for that woman, his mother-in-law, right here in this very building, and on our floor.

LAUDISI. And why not, pray? He was looking for an apartment; the apartment was for rent, so he leased it—for his mother-in-law. You mean to say that a mother-in-law is in duty bound to make advances to the wife and daughter of the man who happens to be her son-in-law's superior on his job?

AMALIA. That is not the way it is, Lamberto. We didn't ask her to call on us. Dina and I took the first step by calling on her and—she *refused* to *receive* us!

LAUDISI. Well, is that any reason why your husband should go and lodge a complaint with the man's boss? Do you expect the government to order him to invite you to tea?

AMALIA. I think he deserves all he gets! That is not the way to treat two ladies. I hope he gets fired! The idea!

LAUDISI. Oh, you women! I say, making that complaint is a dirty trick. By Jove! If people see fit to keep to themselves in their own houses, haven't they a right to?

AMALIA. Yes, but you don't understand! We were trying to do her a favor. She is new in the town. We wanted to make her feel at home.

DINA. Now, now, uncle dear, don't be so cross! Perhaps we did go there out of curiosity more than anything else; but it's all so funny, isn't it! Don't you think it was natural to feel just a little bit curious?

LAUDISI. Natural be damned! It was none of your business!

DINA. Now, see here, uncle, let's suppose—here you are right here minding your own business and quite indifferent to what other people are doing all around you. Very well! I come into the room and right here on this table, under your very nose, and with a long face like an undertaker's, or, rather, with the long face of that jailbird you are defending, I set down—well, what?—anything—a pair of dirty old shoes!

LAUDISI. I don't see the connection.

DINA. Wait, don't interrupt me! I said a pair of old shoes. Well, no, not a pair of old shoes—a flat iron, a rolling pin, or your shaving brush

for instance—and I walk out again without saying a word to anybody!
Now I leave it to you, wouldn't you feel justified in wondering just a
little, little, bit as to what in the world I meant by it?

LAUDISI. Oh, you're irresistible, Dina! And you're clever, aren't you?
But you're talking with old uncle, remember! You see, you have been
putting all sorts of crazy things on the table here; and you did it with
the idea of making me ask what it's all about; and, of course, since you
were doing all that on purpose, you can't blame me if I do ask, why those
old shoes just there, on that table, dearie? But what's all that got to do
with it? You'll have to show me now that this Mr. Ponza of ours, that
jailbird as you say, or that rascal, that boor, as your father calls him,
brought his mother-in-law to the apartment next to ours with the idea of
stringing us all! You've got to show me that he did it on purpose!

DINA. I don't say that he did it on purpose—not at all! But you can't
deny that this famous Mr. Ponza has come to this town and done a number of things which are unusual, to say the least; and which he must
have known were likely to arouse a very natural curiosity in everybody.
Look uncle, here is a man: he comes to town to fill an important public
position, and—what does he do? Where does he go to live? He hires an
apartment on the *top* floor, if you please, of that dirty old tenement out
there on the very outskirts of the town. Now, I ask you—did you ever see
the place? Inside?

LAUDISI. I suppose you went and had a look at it?

DINA. Yes, uncle dear, I went—with mamma! And we weren't the
only ones, you know. The whole town has been to have a look at it. It's
a five story tenement with an interior court so dark at noontime you can
hardly see your hand before your face. Well, there is an iron balcony
built out from the fifth story around the courtyard. A basket is hanging
from the railing . . . They let it up and down—on a rope![1]

LAUDISI. Well, what of it?

DINA [*looking at him with astonished indignation*]. What of it? Well,
there, if you please, is where he keeps his wife!

AMALIA. While her mother lives here next door to us!

LAUDISI. A fashionable apartment, for his mother-in-law, in the
residential district!

AMALIA. Generous to the old lady, eh? But he does that to keep her
from seeing her daughter!

LAUDISI. How do you know that? How do you know that the old lady,
rather, does not prefer this arrangement, just to have more elbow room
for herself?

DINA. No, no, uncle, you're wrong. Everybody knows that it is he
who is doing it.

AMALIA. See here, Lamberto, everybody understands, if a girl, when
she marries, goes away from her mother to live with her husband in some

1 Quite customary in Italy.

other town. But supposing this poor mother can't stand being separated from her daughter and follows her to the place, where she herself is also a complete stranger. And supposing now she not only does not live with ~~her? I leave it to you . . . is~~

LAUDISI. Oh say, you have about as much imagination as so many mud turtles. A mother-in-law and a son-in-law! Is it so hard to suppose that either through her fault or his fault or nobody's fault, they should find it hard to get along together and should therefore consider it wiser to live apart?

DINA [*with another look of pitying astonishment at her uncle*]. How stupid of you, uncle! The trouble is not between the mother-in-law and the son-in-law, but between the mother and the daughter.

LAUDISI. How do you know that?

DINA. Because he is as thick as pudding with the old lady; because they are always together, arm in arm, and as loving as can be. Mother-in-law and son-in-law, if you please! Whoever heard the like of that?

AMALIA. And he comes here every evening to see how the old lady is getting on!

DINA. And that is not the worst of it! Sometimes he comes during the daytime, once or twice!

LAUDISI. How scandalous! Do you think he is making love to the old woman?

DINA. Now don't be improper, uncle. No, we will acquit him of that. She is a poor old lady, quite on her last legs.

AMALIA. But he never, never, never brings his wife! A daughter kept from seeing her mother! The idea!

LAUDISI. Perhaps the young lady is not well; perhaps she isn't able to go out.

DINA. Nonsense! The old lady goes to see *her*!

AMALIA. Exactly! And she never gets in! She can see her only from a distance. Now will you explain to me why, in the name of common sense, that poor mother should be forbidden ever to enter her daughter's house?

DINA. And if she wants to talk to her she has to shout up from the courtyard!

AMALIA. Five stories, if you please! . . . And her daughter comes out and looks down from the balcony up there. The poor old woman goes into the courtyard and pulls a string that leads up to the balcony; a bell rings; the girl comes out and her mother talks up at her, her head thrown back, just as though she were shouting from out of a well. . . .

[*There is a knock at the door and the* BUTLER *enters.*]

BUTLER. Callers, madam!

AMALIA. Who is it, please?

BUTLER. Signor Sirelli, and the Signora with another lady, madam.

AMALIA. Very well, show them in.

[*The* BUTLER *bows and withdraws.*]

SIRELLI, SIGNORA SIRELLI, SIGNORA CINI *appear in the doorway, rear.*

SIRELLI, *also a man of about forty, is a bald, fat gentleman with some pretensions to stylish appearance that do not quite succeed: the overdressed provincial.*

SIGNORA SIRELLI, *his wife, plump, petite, a faded blonde, still young and girlishly pleasing. She, too, is somewhat overdressed with the provincial's fondness for display. She has the aggressive curiosity of the small-town gossip. She is chiefly occupied in keeping her husband in his place.*

SIGNORA CINI *is the old provincial lady of affected manners, who takes malicious delight in the failings of others, all the while affecting innocence and inexperience regarding the waywardness of mankind.*

AMALIA [*as the visitors enter, and taking* SIGNORA SIRELLI's *hands effusively*]. Dearest! Dearest!

SIGNORA SIRELLI. I took the liberty of bringing my good friend, Signora Cini, along. She was so anxious to know you!

AMALIA. So good of you to come, Signora! Please make yourself at home! My daughter Dina, Signora Cini, and this is my brother, Lamberto Laudisi.

SIRELLI [*bowing to the ladies*]. Signora, Signorina. [*He goes over and shakes hands with* LAUDISI.]

SIGNORA SIRELLI. Amalia dearest, we have come here as to the fountain of knowledge. We are two pilgrims athirst for the truth!

AMALIA. The truth? Truth about what?

SIGNORA SIRELLI. Why . . . about this blessed Mr. Ponza of ours, the new secretary at the prefecture. He is the talk of the town, take my word for it, Amalia.

SIGNORA CINI. And we are all just dying to find out!

AMALIA. But we are as much in the dark as the rest of you, I assure you, madam.

SIRELLI [*to his wife*]. What did I tell you? They know no more about it than I do. In fact, I think they know less about it than I do. Why is it this poor woman is not allowed to see her daughter? Do you know the reason, you people, the real reason?

AMALIA. Why, I was just discussing the matter with my brother.

LAUDISI. And my view of it is that you're all a pack of gossips!

DINA. The reason is, they say, that Ponza will not allow her to.

SIGNORA CINI. Not a sufficient reason, if I may say so, Signorina.

SIGNORA SIRELLI. Quite insufficient! There's more to it than that!

SIRELLI. I have a new item for you, fresh, right off the ice: he keeps her locked up at home!

AMALIA. His mother-in-law?

SIRELLI. No, no, his wife!

SIGNORA CINI. Under lock and key!

DINA. There, uncle, what have you to say to that? And you've been trying to defend him all along!

SIRELLI [*staring in astonishment at* LAUDISI]. Trying to defend that man? Really . . .

LAUDISI. Defending him? No! I am not defending anybody. All I'm saying, if you ladies will excuse me, is that your curiosity is unbearable if only because it's quite useless.

SIRELLI. Useless? Useless?

LAUDISI. Useless!

SIGNORA CINI. But we're trying to get somewhere—we are trying to find out!

LAUDISI. Excuse me, what can you find out? What can we really know about other people—who they are—what they are—what they are doing, and why they are doing it?

SIGNORA SIRELLI. How can we know? Why not? By asking, of course! You tell me what you know, and I tell you what I know.

LAUDISI. In that case, madam, you ought to be the best informed person in the world. Why, your husband knows more about what others are doing than any other man—or woman, for that matter—in this neighborhood.

SIRELLI [*deprecating but pleased*]. Oh I say, I say . . .

SIGNORA SIRELLI [*to her husband*]. No dear, he's right, he's right. [*Then turning to* AMALIA.] The real truth, Amalia, is this: for all my husband says he knows, I never manage to keep posted on anything!

SIRELLI. And no wonder! The trouble is—that woman never trusts me! The moment I tell her something she is convinced it is not *quite* as I say. Then, sooner or later, she claims that it *can't* be as I say. And at last she is certain it is the exact opposite of what I say!

SIGNORA SIRELLI. Well, you ought to hear all he tells me!

LAUDISI [*laughing aloud*]. May I speak, madam? Let me answer your husband. My dear Sirelli, how do you expect your wife to be satisfied with things as you explain them to her, if you, as is natural, represent them as they seem to you?

SIGNORA SIRELLI. And that means—as they cannot possibly be!

LAUDISI. Why no, Signora, now you are wrong. From your husband's point of view things are, I assure you, exactly as he represents them.

SIRELLI. As they are in reality!

SIGNORA SIRELLI. Not at all! You are always wrong.

SIRELLI. No, not a bit of it! It is you who are always wrong. I am always right.

LAUDISI. The fact is that neither of you is wrong. May I explain? I will prove it to you. Now here you are, you, Sirelli, and Signora Sirelli, your wife, there; and here I am. You see me, don't you?

SIRELLI. Well . . . er . . . yes.

LAUDISI. Do you see me, or do you not?

SIRELLI. Oh, I'll bite! Of course I see you.

LAUDISI. So you see me! But that's not enough. Come here!

SIRELLI [*smiling, he obeys, but with a puzzled expression on his face as though he fails to understand what* LAUDISI *is driving at*]. Well, here I am!

LAUDISI. Yes! Now take a better look at me . . . Touch me! That's it—that's it! Now you are touching me, are you not? And you see me! You're sure you see me?

SIRELLI. Why, I should say . . .

LAUDISI. Yes, but the point is, you're sure! Of course you're sure! Now if you please, Signora Sirelli, you come here—or rather . . . no . . . [*Gallantly.*] it is my place to come to you! [*He goes over to* SIGNORA SIRELLI *and kneels chivalrously on one knee.*] You see me, do you not, madam? Now that hand of yours . . . touch me! A pretty hand, on my word! [*He pats her hand.*]

SIRELLI. Easy! Easy!

LAUDISI. Never mind your husband, madam! Now, you have touched me, have you not? And you see me? And you are absolutely sure about me, are you not? Well now, madam, I beg of you; do not tell your husband, nor my sister, nor my niece, nor Signora Cini here, what you think of me; because, if you were to do that, they would all tell you that you are completely wrong. But, you see, you are really right; because I am really what you take me to be; though, my dear madam, that does not prevent me from also being really what your husband, my sister, my niece, and Signora Cini take me to be—because they also were absolutely right!

SIGNORA SIRELLI. In other words you are a different person for each of us.

LAUDISI. Of course I'm a different person! And you, madam, pretty as you are, aren't you a different person, too?

SIGNORA SIRELLI [*hastily*]. No siree! I assure you, as far as I'm concerned, I'm always the same always, yesterday, today, and forever!

LAUDISI. Ah, but so am I, from my point of view, believe me! And, I would say that you are all mistaken unless you see me as I see myself; but that would be an inexcusable presumption on my part—as it would be on yours, my dear madam!

SIRELLI. And what has all this rigmarole got to do with it, may I ask?

LAUDISI. What has it go to do with it? Why . . . I find all you people here at your wits' ends trying to find out who and what other people are; just as though other people had to be this, or that, and nothing else.

SIGNORA SIRELLI. All you are saying is that we can never find out the truth! A dreadful idea!

SIGNORA CINI. I give up! I give up! If we can't believe even what we see with our eyes and feel with our fingers . . .

LAUDISI. But you must understand, madam! All I'm saying is that you should show some respect for what other people see and feel, even though it be the exact opposite of what you see and feel.

SIGNORA SIRELLI. The way to answer you is to refuse to talk with you. See, I turn my back on you! You're driving me mad!

LAUDISI. Oh, I beg your pardon. Don't let me interfere with your party. Please go on! Pray continue your argument about Signora Frola and Signor Ponza—I promise not to interrupt again!

AMALIA. You're right for once, Lamberto; and I think it would be even better if you should go into the other room.

DINA. Serves you right, uncle! Into the other room with you, into the other room!

LAUDISI. No, I refuse to budge! Fact is, I enjoy hearing you gossip; but I promise not to say anything more, don't fear! At the very most, with your permission, I shall indulge in a laugh or two.

SIGNORA SIRELLI. How funny . . . and our idea in coming here was to find out . . . But really, Amalia, I thought this Ponza man was your husband's secretary at the Provincial building.

AMALIA. He is his secretary—in the office. But here at home what authority has Agazzi over the fellow?

SIGNORA SIRELLI. Of course! I understand! But may I ask . . . haven't you even tried to see Signora Frola, next door?

DINA. Tried? I should say we had! Twice, Signora!

SIGNORA CINI. Well . . . so then . . . you have probably talked to her . . .

DINA. We were not *received,* if you please!

SIGNORA SIRELLI, SIRELLI, SIGNORA CINI [*in chorus*]. Not received? Why! Why! Why!

DINA. This very forenoon!

AMALIA. The first time we waited fully fifteen minutes at the door. We rang and rang and rang, and no one came. Why, we weren't even able to leave our cards! So we went back today . . .

DINA [*throwing up her hands in an expression of horror*]. And *he* came to the door.

SIGNORA SIRELLI. Why yes, with that face of his . . . you can tell by just looking at the man . . . Such a face! Such a face! You can't blame people for talking! And then, with that black suit of his . . . Why, they all dress in black. Did you ever notice? Even the old lady! And the man's eyes, too! . . .

SIRELLI [*with a glance of pitying disgust at his wife*]. What do you know about his eyes? You never saw his eyes! And you never saw the woman. How do you know she dresses in black? *Probably* she dresses in black . . . By the way, they come from a village in the next county. Had you heard that? A village in Marsica![2]

AMALIA. Yes, the village that was destroyed a short time ago.

2 A region in Abruzzi. In 1915 there was a great earthquake there; the town of Avezzano, e.g. was destroyed.

SIRELLI. Exactly! By an earthquake! Not a house left standing in the place.

DINA. And all their relatives were lost, I have heard. Not one of them left in the world!

SIGNORA CINI [impatient to get on with the story]. Very well, very well, so then . . . he came to the door . . .

AMALIA. Yes . . . And the moment I saw him in front of me with that weird face of his I had hardly enough gumption left to tell him that we had just come to call on his mother-in-law, and he . . . well . . . not a word, not a word . . . not even a "thank you," if you please!

DINA. That is not quite fair, mama: . . . he did bow!

AMALIA. Well, yes, a bow . . . if you want to call it that. Something like this! . . .

DINA. And his eyes! You ought to see his eyes—the eyes of a devil, and then some! You never saw a man with eyes like that!

SIGNORA CINI. Very well, what did he say, finally?

DINA. He seemed quite taken aback.

AMALIA. He was all confused like; he hitched about for a time; and at last he said that Signora Frola was not feeling well, but that she would appreciate our kindness in having come; and then he just stood there, and stood there, apparently waiting for us to go away.

DINA. I never was more mortified in my life!

SIRELLI. A boor, a plain boor, I say! Oh, it's his fault, I am telling you. And . . . who knows? Perhaps he has got the old lady under lock and key.

SIGNORA SIRELLI. Well, I think something should be done about it! . . . After all, you are the wife of a superior of his. You can refuse to be treated like that.

AMALIA. As far as that goes, my husband did take it rather badly— as a lack of courtesy on the man's part; and he went straight to the prefect with the matter, insisting on an apology.

[SIGNOR AGAZZI, commendatore and provincial councillor, appears
in the doorway rear.]

DINA. Oh goody, here's papa now!

[AGAZZI is well on toward fifty. He has the harsh, authoritarian
manner of the provincial of importance. Red hair and beard, rather
unkempt; gold-rimmed eyeglasses.]

AGAZZI. Oh Sirelli, glad to see you! [He steps forward and bows to the company.]

AGAZZI. Signora! . . .[He shakes hands with SIGNORA SIRELLI.]

AMALIA [introducing SIGNORA CINI]. My husband, Signora Cini!

AGAZZI [with a bow and taking her hand]. A great pleasure, madam! [Then turning to his wife and daughter in a mysterious voice.] I have come back from the office to give you some real news! Signora Frola will be here shortly.

SIGNORA SIRELLI [clapping her hands delightedly]. Oh, the mother-in-law! She is coming? Really? Coming here?

SIRELLI [*going over to* AGAZZI *and pressing his hand warmly as an expression of admiration*]. That's the talk, old man, that's the talk. What's needed here is some show of authority.

AGAZZI. Why I had to, you see, I had to! . . . I can't let a man treat my wife and daughter that way! . . .

SIRELLI. I should say not! I was just expressing myself to that effect right here.

SIGNORA SIRELLI. And it would have been entirely proper to inform the prefect also . . .

AGAZZI [*anticipating*]. . . . of all the talk that is going around on this fine gentleman's account? Oh, leave that to me! I didn't miss the opportunity.

SIRELLI. Fine! Fine!

SIGNORA CINI. And such talk!

AMALIA. For my part, I never heard of such a thing. Why, do you know, he has them both under lock and key!

DINA. No, mamma, we not *quite* sure of that. We are not *quite* sure about the old lady, yet.

AMALIA. Well, we know it about his wife, anyway.

SIRELLI. And what did the prefect have to say?

AGAZZI. Oh the prefect . . . well, the prefect . . . he was very much impressed, *very* much impressed, with what I had to say.

SIRELLI. I should hope so!

AGAZZI. You see, some of the talk had reached his ears already. And he agrees that it is better, as a matter of his own official prestige, for all this mystery in connection with one of his assistants to be cleared up, so that once and for all we shall know the truth.

LAUDISI [*bursts out laughing*].

AMALIA. That is Lamberto's usual contribution. He laughs!

AGAZZI. And what is there to laugh about?

SIGNORA SIRELLI. Why he says that no one can ever know the truth.

[*The* BUTLER *appears at the door in back set.*]

THE BUTLER. Excuse me, Signora Frola!

SIRELLI. Ah, here she is now!

AGAZZI. Now we'll see if we can settle it!

SIGNORA SIRELLI. Splendid! Oh, I am so glad I came.

AMALIA [*rising*]. Shall we have her come in?

AGAZZI. Wait, you keep your seat, Amalia! Let's have her come right in here. [*Turning to the butler.*] Show her in!

[*Exit* BUTLER.]

[*A moment later all rise as* SIGNORA FROLA *enters, and* AMALIA *steps forward, holding out her hand in greeting.* SIGNORA FROLA *is a slight, modestly but neatly dressed old lady, very eager to talk and apparently fond of people. There is a world of sadness in her eyes, tempered however, by a gentle smile that is constantly playing about her lips.*]

AMALIA. Come right in, Signora Frola! [*She takes the old lady's hand and begins the introduction.*] Mrs. Sirelli, a good friend of mine; Signora Cini; my husband; Mr. Sirelli; and this is my daughter, Dina; my brother Lamberto Laudisi. Please take a chair, Signora!

SIGNORA FROLA. Oh, I am so very, very sorry! I have come to excuse myself for having been so negligent of my social duties. You, Signora Agazzi, were so kind, so very kind, to have honored me with a first call— when really it was my place to leave my card with you!

AMALIA. Oh, we are just neighbors, Signora Frola! Why stand on ceremony? I just thought that you, being new in town and all alone by yourself, would perhaps like to have a little company.

SIGNORA FROLA. Oh, how very kind of you it was!

SIGNORA SIRELLI. And you are quite alone, aren't you?

SIGNORA FROLA. Oh no! No! I have a daughter, married, though she hasn't been here very long, either.

SIRELLI. And your daughter's husband is the new secretary at the prefecture, Signor Ponza, I believe?

SIGNORA FROLA. Yes, yes, exactly! And I hope that Signor Agazzi, as his superior, will be good enough to excuse me—and him, too!

AGAZZI. I will be quite frank with you madam! I was a bit put out.

SIGNORA FROLA [*interrupting*]. And you were quite right! But I do hope you will forgive him. You see, we are still—what shall I say—still so upset by the terrible things that have happened to us . . .

AMALIA. You went through the earthquake, didn't you?

SIGNORA SIRELLI. And you lost all your relatives?

SIGNORA FROLA. Every one of them! All our family—yes, madam. And our village was left just a miserable ruin, a pile of bricks and stones and mortar.

SIRELLI. Yes, we heard about it.

SIGNORA FROLA. It wasn't so bad for me, I suppose. I had only one sister and her daughter, and my niece had no family. But my poor son-in-law had a much harder time of it. He lost his mother, two brothers, and their wives, a sister and her husband, and there were two little ones, his nephews.

SIRELLI. A massacre!

SIGNORA FROLA. Oh, one doesn't forget such things! You see, it sort of leaves you with your feet off the ground.

AMALIA. I can imagine.

SIGNORA SIRELLI. And all over-night with no warning at all! It's a wonder you didn't go mad.

SIGNORA FROLA. Well, you see, we haven't quite gotten our bearings yet; and we do things that may seem impolite, without in the least intending to. I hope you understand!

AGAZZI. Oh please, Signora Frola, of course!

AMALIA. In fact it was partly on account of your trouble that my daughter and I thought we ought to go to see you first.

SIGNORA SIRELLI [*literally writhing with curiosity*]. Yes, of course, since they saw you all alone by yourself, and yet . . . excuse me, Signora Frola . . . if the question doesn't seem impertinent . . . how is that when you have a daughter here in town and after a disaster like the one you have been through . . . I should think you people would all stand together, that you would need one another.

SIGNORA FROLA. Whereas I am left here all by myself?

SIRELLI. Yes, exactly. It does seem strange, to tell the honest truth.

SIGNORA FROLA. Oh, I understand—of course! But you know, I have a feeling that a young man and a young woman who have married should be left a good deal to themselves.

LAUDISI. Quite so, quite so! They should be left to themselves. They are beginning a life of their own, a life different from anything they have led before. One should not interfere in these relations between a husband and a wife!

SIGNORA SIRELLI. But there are limits to everything, Laudisi, if you will excuse me! And when it comes to shutting one's own mother out of one's life . . .

LAUDISI. Who is shutting her out of the girl's life? Here, if I have understood the lady, we see a mother who understands that her daughter cannot and must not remain so closely associated with her as she was before, for now the young woman must begin a new life on her own account.

SIGNORA FROLA [with evidence of keen gratitude and relief]. You have hit the point exactly, sir. You have said what I would like to have said. You are exactly right! Thank you!

SIGNORA CINI. But your daughter, I imagine, often comes to see you . . .

SIGNORA FROLA [hesitating, and manifestly ill at ease]. Why yes . . . I . . . I . . . we do see each other, of course!

SIRELLI [quickly pressing the advantage]. But your daughter never goes out of her house! At least no one in town has ever seen her.

SIGNORA CINI. Oh, she probably has her little ones to take care of.

SIGNORA FROLA [speaking up quickly]. No, there are no children yet, and perhaps there won't be any, now. You see, she has been married seven years. Oh, of course, she has a lot to do about the house; but that is not the reason, really. You know, we women who come from the little towns in the country—we are used to staying indoors much of the time.

AGAZZI. Even when your mothers are living in the same town, but not in your house? You prefer staying indoors to going and visiting your mothers?

AMALIA. But it's Signora Frola probably who visits her daughter.

SIGNORA FROLA [quickly]. Of course, of course, why not! I go there once or twice a day.

SIRELLI. And once or twice a day you climb all those stairs up to the fifth story of that tenement, eh?

SIGNORA FROLA [growing pale and trying to conceal under a laugh *the torture of that cross-examination*]. Why . . . er . . . to tell the truth, I don't go up. You're right, five flights would be quite too much for me. No, I don't go up. My daughter comes out on the balcony in the court-yard and . . . well . . . we see each other . . . and we talk!

SIGNORA SIRELLI. And that's all, eh? How terrible! You never see each other more intimately than that?

DINA. I have a mamma and certainly I wouldn't expect her to go up five flights of stairs to see me, either; but at the same time I could never stand talking to her that way, shouting at the top of my lungs from a balcony on the fifth story. I am sure I should want a kiss from her occa-sionally, and feel her near me, at least.

SIGNORA FROLA [*with evident signs of embarrassment and confu-sion*]. And you're right! Yes, exactly . . . quite right! I must explain. Yes . . . I hope you people are not going to think that my daughter is some-thing she really is not. You must not suspect her of having so little regard for me and for my years, and you mustn't believe that I, her mother, am . . . well . . . five, six, even more stories to climb would never prevent a real mother, even if she were as old and infirm as I am, from going to her daughter's side and pressing her to her heart with a real mother's love . . . oh no!

SIGNORA SIRELLI [*triumphantly*]. There you have it, there you have it, just as we were saying!

SIGNORA CINI. But there must be a reason, there must be a reason!

AMALIA [*pointedly to her brother*]. Aha, Lamberto, now you see, there *is* a reason, after all!

SIRELLI [*insisting*]. Your son-in-law, I suppose?

SIGNORA FROLA. Oh please, please, please, don't think badly of *him*. He is such a very good boy. Good is no name for it, my dear sir. You can't imagine all he does for me! Kind, attentive, solicitous for my comfort, everything! And as for my daughter—I doubt if any girl ever had a more affectionate and well-intentioned husband. No, on that point I am proud of myself! I could not have found a better man for her.

SIGNORA SIRELLI. Well then . . . What? What? *What?*

SIGNORA CINI. So your son-in-law is not the reason?

AGAZZI. I never thought it was his fault. Can you imagine a man forbidding his wife to call on her mother, or preventing the mother from paying an occasional visit to her daughter?

SIGNORA FROLA. Oh, it's not a case of forbidding! Who ever dreamed of such a thing! No, it's we, Commendatore, I and my daughter, that is. Oh, please, believe me! We refrain from visiting each other of our own accord, out of consideration for him, you understand.

AGAZZI. But excuse me . . . how in the world could he be offended by such a thing? I *don't* understand.

SIGNORA FROLA. Oh, please don't be angry, Signor Agazzi. You see it's a . . . what shall I say . . . a feeling . . . that's it, a feeling, which it would perhaps be very hard for anyone else to understand; and yet, when you do understand it, it's all so simple, I am sure . . . so simple . . . and believe me, my dear friends, it is no slight sacrifice that I am making, and that my daughter is making, too.

AGAZZI. Well, one thing you will admit, madam. This is a very, very unusual situation.

SIRELLI. Unusual, indeed! And such as to justify a curiosity even more persistent than ours.

AGAZZI. It is not only unusual, madam. I might even say it is suspicious.

SIGNORA FROLA. Suspicious? You mean you suspect Signor Ponza? Oh please, Commendatore, don't say that. What fault can you possibly find with him, Signor Agazzi?

AGAZZI. I didn't say just that . . . Please don't misunderstand! I said simply that the situation is so very strange that people might legitimately suspect . . .

SIGNORA FROLA. Oh, no, no, no! What could they suspect. We are in perfect agreement, all of us; and we are really quite happy, very happy, I might even say . . . both I and my daughter.

SIGNORA SIRELLI. Perhaps it's a case of jealousy?

SIGNORA FROLA. Jealousy of me? It would be hardly fair to say that, although . . . really . . . oh, it is so hard to explain! . . . You see, he is in love with my daughter . . . so much so that he wants her whole heart, her every thought, as it were, for himself; so much so that he insists that the affections which my daughter must have for me, her mother—he finds that love quite natural of course, why not? Of course he does!— should reach me through him—that's it, through him—don't you understand?

AGAZZI. Oh, that is going pretty strong! No, I don't understand. In fact it seems to me a case of downright cruelty!

SIGNORA FROLA. Cruelty? No, no, please don't call it cruelty, Commendatore. It is something else, believe me! You see it's so hard for me to explain the matter. Nature, perhaps . . . but no, that's hardly the word. What shall I call it? Perhaps a sort of disease. It's a fullness of love, of a love shut off from the world. There, I guess that's it . . . a fullness . . . a completeness of devotion in which his wife must live without ever departing from it, and into which no other person must ever be allowed to enter.

DINA. Not even her mother, I suppose?

SIRELLI. It is the worst case of selfishness I ever heard of, if you want my opinion!

SIGNORA FROLA. Selfishness? Perhaps! But a selfishness, after all, which offers itself wholly in sacrifice. A case where the selfish person gives all he has in the world to the one he loves. Perhaps it would be fairer to call me selfish; for selfish it surely is for me to be always trying to break into this closed world of theirs, break in by force if necessary; when I know that my daughter is really so happy, so passionately adored —you ladies understand, don't you? A true mother should be satisfied when she knows her daughter is happy, oughtn't she? Besides I'm not completely separated from my daughter, am I? I see her and I speak to her [*She assumes a more confidential tone.*] You see, when she lets down the basket there in the courtyard I always find a letter in it—a short note, which keeps me posted on the news of the day; and I put in a little letter that I have written. That is some consolation, a great consolation indeed, and now, in course of time, I've grown used to it. I am resigned, there! Resignation, that's it! And I've ceased really to suffer from it at all.

AMALIA. Oh well then, after all, if you people are satisfied, why should . . .

SIGNORA FROLA [*rising*]. Oh yes, yes! But, remember, I told you he is such a good man! Believe me, he couldn't be better, really! We all have our weaknesses in this world, haven't we! And we get along best by having a little indulgence, for one another. [*She holds out her hand to* AMALIA.] Thank you for calling, madam. [*She bows to* SIGNORA SIRELLI, SIGNORA CINI, *and* DINA; *then turning to* AGAZZI, *she continues.*] And I do hope you have forgiven me!

AGAZZI. Oh, my dear madam, please, please! And we are extremely grateful for your having come to call on us.

SIGNORA FROLA [*offering her hand to* SIRELLI *and* LAUDISI *and again turning to* AMALIA *who has risen to show her out*]. Oh no, please, Signora Agazzi, please stay here with your friends! Don't put yourself to any trouble!

AMALIA. No, no, I will go with you; and believe me, we were very, very glad to see you!

[*Exit* SIGNORA FROLA *with* AMALIA *showing her the way.* AMALIA *returns immediately.*]

SIRELLI. Well, there you have the story, ladies and gentlemen! Are you satisfied with the explanation?

AGAZZI. An explanation, you call it? So far as I can see she has explained nothing. I tell you there is some big mystery in all this business.

SIGNORA SIRELLI. That poor woman! Who knows what torment she must be suffering?

DINA. And to think of that poor girl!

SIGNORA CINI. She could hardly keep in her tears as she talked.

AMALIA. Yes, and did you notice when I mentioned all those stairs she would have to climb before really being able to see her daughter?

LAUDISI. What impressed me was her concern, which amounted to a steadfast determination, to protect her son-in-law from the slightest suspicion.

SIGNORA SIRELLI. Not at all, not at all! What could she say for him? She couldn't really find a single word to say for him.

SIRELLI. And I would like to know how anyone could condone such violence, such downright cruelty!

THE BUTLER [*appearing again in the doorway*]. Beg pardon, sir! Signor Ponza calling.

SIGNORA SIRELLI. The man himself, upon my word!

[*An animated ripple of surprise and curiosity, not to say of guilty
self-consciousness, sweeps over the company.*]

AGAZZI. Did he ask to see me?

BUTLER. He asked simply if he might be received. That was all he
said.

SIGNORA SIRELLI. Oh please, Signor Agazzi, please let him come in!
I am really afraid of the man; but I confess the greatest curiosity to have
a close look at the monster.

AMALIA. But what in the world can he be wanting?

AGAZZI. The way to find that out is to have him come in. [*To the*
BUTLER.] Show him in, please.

[*The* BUTLER *bows and goes out. A second later* PONZA *appears,
aggressively, in the doorway.*]

[PONZA *is a short, thick set, dark complexioned man of a distinctly
unprepossessing appearance; black hair, very thick and coming
down low over his forehead; a black mustache upcurling at the
ends, giving his face a certain ferocity of expression. He is dressed
entirely in black. From time to time he draws a black-bordered
handkerchief and wipes the perspiration from his brow. When he
speaks his eyes are invariably hard, fixed, sinister.*]

AGAZZI. This way please, Ponza, come right in! [*Introducing him.*]
Signor Ponza; our new provincial secretary; my wife; Signora Sirelli;
Signora Cini; my daughter Dina. This is Signor Sirelli; and here is
Laudisi, my brother-in-law. Please join our party, won't you, Ponza?

PONZA. So kind of you! You will pardon the intrusion. I shall disturb
you only a moment, I hope.

AGAZZI. You had some private business to discuss with me?

PONZA. Why yes, but I could discuss it right here. In fact, perhaps
as many people as possible should hear what I have to say. You see it is
a declaration that I owe, in a certain sense, to the general public.

AGAZZI. Oh my dear Ponza, if it is that little matter of your mother-
in-law's not calling on us, it is quite all right; because you see . . .

PONZA. No, that was not what I came for, Commendatore. It was not
to apologize for her. Indeed I may say that Signora Frola, my wife's
mother, would certainly have left her cards with Signora Agazzi, your
wife, and Signorina Agazzi, your daughter, long before they were so kind
as to honor her with their call, had I not exerted myself to the utmost to
prevent her coming, since I am absolutely unable to consent to her paying
or receiving visits!

AGAZZI [*drawing up into an authoritative attitude and speaking
with some severity*] Why? If you will be so kind as to explain, Ponza?

PONZA [*with evidences of increasing excitement in spite of his
efforts to preserve his self-control*]. I suppose my mother-in-law has been
talking to you people about her daughter, my wife. Am I mistaken? And
I imagine she told you further that I have forbidden her entering my
house and seeing her daughter intimately.

AMALIA. Oh not at all, not at all, Signor Ponza! Signora Frola had only the nicest things to say about you. She could not have spoken of you with greater respect and kindness.

DINA. She seems to be very fond of you indeed.

AGAZZI. She says that she refrains from visiting your house of her own accord, out of regard for feelings of yours which we frankly confess we are unable to understand.

SIGNORA SIRELLI. Indeed, if we were to express our honest opinion . . .

AGAZZI. Well, yes, why not be honest? We think you are extremely harsh with the woman, extremely harsh, perhaps cruel would be an exacter word.

PONZA. Yes, that is what I thought; and I came here for the express purpose of clearing the matter up. The condition this poor woman is in is a pitiable one indeed—not less pitiable than my own perhaps; because, as you see, I am compelled to come here and make apologies—a public declaration—which only such violence as has just been used upon me could ever bring me to make in the world . . . [*He stops and looks about the room. Then he says slowly with emphatic emphasis on the important syllables.*] Signora Frola is mad.

ALL [*with a start*]. Mad?

PONZA. She's been mad for four years.

SIGNORA SIRELLI [*with a cry*]. Dear me, she doesn't seem mad in the least!

AGAZZI [*amazed*]. What? Mad?

PONZA. She doesn't seem mad: she *is* mad. And her madness consists precisely in believing that I don't want to let her see her daughter. [*His face takes on an expression of cruel suffering mingled with a sort of ferocious excitement*]. What daughter, for God's sake? Why her daughter died four years ago! [*A general sensation*].

EVERYONE AT ONCE. Died? She is dead? What do you mean? Oh, really? Four years ago? Why! Why!

PONZA. Four years ago! In fact it was the death of the poor girl that drove her mad.

SIRELLI. Are we to understand that the wife with whom you are now living . . .

PONZA. Exactly! She is my second wife. I married her two years ago.

AMALIA. And Signora Frola believes that her daughter is still living, that she is your wife still?

PONZA. Perhaps it was best for her that way. She was in the charge of a nurse in her own room, you see. Well, when she chanced to see me passing by inadvertence on her street one day, with this woman, my second wife, she suddenly began to laugh and cry and tremble all over in an extreme of happiness. She was sure her daughter, whom she had believed dead, was alive and well; and from a condition of desperate despondency which was the first form of her mental disturbance, she entered on a second obsession, believing steadily that her daughter was not dead at all; but that I, the poor girl's husband, am so completely in love with her that I want her wholly for myself and will not allow anyone to approach her. She became otherwise quite well, you might say. Her nervousness disappeared. Her physical condition improved, and her powers of reasoning returned quite clear. Judge for yourself, ladies and gentlemen! You have seen her and talked with her. You would never suspect in the world that she is mad.

AMALIA. Never in the world! Never!

SIGNORA SIRELLI. And the poor woman says she is so happy, so happy!

PONZA. That is what she says to everybody; and for that matter she really has a wealth of affection and gratitude for me; because, as you may well suppose, I do my very best, in spite of the sacrifices entailed, to keep up this beneficial illusion in her. The sacrifices you can readily understand. In the first place I have to maintain two homes on my small salary. Then it is very hard on my wife, isn't it? But she, poor thing, does the very best she can to help me out! She comes to the window when the old lady appears. She talks to her from the balcony. She writes letters to her. But you people will understand that there are limits to what I can ask of my poor wife. Signora Frola, meanwhile, lives practically in confinement. We have to keep a pretty close watch on her. We have to lock her up, virtually. Otherwise, some fine day she would be walking right into my house. She is of a gentle, placid disposition fortunately; but you understand that my wife, good as she is, could never bring herself to accepting caresses intended for another woman, a dead woman! That would be a torment beyond conception.

AMALIA. Oh, of course! Poor woman! Just imagine!

SIGNORA SIRELLI. And the old lady herself consents to being locked up all the time?

PONZA. You, Commendatore, will understand that I couldn't permit her calling here except under absolute constraint.

AGAZZI. I understand perfectly, my dear Ponza, and you have my deepest sympathy.

PONZA. When a man has a misfortune like this fall upon him he must not go about in society; but of course when, by complaining to the prefect, you practically compelled me to have Signora Frola call, it was my duty to volunteer this further information; because, as a public official, and with due regard for the post of responsibility I occupy, I could not allow any discredible suspicions to remain attached to my reputation. I could not have you good people suppose for a moment that, out of jealousy or for any other reason, I could ever prevent a poor suffering mother from seeing her own daughter. [*He rises.*] Again my apologies for having intruded my personal troubles upon your party. [*He bows.*] My compliments, Commendatore. Good afternoon, good afternoon! Thank you! [*Bowing to* LAUDISI, SIRELLI, *and the others in turn, he goes out through the door, rear.*]

AMALIA [*with a sigh of sympathy and astonishment*]. Uhh! Mad! What do you think of that?

SIGNORA SIRELLI. The poor old thing! But you wouldn't have believed it, would you?

DINA. I always knew there was something under it all.

SIGNORA CINI. But who could ever have guessed . . .

AGAZZI. Oh, I don't know, I don't know! You could tell from the way she talked . . .

LAUDISI. You mean to say that you thought . . . ?

AGAZZI. No, I can't say that. But at the same time, if you remember, she could never quite find her words.

SIGNORA SIRELLI. How could she, poor thing, out of her head like that?

SIRELLI. And yet, if I may raise the question, it seems strange to me that an insane person . . . ah, I admit that she couldn't really talk rationally . . . but what surprises me is her trying to find a reason to explain why her son-in-law should be keeping her away from her daughter. This effort of hers to justify it and then to adapt herself to excuses of her own invention . . .

AGAZZI. Yes, but that is only another proof that she's mad. You see, she kept offering excuses for Ponza that really were not excuses at all.

AMALIA. Why, yes! She'd say a thing and then take it right back again.

AGAZZI. If she weren't downright mad, how could she or any other woman ever accept such a situation from a man? How could she ever consent to talk with her own daughter only by shouting up from the bottom of a well five stories deep?

SIRELLI. But if I remember rightly she has you there! Notice, she doesn't accept the situation. She says she is resigned to it. That's different! No, I tell you, there is still something funny about this business. What do you say, Laudisi?

LAUDISI. Why, I say nothing, nothing at all!

THE BUTLER [*appearing at the door and visibly excited*]. Beg pardon, Signora Frola is here again!

AMALIA [*with a start*]. Oh dear me, again? Do you suppose she'll be pestering us all the time now?

SIGNORA SIRELLI. I understand how you feel now that you know she's mad.

SIGNORA CINI. My, my, what do you suppose she is going to say now?

SIRELLI. For my part I'd really like to hear what she's got to say.

DINA. Oh yes, mamma, don't be afraid! Ponza said she was quite harmless. Let's have her come in.

AGAZZI. Of course, we can't send her away. Let's have her come in; and, if she makes any trouble, why . . . [*Turning to the* BUTLER.] Show her in. [*The* BUTLER *bows and withdraws.*]

AMALIA. You people stand by me, please! Why, I don't know what I am ever going to say to her now!

[SIGNORA FROLA *appears at the door.* AMALIA *rises and steps forward to welcome her. The others look on in astonished silence.*]

SIGNORA FROLA. May I please . . . ?

AMALIA. Do come in, Signora Frola, do come in! You know all these ladies. They were here when you came before.

SIGNORA FROLA [*with an expression of sadness on her features, but still smiling gently*]. How you all look at me—and even you, Signora Agazzi! I am sure you think I am mad, don't you!

AMALIA. My dear Signora Frola, what in the world are you talking about?

SIGNORA FROLA. But I am sure you will forgive me if I disturb you for a moment. [*Bitterly.*] Oh, my dear Signora Agazzi, I wish I had left things as they were. It was hard to feel that I had been impolite to you by not answering the bell when you called that first time; but I could never have supposed that you would come back and force me to call upon you. I could foresee the consequences of such a visit from the very first.

AMALIA. Why, not at all, not at all! I don't understand. Why?

DINA. What consequences could you foresee, madam?

SIGNORA FROLA. Why, my son-in-law, Signor Ponza, has just been here, hasn't he?

AGAZZI. Why, yes, he was here! He came to discuss certain office matters with me . . . just ordinary business, you understand!

SIGNORA FROLA [*visibly hurt and quite dismayed*]. Oh, I know you are saying that just to spare me, just in order not to hurt my feelings.

AGAZZI. Not at all, not at all! That was really why he came.

SIGNORA FROLA [*with some alarm*]. But he was quite calm, I hope, quite calm?

AGAZZI. Calm? As calm as could be! Why not? Of course!

[*The members of the company all nod in confirmation.*]

SIGNORA FROLA. Oh, my dear friends, I am sure you are trying to reassure me; but as a matter of fact I came to set you right about my son-in-law.

SIGNORA SIRELLI. Why no, Signora, what's the trouble?

AGAZZI. Really, it was just a matter of politics we talked about . . .

SIGNORA FROLA. But I can tell from the way you all look at me . . . Please excuse me, but it is not a question of me at all. From the way you all look at me I can tell that he came here to prove something that I would never have confessed for all the money in the world. You will all bear me out, won't you? When I came here a few moments ago you all asked me questions that were very cruel questions to me, as I hope you will understand. And they were questions that I couldn't answer very well; but anyhow I gave an explanation of our manner of living which can be satisfactory to nobody, I am well aware. But how could I give you the real reason? How could I tell you people, as he's doing, that my daughter has been dead for four years and that I'm a poor mad mother who believes that her daughter is still living and that her husband will not allow me to see her?

AGAZZI [*quite upset by the ring of deep sincerity he finds in* SIGNORA FROLA's *manner of speaking*]. What do you mean, your daughter?

SIGNORA FROLA [*hastily and with anguished dismay written on her features*]. You know that's so. Why do you try to deny it? He did say that to you, didn't he?

SIRELLI [*with some hesitation and studying her features warily*]. Yes . . . in fact . . . he did say that.

SIGNORA FROLA. I know he did; and I also know now it pained him to be obliged to say such a thing of me. It is a great pity, Commendatore! We have made continual sacrifices, involving unheard of suffering, I assure you; and we could endure them only by living as we are living now. Unfortunately, as I well understand, it must look very strange to people, seem even scandalous, arouse no end of gossip! But after all, if he is an excellent secretary, scrupulously honest, attentive to his work, why should people complain? You have seen him in the office, haven't you? He is a good worker, isn't he?

AGAZZI. To tell the truth, I have not watched him particularly, as yet.

SIGNORA FROLA. Oh he really is, he really is! All the men he ever worked for say he's most reliable; and I beg of you, please don't let this other matter interfere. And why then should people go tormenting him with all this prying into his private life, laying bare once more a misfortune which he has succeeded in mastering and which, if it were widely talked about, might upset him again personally, and even hurt him in his career?

AGAZZI. Oh no, no, Signora, no one is trying to hurt him. Nor would we hurt you either.

SIGNORA FROLA. But my dear sir, how can you help hurting me when you force him to give almost publicly an explanation which is quite absurd—ridiculous I might even say! Surely people like you can't seriously believe what he says? You can't possibly be taking me for mad. You don't really think that this woman is his second wife? And yet it is all so necessary! He needs to have it that way. It is the only way he can pull himself together; get down to his work again . . . the only way . . . the only way! Why he gets all wrought up, all excited, when he is forced to talk of this other matter; because he knows himself how hard it is for him to say certain things. You may have noticed it . . .

AGAZZI. Yes, that is quite true. He did seem very much excited.

SIGNORA SIRELLI. Well, well, well, so then it's he!

SIRELLI [*triumphantly*]. I always said it was he.

AGAZZI. Oh, I say! Is that really possible? [*He motions to the company to be quiet.*]

SIGNORA FROLA [*joining her hands beseechingly*]. My dear friends, what are you really thinking? It is only on this subject that he is a little queer. The point is, you must simply not mention this particular matter to him. Why, really now, you could never suppose that I would leave my daughter shut up with him all alone like that? And yet just watch him at his work and in the office. He does everything he is expected to do and no one in the world could do it better.

AGAZZI. But this is not enough, madam, as you will understand. Do you mean to say that Signor Ponza, your son-in-law, came here and made up a story out of whole cloth?

SIGNORA FROLA. Yes, sir, yes sir, exactly . . . only I will explain. You must understand—you must look at things from his point of view.

AGAZZI. What do you mean? Do you mean that your daughter is not dead?

SIGNORA FROLA. God forbid! Of course she is not dead!

AGAZZI. Well, then, he is mad!

SIGNORA FROLA. No, no, look, look! . . .

SIRELLI. I always said it was he! . . .

SIGNORA FROLA. No, look, look, not that, not that! Let me explain . . . You have noticed him, haven't you? Fine, strong looking man . . . violent . . . when he married my daughter he was seized with a veritable frenzy of love . . . he risked my little daughter's life almost, she was frail . . . On the advice of doctors and relatives, even *his* relatives—dead now, poor things—they had to take his wife off in secret and shut her up in a sanatorium. And he came to think she was dead.

Just imagine when we brought my daughter back to him—and a pretty thing she was to look at, too—he began to scream and say, no, no, no, she wasn't his wife, his wife was dead! He looked at her: No, no, no, not at all! She wasn't the woman! Imagine my dear friends, how terrible it all was. Finally he came up close to her and for a moment it seemed that he was going to recognize her again; but once more it was "No, no, no, she is not my wife!" And do you know, to get him to accept my daughter at all again, we were obliged to pretend having a second wedding, with the collusion of his doctors and his friends, you understand!

SIGNORA SIRELLI. Ah, so that is why he says that . . .

SIGNORA FROLA. Yes, but he doesn't really believe it, you know; and he hasn't for a long time, I am sure. But he seems to feel a need for maintaining the pretense. He can't do without it. He feels surer of himself that way. He is seized with a terrible fear, from time to time, that this little wife he loves may be taken from him again. [*Smiling and in a low, confidential tone.*] So he keeps her locked up at home where he can have her all for himself. But he worships her—he worships her; and I am really quite convinced that my daughter is happy. [*She gets up.*] And now I must be going. You see, my son-in-law is in a terrible state of mind at present. I wouldn't like to have him call, and find me not at home. [*With a sigh, and gesturing with her joined hands.*] Well, I suppose we must get along as best we can; but it is hard on my poor girl. She has to pretend all along that she is not herself, but another, his second wife; and I . . . oh, as for me, I have to pretend that I am mad when he's around, my dear friends; but I'm glad to, I'm glad to, really, so long as it does him some good. [*The* LADIES *rise as* SHE *steps nearer to the door.*] No, no, don't let me interrupt your party. I know the way out! Good afternoon! Good afternoon! [*Bowing and smiling, she hurries out through the rear door.* THEY *all remain standing, astonished, stunned, looking into each other's eyes. Silence.*]

LAUDISI [*coming forward among them*]. So you're having a look at each other? Well! And the truth? [*He bursts out laughing.*]


## ACT II

COUNCILLOR AGAZZI'S *study in the same house. Antique furnishings with old paintings on the walls. A portière over the rear entrance and over the door to the left which opens into the drawing room shown in the first act. To the right a substantial fireplace with a big mirror above the mantel. A flat top desk with a telephone. A sofa, armchairs, straight back chairs, etc.*

*As the curtain rises* AGAZZI *is shown standing beside his desk with the telephone receiver pressed to his ear.* LAUDISI *and* SIRELLI *sit looking at him expectantly.*

AGAZZI. Yes, I want Centuri. Hello . . . hello . . . Centuri? Yes, Agazzi speaking. That you, Centuri? It's me, Agazzi. Well? [*He listens for some time.*] What's that? Really? [*Again he listens at length.*] I understand, but you might go at the matter with a little more speed . . . [*Another long pause.*] Well, I give up! How can that possibly be? [*A pause.*] Oh, I see, I see . . . [*Another pause.*] Well, never mind, I'll look into it myself. Goodbye, Centuri, goodbye! [*He lays down the receiver and steps forward on the stage.*]

SIRELLI [*eagerly*]. Well?

AGAZZI. Nothing! Absolutely nothing!

SIRELLI. Nothing at all?

AGAZZI. You see the whole blamed village was wiped out. Not a house left standing! In the collapse of the town hall, followed by a fire, all the records of the place seem to have been lost—births, deaths, marriages, everything.

SIRELLI. But not everybody was killed. They ought to be able to find somebody who knows them.

AGAZZI. Yes, but you see they didn't rebuild the place. Everybody moved away, and no record was ever kept of the people, of course. So far they have found nobody who knows the Ponzas. To be sure, if the police really went at it, they might find somebody; but it would be a tough job.

SIRELLI. So we can't get anywhere along that line! We have got to take what they say and let it go at that.

AGAZZI. That, unfortunately, is the situation.

LAUDISI [*rising*]. Well, you fellows take a piece of advice from me: believe them both!

AGAZZI. What do you mean—"believe them both"? . . .

SIRELLI. But if she says one thing, and he says another . . .

LAUDISI. Well, in that case, you needn't believe either of them!

SIRELLI. Oh, you're just joking. We may not be able to verify the stories; but that doesn't prove that either one or the other may not be telling the truth. Some document or other . . .

LAUDISI. Oh, documents! Documents! Suppose you had them? What good would they do you?

AGAZZI. Oh, I say! Perhaps we can't get them now, but there were such documents once. If the old lady is mad, there was, as there still may be somewhere, the death certificate of the daughter. Or look at it from the other angle: if we found all the records, and the death certificate were not there for the simple reason that it never existed, why then, it's Ponza, the son-in-law. He would be mad.

SIRELLI. You mean to say you wouldn't give in if we stuck that certificate under your nose tomorrow or the next day? Would you still deny . . .

LAUDISI. Deny? Why . . . why . . . I'm not denying anything! In fact, I'm very careful not to be denying anything. You're the people who are looking up the records to be able to affirm or deny something. Personally, I don't give a rap for the documents; for the truth in my eyes is not in them but in the mind. And into their minds I can penetrate only through what they say to me of themselves.

SIRELLI. Very well— She says he's mad and he says she's mad. Now one of them must be mad. You can't get away from that. Well which is it, she or he?

AGAZZI. There, that's the way to put it!

LAUDISI. But just observe; in the first place, it isn't true that they are accusing each other of madness. Ponza, to be sure, says his mother-in-law is mad. She denies this, not only of herself, but also of him. At the most, she says that he was a little off once, when they took her daughter from him; but that now he is quite all right.

SIRELLI. I see! So you're rather inclined, as I am, to trust what the old lady says.

AGAZZI. The fact is, indeed, that if you accept his story, all the facts in the case are explained.

LAUDISI. But all the facts in the case are explained if you take her story, aren't they?

SIRELLI. Oh, nonsense! In that case neither of them would be mad! Why, one of them must be, damn it all!

LAUDISI. Well, which one? You can't tell, can you? Neither can anybody else! And it is not because those documents you are looking for have been destroyed in an accident—a fire, an earthquake—what you will; but because those people have concealed those documents in themselves, in their own souls. Can't you understand that? She has created for him, or he for her, a world of fancy which has all the earmarks of reality itself. And in this fictitious reality they get along perfectly well, and in full accord with each other; and this world of fancy, this reality of theirs, no document can possibly destroy because the air they breathe is of that world. For them it is something they can see with their eyes, hear with their ears, and touch with their fingers. Oh, I grant you—if you could get a death cerificate or a marriage certificate or something of the kind, you might be able to satisfy that stupid curiosity of yours. Unfortunately, you can't get it. And the result is that you are in the extraordinary fix of having before you, on the one hand, a world of fancy, and on the other, a world of reality, and you, for the life of you, are not able to distinguish one from the other.

AGAZZI. Philosophy, my dear boy, philosophy! And I have no use for philosophy. Give me facts, if you please! Facts! So, I say, keep at it; and I'll bet you we get to the bottom of it sooner or later.

SIRELLI. First we got her story and then we got his; and then we got a new one from her. Let's bring the two of them together—and you think that then we won't be able to tell the false from the true?

LAUDISI. Well, bring them together if you want to! All I ask is permission to laugh when you're through.

AGAZZI. Well, we'll let you laugh all you want. In the meantime let's see . . . [*He steps to the door at the left and calls.*] Amalia, Signora Sirelli, won't you come in here a moment?

[*The* LADIES *enter with* DINA.]

SIGNORA SIRELLI [*catching sight of* LAUDISI *and shaking a finger at him*]. But how is it a man like you, in the presence of such an extraordinary situation, can escape the curiosity we all feel to get at the bottom of this mystery? Why, I lie awake nights thinking of it!

AGAZZI. As your husband says, that man's impossible! Don't bother about him, Signora Sirelli.

LAUDISI. No, don't bother with me; you just listen to Agazzi! He'll keep you from lying awake tonight.

AGAZZI. Look here, ladies. This is what I want—I have an idea: won't you just step across the hall to Signora Frola's?

AMALIA. But will she come to the door?

AGAZZI. Oh I imagine she will!

DINA. We're just returning the call, you see . . .

AMALIA. But didn't he ask us not to call on his mother-in-law? Hasn't he forbidden her to receive visits?

SIRELLI. No, not exactly! That's how he explained what had happened; but at that time nothing was known. Now that the old lady, through force of circumstance, has spoken, giving her version at least of her strange conduct. I should think that . . .

SIGNORA SIRELLI. I have a feeling that she'll be awfully glad to see us, if for nothing else, for the chance of talking about her daughter.

DINA. And she really is a jolly old lady. There is no doubt in my mind, not the slightest: Ponza is mad!

AGAZZI. Now, let's not go too fast. You just listen to me [*He looks at his wife.*]—don't stay too long—five or ten minutes at the outside!

SIRELLI [*to his wife*]. And for heaven's sake, keep your mouth shut!

SIGNORA SIRELLI. And why such considerate advice to me?

SIRELLI. Once *you* get going . . .

DINA [*with the idea of preventing a scene*]. Oh, we are not going to stay very long, ten minutes—fifteen, at the outside. I'll see that no breaks are made.

AGAZZI. And I'll just drop around to the office, and be back at eleven o'clock—ten or twenty minutes at the most.

SIRELLI. And what can I do?

AGAZZI. *Wait!* [*Turning to the* LADIES.] Now, here's the plan! You people invent some excuse or other so as to get Signora Frola in here.

AMALIA. What? How can we possibly do that?

AGAZZI. Oh, find some excuse! You'll think of something in the course of your talk; and if you don't, there's Dina and Signora Sirelli. But when you come back, you understand, go into the drawing room. [*He steps to the door on the left, makes sure that it is wide open, and draws aside the portière.*] This door must stay open, wide open, so that we can hear you talking from in here. Now, here are some papers that I ought to take with me to the office. However, I forget them here. It is a brief that requires Ponza's immediate personal attention. So then, I forget it. And when I get to the office I have to bring him back here to find them— See?

SIRELLI. But just a moment. Where do I come in? When am I expected to appear?

AGAZZI. Oh, yes! . . . A moment or two after eleven, when the ladies are again in the drawing room, and I am back here, you just drop in— to take your wife home, see? You ring the bell and ask for me, and I'll have you brought in here. Then I'll invite the whole crowd in! That's natural enough, isn't it?—into my office? . . .

LAUDISI [*interrupting*]. And we'll have the Truth, the whole Truth with a capital T!

DINA. But look, uncle, of course we'll have the truth—once we get them together face to face—capital T and all!

AGAZZI. Don't get into an argument with that man. Besides, it's time you ladies were going. None of us has any too much leeway.

SIGNORA SIRELLI. Come, Amalia, come Dina! And as for you, sir [*Turning to* LAUDISI.], I won't even shake hands with you.

LAUDISI. Permit me to do it for you, madam. [*He shakes one hand with the other.*] Good luck to you, my dear ladies.

[*Exit* DINA, AMALIA, SIGNORA SIRELLI.]

AGAZZI [*to Sirelli.*] And now we'd better go, too. Suppose we hurry!

SIRELLI. Yes, right away. Goodbye, Lamberto!

LAUDISI. Goodbye, good luck, good luck! [AGAZZI *and* SIRELLI *leave.*

LAUDISI, *left alone, walks up and down the study a number of times, nodding his head and occasionally smiling. Finally he draws up in front of the big mirror that is hanging over the mantelpiece. He sees himself in the glass, stops, and addresses his image.*]

LAUDISI. So there you are! [*He bows to himself and salutes, touching his forehead with his fingers.*] I say, old man, who is mad, you or I? [*He levels a finger menacingly at his image in the glass; and, of course, the image in turn levels a finger at him. As he smiles, his image smiles.*] Of course, I understand! I say it's you, and you say it's me. You—you are mad! No? It's me? Very well! It's me! Have it *your* way. Between you and me, we get along very well, don't we! But the trouble is, others don't think of you just as I do; and that being the case, old man, what a fix you're in! As for me, I say that here, right in front of you, I can see myself with my eyes and touch myself with my fingers. But what are you for other people? What are you in their eyes? An image, my dear sir, just an image in the glass! They're all carrying just such a phantom around inside themselves, and here they are racking their brains about the phantoms in other people; and they think all that is quite another thing!

[*The* BUTLER *has entered the room in time to catch* LAUDISI *gesticulating at himself in the glass. He wonders if the man is crazy.*
*Finally he speaks up.*]

BUTLER. Ahem! . . . Signor Laudisi, if you please . . .

LAUDISI [*coming to himself*]. Uff!

BUTLER. Two ladies calling, sir! Signora Cini and another lady!

LAUDISI. Calling to see me?

BUTLER. Really, they asked for the signora; but I said that she was out—on a call next door; and then . . .

LAUDISI. Well, what then?

BUTLER. They looked at each other and said, "Really! Really!" and finally they asked me if anybody else was at home.

LAUDISI. And of course you said that everyone was out!

BUTLER. I said that you were in!

LAUDISI. Why, not at all! I'm miles and miles away! Perhaps that fellow they call Laudisi is here!

BUTLER. I don't understand, sir.

LAUDISI. Why? You think the Laudisi they know is the Laudisi I am?

BUTLER. I don't understand, sir.

LAUDISI. Who are you talking to?

BUTLER. Who am I talking to? I thought I was talking to you.

LAUDISI. Are you really sure the Laudisi you are talking to is the Laudisi the ladies want to see?

BUTLER. Why, I think so, sir. They said they were looking for the brother of Signora Agazzi.

LAUDISI. Ah, in that case you are right! [*Turning to the image in the glass.*] You are not the brother of Signora Agazzi? No, it's me! [*To the* BUTLER.] Right you are! Tell them I am in. And show them in here, won't you? [*The* BUTLER *retires.*]

SIGNORA CINI. May I come in?

LAUDISI. Please, please, this way, madam!

SIGNORA CINI. I was told Signora Agazzi was not at home, and I brought Signora Nenni along. Signora Nenni is a friend of mine, and she was most anxious to make the acquaintance of . . .

LAUDISI. . . . of Signora Frola?

SIGNORA CINI. Of Signora Agazzi, your sister!

LAUDISI. Oh, she will be back very soon, and Signora Frola will be here, too.

SIGNORA CINI. Yes, we thought as much.

[SIGNORA NENNI *is an oldish woman of the type of* SIGNORA CINI, *but with the mannerisms of the latter somewhat more pronounced. She, too, is a bundle of concentrated curiosity, but of the sly, cautious type, ready to find something frightful under everything.*]

LAUDISI. Well, it's all planned in advance! It will be a most interesting scene! The curtain rises at eleven, precisely!

SIGNORA CINI. Planned in advance? What is planned in advance?

LAUDISI [*mysteriously, first with a gesture of his finger and then aloud*]. Why, bringing the two of them together! [*A gesture of admiration.*] Great idea, I tell you!

SIGNORA CINI. The two of them—together—who?

LAUDISI. Why, the two of them. He—in here! [*Pointing to the room about him.*]

SIGNORA CINI. Ponza, you mean?

LAUDISI. And she—in there! [*He points toward the drawing room.*]

SIGNORA CINI. Signora Frola?

LAUDISI. Exactly! [*With an expressive gesture of his hands and even more mysteriously.*] But afterwards, all of them—in here! Oh, a great idea, a great idea!

SIGNORA CINI. In order to get . . .

LAUDISI. The truth! But it's already known: all that remains is the unmasking.

SIGNORA CINI [*with the greatest surprise*]. Oh, really? So they know the truth! And which is it— He or she?

LAUDISI. Well, I'll tell you . . . you just guess! Who do you think it is?

SIGNORA CINI [*ahemming*]. Well . . . I say . . . really . . . you see . . .

LAUDISI. Is it she or is it he? You don't mean to say you don't know! Come now, give a guess!

SIGNORA CINI. Why, for my part I should say . . . well, I'd say . . . it's *he.*

LAUDISI [*looks at her admiringly*]. Right you are! It *is* he!

SIGNORA CINI. Really? I always thought so! Of course, it was perfectly plain all along. It had to be he!

SIGNORA NENNI. All of us women in town said it was he. We always said so!

SIGNORA CINI. But how did you get it? I suppose Signor Agazzi ran down the documents, didn't he—the birth certificate, or something?

SIGNORA NENNI. Through the prefect, of course! There was no getting away from those people. Once the police start investigating . . . !

LAUDISI [motions to them to come closer to him; then in a low voice and in the same mysterious manner, and stressing each syllable]. The certificate!—Of the second marriage!

SIGNORA CINI [starting back with astonishment]. What?

SIGNORA NENNI [likewise taken aback]. What did you say? The second marriage?

SIGNORA CINI. Well, in that case he was right.

LAUDISI. Oh, documents, ladies, documents! This certificate of the second marriage, so it seems, talks as plain as day.

SIGNORA NENNI. Well, then, she is mad.

LAUDISI. Right! She must be, mustn't she?

SIGNORA CINI. But I thought you said . . .

LAUDISI. Yes, I did say . . . but this certificate of the second marriage may very well be, as Signora Frola said, a fictitious document, gotten up through the influence of Ponza's doctors and friends to pamper him in the notion that his wife was not his first wife, but another woman.

SIGNORA CINI. But it's a public document. You mean to say a public document can be a fraud?

LAUDISI. I mean to say—well, it has just the value that each of you chooses to give it. For instance, one could find somewhere, possibly, those letters that Signora Frola said she gets from her daughter, who lets them down in the basket in the courtyard. There are such letters, aren't there?

SIGNORA CINI. Yes, of course!

LAUDISI. They are documents, aren't they? Aren't letters documents? But it all depends on how you read them. Here comes Ponza, and he says they are just made up to pamper his mother-in-law in her obsession . . .

SIGNORA CINI. Oh, dear, dear, so then we're never sure about anything?

LAUDISI. Never sure about anything? Why not at all, not at all! Let's be exact. We are sure of many things, aren't we? How many days are there in the week? Seven—Sunday, Monday, Tuesday, Wednesday . . . How many months in the year are there? Twelve: January, February, March . . .

SIGNORA CINI. Oh, I see, you're just joking! You're just joking! [DINA appears, breathless, in the doorway, at the rear.]

DINA. Oh, uncle, won't you please . . . [She stops at the sight of SIGNORA CINI.] Oh, Signora Cini, you here?

SIGNORA CINI. Why, I just came to make a call! . . .

LAUDISI. . . . with Signora Cenni.

SIGNORA NENNI. No, my name is Nenni.

LAUDISI. Oh yes, pardon me! She was anxious to make Signora Frola's acquaintance . . .

SIGNORA NENNI. Why, not at all!

SIGNORA CINI. He has just been making fun of us! You ought to see what fools he made of us!

DINA. Oh, he's perfectly insufferable, even with mamma and me. Will you excuse me for just a moment? No, everything is all right. I'll just run back and tell mamma that you people are here and I think that will be enough. Oh, uncle, if you had only heard her talk! Why, she is a perfect *dear*, and what a good, kind soul! . . . She showed us all those letters her daughter wrote . . .

SIGNORA CINI. Yes, but as Signor Laudisi was just saying . . .

DINA. He hasn't even seen them!

SIGNORA NENNI. You mean they are not really fictitious?

DINA. Fictitious nothing! They talk as plain as day. And such things! You can't fool a mother when her own daughter talks to her. And you know—the letter she got yesterday! . . . [*She stops at the sound of voices coming into the study from the drawing room.*] Oh, here they are, here they are, already! [*She goes to the door and peeps into the room.*]

SIGNORA CINI [*following her to the door*]. Is *she* there, too?

DINA. Yes, but you had better come into the other room. All of us women must be in the drawing room. And it is just eleven o'clock, uncle!

AMALIA [*entering with decision from the door on the left*]. I think this whole business is quite unnecessary! We have absolutely no further need of proofs . . .

DINA. Quite so! I thought of that myself. Why bring Ponza here?

AMALIA [*taken somewhat aback by* SIGNORA CINI'S *presence*]. Oh, my dear Signora Cini! . . .

SIGNORA CINI [*introducing* SIGNORA NENNI]. A friend of mine, Signora Nenni! I ventured to bring her with me . . .

AMALIA [*bowing, but somewhat coolly, to the visitor*]. A great pleasure, Signora! [*After a pause.*] There is not the slightest doubt in the world: . . . it's he!

SIGNORA CINI. It's he? Are you sure it's he?

DINA. And such a trick on the poor old lady!

AMALIA. Trick is not the name for it! It's downright dishonest!

LAUDISI. Oh, I agree with you: it's outrageous! Quite! So much so, I'm quite convinced it must be *she!*

AMALIA. She? What do you mean? How can you say that?

LAUDISI. I say, it is *she*, it is *she*, it's *she!*

AMALIA. Oh, I say! If you had heard her talk . . . !

DINA. It is absolutely clear to us now.

SIGNORA CINI and SIGNORA NENNI [*swallowing*]. Really? You are sure?

LAUDISI. Exactly! Now that you are sure it's he, why, obviously—it must be she.

DINA. Oh dear me, why talk to that man? He is just impossible.

AMALIA. Well, we must go into the other room . . . This way, if you please!

[SIGNORA CINI, SIGNORA NENNI *and* AMALIA *withdraw through the door on the left.* DINA *starts to follow, when* LAUDISI *call her back.*]

LAUDISI. Dina!

DINA. I refuse to listen to you! I refuse!

LAUDISI. I was going to suggest that, since the whole matter is closed, you might close the door also.

DINA. But papa . . . he told us to leave it open. Ponza will be here soon; and if papa finds it closed—well, you know how papa is!

LAUDISI. But you can convince him! . . . You especially. You can show him that there really was no need of going any further. You are convinced yourself, aren't you?

DINA. I am as sure of it, as I am that I'm alive!

LAUDISI [*putting her to the test with a smile*]. Well, close the door then!

DINA. I see, you're trying to make me say that I'm not really sure. Well, I won't close the door, but it's just on account of papa.

LAUDISI. Shall I close it for you?

DINA. If you take the responsibility yourself! . . .

LAUDISI. But you see, *I* am sure! I *know* that Ponza is mad!

DINA. The thing for you to do is to come into the other room and just hear her talk a while. Then you'll be sure, absolutely sure. Coming?

LAUDISI. Yes, I'm coming, and I'll close the door behind me—on my own responsibility, of course.

DINA. Ah, I see. So you're convinced even before you hear her talk.

LAUDISI. No, dear, it's because I'm sure that your papa, who has been with Ponza, is just as certain as you are that any further investigation is unnecessary.

DINA. How can you say that?

LAUDISI. Why, of course, if you talk with Ponza, you're sure the old lady is mad. [*He walks resolutely to the door.*] I am going to shut this door.

DINA [*restraining him nervously, then hesitating a moment*]. Well, why not . . . if you're really sure? What do you say—let's leave it open!

LAUDISI [*bursts out laughing*].

DINA. But just because papa told us to!

LAUDISI. And papa will tell you something else by and by. Say . . . let's leave it open!

[*A piano starts playing in the adjoining room—an ancient tune, sweet, graceful, full of pain, from "Nina Mad Through Love" by Paisiello.*]

DINA. Oh, there she is. She's playing! Do you hear? Actually playing the piano!

LAUDISI. The old lady?

DINA. Yes! And you know? She told us that her daughter used to

play this tune, always the same tune. How well she plays! Come! Come!
[THEY *hurry through the door.*]

*The stage, after the exit of* LAUDISI *and* DINA, *remains empty for a
space of time while the music continues from the other room.* PONZA,
*appearing at the door with* AGAZZI, *catches the concluding notes and his
face changes to an expression of deep emotion—an emotion that will
develop into a virtual frenzy as the scene proceeds.*

AGAZZI [*in the doorway*]. After you, after you, please! [*He takes*
PONZA'S *elbow and motions him into the room. He goes over to his desk,
looks about for the papers which he pretends he had forgotten, finds
them eventually and says.*] Why, here they are! I was sure I had left them
here. Won't you take a chair, Ponza? [PONZA *seems not to hear. He stands
looking excitedly at the door into the drawing room, through which the
sound of the piano is still coming.*]

AGAZZI. Yes, they are the ones! [HE *takes the papers and steps to*
PONZA'S *side, opening the folder.*] It is an old case, you see. Been running
now for years and years! To tell you the truth I haven't made head or
tail of the stuff myself. I imagine you'll find it one big mess. [*He, too,
becomes aware of the music and seems somewhat irritated by it. His eyes
also rest on the door to the drawing room.*] That noise, just at this moment! [*He walks with a show of anger to the door.*] Who is that at the
piano anyway? [*In the doorway he stops and looks, and an expression
of astonishment comes into his face.*] Ah!

PONZA [*going to the door also. On looking into the next room he
can hardly restrain his emotion*]. In the name of God, is *she* playing?

AGAZZI. Yes—Signora Frola! And how well she does play!

PONZA. How is this? You people have brought her in here, again!
And you're letting her play!

AGAZZI. Why not? What's the harm?

PONZA. Oh, please, please, no, not that song! It is the one her
daughter used to play.

AGAZZI. Ah, I see! And it hurts you?

PONZA. Oh, no, not me—but her—it hurts her—and you don't
know how much! I thought I had made you and those women understand
just how that poor old lady was!

AGAZZI. Yes, you did . . . quite true! But you see . . . but see here,
Ponza! [*Trying to pacify the man's growing emotion.*]

PONZA [*continuing*]. But you *must* leave her alone! You *must* not go
to her house! She *must* not come in here! I am the only person who can
deal with her. You are killing her . . . killing her!

AGAZZI. No, I don't think so. It is not so bad as that. My wife and
daughter are surely tactful enough . . . [*Suddenly the music ceases.
There is a burst of applause.*]

AGAZZI. There, you see. Listen! Listen!

[*From the next room the following conversation is distinctly heard.*]

DINA. Why, Signora Frola, you are perfectly *marvelous* at the piano!

SIGNORA FROLA. But you should hear how my Lena plays!

[PONZA *digs his nails into his hands.*]

AGAZZI. Her daughter, of course!

PONZA. Didn't you hear? "How my Lena plays! How my Lena *plays!*"

[*Again from inside.*]

SIGNORA FROLA. Oh, no, not now! . . . She hasn't played for a long time—since that happened. And you know, it is what she takes hardest, poor girl!

AGAZZI. Why, that seems quite natural to me! Of course, she thinks the girl is still alive!

PONZA. But she shouldn't be allowed to say such things. She *must* not—she *must* not say such things! Didn't you hear? "She hasn't played since that happened"! She said "she *hasn't* played since that happened"! Talking of the piano, you understand! Oh, you don't understand, no, of course! My first wife had a piano and played that tune. Oh, oh, oh! You people are determined to ruin me!

[SIRELLI *appears at the back door at this moment, and hearing the concluding words of* PONZA *and noticing his extreme exasperation, stops short, uncertain as to what to do.* AGAZZI *is himself very much affected and motions to* SIRELLI *to come in.*]

AGAZZI. Why, no, my dear fellow, I don't see any reason . . . [*To* SIRELLI.] Won't you just tell the ladies to come in here?

[SIRELLI, *keeping at a safe distance from* PONZA, *goes to the door at the left and calls.*]

PONZA. The ladies in here? In here with me? Oh, no, no, please, rather . . .

[*At a signal from* SIRELLI, *who stands in the doorway to the left, his face taut with intense emotion, the* LADIES *enter. They all show various kinds and degrees of excitement and emotion.* SIGNORA FROLA *appears, and catching sight of* PONZA *trembling from head to foot, worked up into a state of positively animal passion, stops, quite overwhelmed. As* HE *assails her during the lines that follow,* SHE *exchanges glances of understanding from time to time with the* LADIES *about her. The action here is rapid, nervous, tense with excitement, and extremely violent.*]

PONZA. You? Here? How is this? You! Here! Again! What are you doing here?

SIGNORA FROLA. Why, I just came . . . don't be cross!

PONZA. You come here to tell these ladies . . . What did you tell these ladies?

SIGNORA FROLA. Nothing! I swear to God, nothing!

PONZA. Nothing? What do you mean, nothing? I heard you with my own ears, and this gentleman here heard you also. You said "she plays."

Who plays? Lena plays! And you know very well that Lena has been dead for four years. Dead, do you hear! Your daughter has been dead—for four years!

SIGNORA FROLA. Yes, yes, I know . . . Don't get excited, my dear . . . Oh, yes, oh yes. I know . . .

PONZA. And you said "she hasn't been able to play since that happened." Of course she hasn't been able to play since that happened. How could she, if she's dead?

SIGNORA FROLA. Why, of course, certainly. Isn't that what I said? Ask these ladies. I said that she hasn't been able to play since that happened. Of course. How could she, if she's dead?

PONZA. And why were you worrying about that piano, then?

SIGNORA FROLA. No, no! I'm not worrying about any piano . . .

PONZA. I broke that piano up and destroyed it. You know that, the moment your daughter died, so that my second wife couldn't touch it. She can't play in any case. You know she doesn't play.

SIGNORA FROLA. Why, of course, dear! Of course! She doesn't know how to play!

PONZA. And one thing more: Your daughter was Lena, wasn't she? Her name was Lena. Now, see here! You just tell these people what my second wife's name is. Speak up! You know very well what her name is! What is it? What is it?

SIGNORA FROLA. Her name is Julia! Yes, yes, of course, my dear friends, her name is Julia! [*Winks at someone in the company.*]

PONZA. Exactly! Her name is Julia, and not Lena! Who are you winking at? Don't you go trying to suggest by those winks of yours that she's not Julia!

SIGNORA FROLA. Why, what do you mean? I wasn't winking! Of course I wasn't!

PONZA. I saw you! I saw you very distinctly! You are trying to ruin me! You are trying to make these people think that I am keeping your daughter all to myself, just as though she were not dead. [*He breaks into convulsive sobbing.*] . . . just as though she were not dead!

SIGNORA FROLA [*hurrying forward and speaking with infinite kindness and sympathy*]. Oh no! Come, come, my poor boy. Come! Don't take it so hard. I never said any such thing, did I, madam!

AMALIA, SIGNORA SIRELLI, DINA. Of course she never said such a thing! She always said the girl was dead! Yes! Of course! No!

SIGNORA FROLA. I did, didn't I? I said she's dead, didn't I? And that you are so very good to me. Didn't I, didn't I? I, trying to ruin you? I, trying to get you into trouble?

PONZA. And you, going into other people's houses where there are pianos, playing your daughter's tunes on them! Saying that Lena plays them that way, or even better!

SIGNORA FROLA. No, it was . . . why . . . you see . . . it was . . . well . . . just to see whether . . .

PONZA. But you *can't* . . . you *mustn't!* How could you ever dream of trying to play a tune that your dead daughter played!

SIGNORA FROLA. You are quite right! . . . Oh, yes! Poor boy! Poor boy! [*She also begins to weep.*] I'll never do it again: Never, never, never again!

PONZA [*advancing upon her threateningly*]. What are you doing here? Get out of here! Go home at once! Home! Home! Go home!

SIGNORA FROLA. Yes, yes! Home! I am going home! Oh dear, oh dear!

[*She backs out the rear door, looking beseechingly at the company, as though urging everyone to have pity on her son-in-law. She retires, sobbing. The others stand there looking at* PONZA *with pity and terror; but the moment* SIGNORA FROLA *has left the room, he regains his normal composure.*]

PONZA. I beg pardon for the sad spectacle I've had to present before all you ladies and gentlemen to remedy the evil which, without wanting, without knowing, you are doing to this unhappy woman— with your compassion.

AGAZZI [*astonished like all the others*]. What? You were only pretending?

PONZA. I had to, my good people! It's the only way to keep up the illusion for her, don't you see? I have to roar out the truth that way—as if it were madness, *my* madness! Forgive me, I must be going, I must go to her. [*He hurries out through the rear door. Once more* THEY *stand astonished and silent looking at each other.*]

LAUDISI [*coming forward*]. And so, ladies and gentlemen, we learn the truth! [*He bursts out laughing*].


## ACT III

*The same scene. As the curtain rises,* LAUDISI *is sprawling in an easy chair, reading a book. Through the door that leads into the parlor on the left comes the confused murmur of many voices.*

*The* BUTLER *appears in the rear door, introducing the police commissioner,* CENTURI. CENTURI *is a tall, stiff, scowling official, with a decidedly professional air. He is in the neighborhood of forty.*

THE BUTLER. This way, sir. I will call Signor Agazzi at once.

LAUDISI [*drawing himself up in his chair and looking around*]. Oh, it's you, Commissioner! [*He rises hastily and recalls the butler, who has stepped out through the door.*] One moment, please, Wait! [*To* CENTURI.] Anything new, Commissioner?

COMMISSIONER [*stiffly*]. Yes, something new!

LAUDISI. Ah! very well. [*To the* BUTLER.] Never mind. I'll call him myself. [*He motions with his hand toward the door on the left. The* BUT-

LER *bows and withdraws*.] You have worked miracles, Commissioner! You're the savior of this town. Listen! Do you hear them! You are the lion of the place! How does it feel to be the father of your country? But say, what you've discovered is all solid fact?

COMMISSIONER. We've managed to unearth a few people.

LAUDISI. From Ponza's town? People who know all about him?

COMMISSIONER. Yes! And we have gathered from them a few facts —not many, perhaps, but well authenticated.

LAUDISI. Ah, that's nice. Congratulations! For example . . .

COMMISSIONER. For example? Why, for instance, here . . . well, here are all the communications I have received. Read 'em yourself! [*From an inner pocket he draws a yellow envelope, opened at one end, from which he takes a document and hands it to* LAUDISI.]

LAUDISI. Interesting, I am sure. Very interesting! . . . [*He stands, reading the document carefully, commenting from time to time with exclamations in different tones. First an "ah" of satisfaction, then another "ah" which attenuates this enthusiasm very much. Finally an "eh" of disappointment, which leads to another "eh" of complete disgust.*] Why, no, what's all this amount to, Commissioner?

COMMISSIONER. Well, it's what we were able to find out.

LAUDISI. But this doesn't prove anything, you understand! It leaves everything just where it was. There's nothing of any significance whatever here. [*He looks at the* COMMISSIONER *for a moment and then, as though suddenly making up his mind, he says:*] I wonder, Commissioner, would you like to do something really great—render a really distinguished service to this town; and meanwhile lay up a treasure in heaven?

COMMISSIONER [*looking at him in perplexity*]. What are you thinking of, sir?

LAUDISI. I'll explain. Here, please, take this chair! [*He sets the chair in front of* AGAZZI's *desk.*] I advise you, Mr. Commissioner, to tear up this sheet of paper that you've brought and which has absolutely no significance at all. But here on this other piece of paper, why don't you write down something that will be precise and clear?

COMMISSIONER. Why . . . why . . . myself? What do you mean? What should I write?

LAUDISI [*insisting*]. Just say something—anything—that these two old acquaintances of Ponza's whom you managed to get hold of might have said. Come, Commissioner, rise to the occasion! Do something for the commonwealth! Bring this town back to normal again! Don't you see what they are after? They all want the truth—*a* truth that is: Something specific; something concrete! They don't care what it is All they want is something categorical, something that speaks plainly! Then they'll quiet down.

COMMISSIONER. *The* truth—*a* truth? Excuse me, have I understood you clearly? You were suggesting that I commit a forgery? I am astonished that you dare propose such a thing, and when I say I am astonished, I'm not saying half what I actually feel. Be so good as to tell the Commendatore that I am here!

LAUDISI [*dropping his arms dejectedly*]. As you will, Commissioner! [*He steps over to the door on the left. As he draws the portières and swings the door more widely open, the voices become louder and more confused. As he steps through, there is a sudden silence. The* POLICE COMMISSIONER *stands waiting with a satisfied air, twirling one of the points of his mustache. All of a sudden, there is commotion and cheering in the next room. Cries of delight and applause, mixed with handclapping. The* POLICE COMMISSIONER *comes out of his reverie and looks up with an expression of surprise on his features, as though not understanding what it's all about. Through the door to the left come* AGAZZI, SIRELLI, LAUDISI, AMALIA, DINA, SIGNORA SIRELLI, SIGNORA CINI, SIGNORA NENNI, *and many other ladies and gentlemen.* AGAZZI *leads the procession. They are all still talking and laughing excitedly, clapping their hands, and crying "I told you so! Fine! Fine! Good! How wonderful! Now we'll know!" etc.*]

AGAZZI [*stepping forward cordially*]. Ah, my dear Centuri, I was sure you could! Nothing ever gets by *our* chief!

COMPANY. Fine! Good! What did you find out! Have you brought something? Is it she? Is it he? Tell us?

COMMISSIONER [*who doesn't yet understand what all the excitement is about. For him it has been a mere matter of routine*]. Why, no . . . why, Commendatore, simply . . . you understand . . .

AGAZZI. Hush! Give him a chance! . . .

COMMISSIONER. I have done my best. I . . . but what did Signor Laudisi tell you?

AGAZZI. He told us that you have brought news, real news!

SIRELLI. Specific data, clear, precise! . . .

LAUDISI [*amplifying*]. . . . not many, perhaps, but well authenticated! The best they've managed to trace! Old neighbors of Ponza, you see; people well acquainted with him . . .

EVERYBODY. Ah! At last! At last! Now we'll know! At last!

[*The* COMMISSIONER *hands the document to* AGAZZI.]

COMMISSIONER. There you have it, Commendatore!

AGAZZI [*opening the sheet, as all crowd around him*]. Let's have a look at it!

COMMISSIONER. But you, Signor Laudisi . . .

LAUDISI. Don't interrupt, please, the document speaks for itself! Agazzi, you read it.

AGAZZI. [*to* LAUDISI]. But give me a chance, won't you? Please! Please! Now! There you are!

LAUDISI. Oh, I don't care. I've read the thing already.

EVERYBODY [*crowding around him*]. You've read it already? What did it say? Is it he? Is it she?

LAUDISI [*speaking very formally*]. There is no doubt whatever, as a former neighbor of Ponza's testifies, that the woman Frola was once in a sanatorium!

THE GROUP [*cries of disappointment*]. Oh really! Too bad! Too bad!

SIGNORA SIRELLI. Signora Frola, did you say?

DINA. Are you sure it was she?

AGAZZI. Why, no! Why, no, it doesn't say anything of the kind. [*Coming forward and waving the document triumphantly.*] It doesn't say anything of the kind! [*General excitement.*]

EVERYBODY. Well, what does it say? What does it say?

LAUDISI [*insisting*]. It does too! It says "the Frola woman"—the Frola woman, categorically.

AGAZZI. Nothing of the kind! The witness says that he *thinks* she was in a sanatorium. He does not assert that she was. Besides, there is another point. He doesn't know whether this Frola woman who was in a sanatorium was the mother or the daughter, the first wife, that is!

EVERYBODY [*with relief*]. Ah!

LAUDISI [*insistingly*]. But I say he does. It must be the mother! Who else could it be?

SIRELLI. No, of course, it's the daughter! It's the daughter!

SIGNORA SIRELLI. Just as the old lady said herself!

AMALIA. Exactly! That time when they took her away by force from her husband! . . .

DINA. Yes, she says that her daughter was taken to a home.

AGAZZI. Furthermore, observe another thing. The witness does not really belong to their town. He says that he used to go there frequently, but that he does not remember particularly. He remembers that he heard something or other! . . .

SIRELLI. Ah! How can you depend on such a man's testimony? Nothing but hearsay!

LAUDISI. But, excuse me! If all you people are so sure that Signora Frola is right, what more do you want? Why do you go looking for documents? This is all nonsense!

SIRELLI. If it weren't for the fact that the prefect has accepted Ponza's side of the story, I'll tell you . . .

COMMISSIONER. Yes, that's true. The prefect said as much to me . . .

AGAZZI. Yes, but that's because the prefect has never talked with the old lady who lives next door.

SIGNORA SIRELLI. You bet he hasn't. He talked only with Ponza.

SIRELLI. But, for that matter, there are other people of the same mind as the prefect.

A GENTLEMAN. That is my situation, my situation exactly. Yes sir! Because I know of just such a case where a mother went insane over the death of her daughter and insists that the daughter's husband will not allow her to see the girl. The same case to a *T*.

A SECOND GENTLEMAN. Not exactly to a T! Not exactly to a T! In the case you mention the man didn't marry again. Here, this man Ponza is living with another woman . . .

LAUDISI [*his face brightening with a new idea that has suddenly come to him*]. I have it, ladies and gentleman! Did you hear that? It's perfectly simple. Dear me, as simple as Columbus's egg!

EVERYBODY. What? What? What? What?

THE SECOND GENTLEMAN. What did I say? I didn't realize it was important.

LAUDISI. Just a moment, ladies and gentlemen! [*Turning to* AGAZZI.] Is the prefect coming here, by chance?

AGAZZI. Yes, we were expecting him. But what's the new idea?

LAUDISI. Why, you were bringing him here to talk with Signora Frola. So far, he is standing by Ponza. When he has talked with the old lady, he'll know whether to believe Ponza or her. That's *your* idea! Well, I've thought of something better that the prefect can do. Something that only he can do.

EVERYBODY. What is it? What is it? What is it?

LAUDISI [*triumphantly*]. Why, this wife of Ponza's, of course . . . at least, the woman he is living with! What this gentleman said suggested the idea to me.

SIRELLI. Get the second woman to talk? Of course! Of course!

DINA. But how can we, when she is kept under lock and key?

SIRELLI. Why, the prefect can use his authority—order her to speak!

AMALIA. Certainly, she is the one who can clear up the whole mystery.

SIGNORA SIRELLI. I don't believe it. She'll say just what her husband tells her to say.

LAUDISI. She must speak before the prefect. Of course!

SIRELLI. She must speak with the prefect privately, all by himself.

AGAZZI. And the prefect, as the final authority over the man, will insist that the wife make a formal explicit statement before him. Of course, of course! What do you say, Commissioner?

COMMISSIONER. Why certainly, there's no doubt that if the prefect were so inclined . . .

AGAZZI. It is the only way out of it, after all. We ought to phone him and explain that he needn't go to the trouble of coming here. You attend to that, will you, Commissioner?

COMMISSIONER. Very glad to! My compliments, ladies! Good afternoon, gentlemen!

SIGNORA SIRELLI. A good idea for once, Laudisi.

DINA. Oh, uncle, how clever of you! Wise old uncle!

THE COMPANY. The only way out of it! Yes! Yes! Fine! At last!

AGAZZI. Curious none of us thought of that before!

SIRELLI. Not so curious! None of us ever set eyes on the woman. She might as well be in another world, poor girl.

LAUDISI [*as though suddenly impressed by this latter reflection*]. In another world? Why yes,—are you really sure there is such a woman?

AMALIA. Oh 1 say! Please, please, Lamberto!

SIRELLI [*with a laugh*]. You mean to say you think there is no such woman?

LAUDISI. How can you be sure there is? You can't guarantee it!

DINA. But the old lady sees her and talks with her every day.

SIGNORA SIRELLI. And Ponza says that, too. They both agree on that point!

LAUDISI. Yes, yes, I don't deny that. But just a moment! To be strictly logical: there must be a phantom in that house.

ALL. A phantom?

AGAZZI. Oh, go on with you!

LAUDISI. Let me finish.—It's the phantom of the second wife, if Signora Frola is right. It's the phantom of the daughter, if Signor Ponza is right. It remains to be seen if what is a phantom for him and her is actually a person for herself. At this point it seems to me there's some reason to doubt it.

AMALIA. Oh, come on! You'd like us all to be as mad as you are!

SIGNORA NENNI. Heavens: how he makes my flesh creep!

SIGNORA CINI. I can't think why you enjoy frightening us like this!

ALL. Nonsense! It's a joke, a joke!

SIRELLI. She's a woman of flesh and bones, rest assured. And we'll have her talk, we'll have her talk!

AGAZZI. You suggested it yourself, didn't you?—having her talk with the prefect?

LAUDISI. Certainly the woman from that house should talk with the prefect—if there is such a woman—and if she *is* a woman!

SIGNORA SIRELLI. Dear me, dear me! That man simply drives me mad.

LAUDISI. Well, supposing we wait and see!

EVERYBODY. Well, who is she then? But people have seen her! His wife! On the balcony! She writes letters!

POLICE COMMISSIONER [*in the heat of the confusion comes into the room, excitedly announcing*]. The prefect is coming! The prefect!

AGAZZI. What do you mean? Coming here? But you went to . . .

COMMISSIONER. Why yes, but I met him hardly a block away. He was coming here; and Ponza is with him.

SIRELLL. Ah, Ponza!

AGAZZI. Oh, if Ponza is with him, I doubt whether he is coming here. They are probably on their way to the old lady's. Please, Centuri, you just wait on the landing there and ask him if he won't step in here as he promised?

COMMISSIONER. Very well! I'll do so! [*He withdraws hurriedly through the door in the rear.*]

AGAZZI. Won't you people just step into the other room?

SIGNORA SIRELLI. But remember now, be sure to make him see the point! It's the only way out, the only way.

AMALIA [*at the door to the left*]. This way, ladies, if you please!

AGAZZI. Won't you just stay here, Sirelli; and you, too, Lamberto?

[*All the others go out through the door to the left.*]

AGAZZI [*to* LAUDISI]. But let me do the talking, won't you!

LAUDISI. Oh, as for that, don't worry. In fact, if you prefer, I'll go into the other room . . .

AGAZZI. No, no, it's better for you to be here. Ah, here he is now!

[THE PREFECT *is a man of about sixty, tall, thick set, good natured, affable.*]

PREFECT. Ah, Agazzi, glad to see you. How goes it, Sirelli? Good to see you again, Laudisi. [*He shakes hands all around.*]

AGAZZI [*motioning toward a chair*]. I hope you won't mind my having asked you to come here.

PREFECT. No, I was coming, just as I promised you!

AGAZZI. [*noticing the* POLICE COMMISSIONER *at the door*]. Oh, I'm sorry, Commissioner! Please come in! Here, have a chair!

PREFECT [*good-naturedly to* SIRELLI]. By the way, Sirelli, they tell me that you've gone half nutty over this blessed affair of our new secretary.

SIRELLI. Oh, no governor, believe me. I'm not the only one! The whole village is worked up.

AGAZZI. And that's putting it very mildly.

PREFECT. What's it all about? What's it all about? Good heavens!

AGAZZI. Of course, governor, you're probably not posted on the whole business. The old lady lives here next door. . . .

PREFECT. Yes, I understand so.

SIRELLI. No, one moment, please, governor. You haven't talked with the poor old lady yet.

PREFECT. I was on my way to see her. [*Turning to* AGAZZI.] I had promised you to see her here, but Ponza came and begged me, almost on his knees, to see her in her own house. His idea was to put an end to all this talk that's going around. Do you think he would have done such a thing if he weren't absolutely sure?

AGAZZI. Of course, he's sure! Because when she's talking in front of him, the poor woman . . .

SIRELLI [*suddenly getting in his oar*]. She says just what he wants her to say, governor; which proves that she is far from being as mad as he claims.

AGAZZI. We had a sample of that, here, yesterday, all of us.

PREFECT. Why, I understand so. You see he's trying all the time to make her believe he's mad. He warned me of that. And how else could he keep the poor woman in her illusion? Do you see any way? All this talk of yours is simply torture to the poor fellow! Believe me, pure torture!

SIRELLI. Very well, governor! But supposing *she* is the one who is trying to keep *him* in the idea that her daughter is dead; so as to reassure him that his wife will not be taken from him again. In that case, you see, governor, it's the old lady who is being tortured, and not Ponza!

AGAZZI. The moment you see the possibility of that, governor . . . Well, you ought to hear her talk; but all by herself, when he's not around. Then you'd see the possibility all right . . .

SIRELLI. Just as we all see it!

PREFECT. Oh, I wonder! You don't seem to me so awfully sure; and for my part, I'm quite willing to confess that I'm not so sure myself. How about you, Laudisi?

LAUDISI. Sorry, governor, I promised Agazzi here to keep my mouth shut.

AGAZZI [*protesting angrily*]. Nothing of the kind! How dare you say that? When the governor asks you a plain question . . . It's true I told him not to talk, but do you know why? He's been doing his best for the past two days to keep us all rattled so that we can't find out anything.

LAUDISI. Don't you believe him, governor. On the contrary. I've been doing my best to bring these people to common sense.

SIRELLI. Common sense! And do you know what he calls common sense? According to him it is not possible to discover the truth; and now he's been suggesting that Ponza is living not with a woman, but with a ghost!

PREFECT [*enjoying the situation*]. That's a new one! Quite an idea! How do you make that out, Laudisi?

AGAZZI. Oh, I say! . . . You know how he is. There's no getting anywhere with him!

LAUDISI. I leave it to you, governor. I was the one who first suggested bringing you here.

PREFECT. And do you think, Laudisi, I ought to see the old lady next door?

LAUDISI. No, I advise no such thing, governor. In my judgment you are doing very well in depending on what Ponza tells you.

PREFECT. Ah, I see! Because you, too, think that Ponza . . .

LAUDISI. No, not at all . . . because I'm also satisfied to have all these people stand on what Signora Frola says, if that does them any good.

AGAZZI. So you see, eh, governor? That's what you call arguing, eh?

PREFECT. Just a moment! Let me understand! [*Turning to* LAUDISI.] So you say we can also trust what the old lady says?

LAUDISI. Of course you can! Implicitly! And so you can depend upon what Ponza says. Implicitly!

PREFECT. Excuse me, I don't follow you!

SIRELLI. But man alive, if they both say the exact opposite of each other! . . .

AGAZZI [*angrily and with heat*]. Listen to me, governor, please. I am prejudiced neither in favor of the old lady nor in favor of Ponza. I recognize that he may be right and that she may be right. But we ought to settle the matter, and there is only one way to do it.

SIRELLI. The way that Laudisi here suggested.

PREFECT. He suggested it? That's interesting? What is it?

AGAZZI. Since we haven't been able to get any positive proof, there is only one thing left. You, as Ponza's final superior, as the man who can fire him if need be, can obtain a statement from his wife.

PREFECT. Make his wife talk, you mean?

SIRELLI. But not in the presence of her husband, you understand.

AGAZZI. Yes, making sure she tells the truth!

SIRELLI. . . . tell whether she's the daughter of Signora Frola, that is, as we think she must be . . .

AGAZZI. . . . or a second wife who is consenting to impersonate the daughter of Signora Frola, as Ponza claims.

PREFECT. . . . and as I believe myself, without a shadow of doubt! [*Thinking a moment.*] Why, I don't see any objection to having her talk. Who could object? Ponza? But Ponza, as I know very well, is more eager than anybody else to have this talk quieted down. He's all upset over this whole business, and said he was willing to do anything I proposed. I'm sure he will raise no objection. So if it will ease the minds of you people here . . . Say, Centuri [*The* POLICE COMMISSIONER *rises*], won't you just ask Ponza to step in here a moment? He's next door with his mother-in-law.

COMMISSIONER. At once, Your Excellency! [*He bows and withdraws through the door at the rear.*]

AGAZZI. Oh well, if he consents . . .

PREFECT. He'll consent, all right. And we'll be through with it in a jiffy. We'll bring her right in here so that you people . . .

AGAZZI. Here, in my house?

SIRELLI. You think he'll let his wife come in here?

PREFECT. Just leave it to me, just leave it to me! I prefer to have her right here because, otherwise you see, you people would always suppose that I and Ponza had . . .

AGAZZI. Oh, please, governor, no! That's not fair!

SIRELLI. Oh, no, governor, we trust you implicitly?

PREFECT. Oh, I'm not offended, not at all. But you know very well that I'm on his side in this matter; and you'd always be thinking that to hush up any possible scandal in connection with a man in my office . . . No, you see. I must insist on having the interview here . . . Where's your wife, Agazzi?

AGAZZI. In the other room, governor, with some other ladies.

PREFECT. Other ladies? Aha, I see! [*Laughing.*] You have a regular detective bureau here, eh? [*The* POLICE COMMISSIONER *enters with* PONZA.]

COMMISSIONER. May I come in? Signor Ponza is here.

PREFECT. Thanks, Centuri. This way, Ponza, come right in! [PONZA *bows.*]

AGAZZI. Have a chair, Ponza. [PONZA *bows and sits down.*]

PREFECT. I believe you know these gentlemen? [PONZA *rises and bows.*]

AGAZZI. Yes, I introduced them yesterday. And this is Laudisi, my wife's brother. [PONZA *bows.*]

PREFECT. I venture to disturb you, my dear Ponza, just to tell you that here with these friends of mine . . . [*At the first words of the prefect,* PONZA *evinces the greatest nervousness and agitation.*]

PREFECT. Was there something you wanted to say, Ponza?

PONZA. Yes, there is something I want to say, governor. I want to present my resignation here and now.

PREFECT. Oh, my dear fellow, I'm so sorry! But just a few moments ago down at the office you were talking . . .

PONZA. Oh, really, this is an outrage, governor! This is just plain persecution, plain persecution!

PREFECT. Oh, now, don't take it that way, old man. See here. These good people . . .

AGAZZI. Persecution, did you say? On my part? . . .

PONZA. On the part of all of you! And I am sick and tired of it! I am going to resign, governor. I refuse to submit to this ferocious prying into my private affairs which will end by undoing a work of love that has cost me untold sacrifice these past two years. You don't know, governor! Why, I've treated that dear old lady in there just as tenderly as though she were my own mother. And yesterday I had to shout at her in the most cruel and terrible way! Why, I found her just now so worked up and excited that . . .

AGAZZI. That's queer! While she was in her Signora Frola was quite mistress of herself. If anybody was worked up, Ponza, it was you. And even now, if I might say . . .

PONZA. But you people don't know what you're making me go through!

PREFECT. Oh, come, come, my dear fellow, don't take it so hard. After all, I'm here, am I not? And you know I've always stood by you! And I always will!

PONZA. Yes, governor, and I appreciate your kindness, really!

PREFECT. And then you say that you're as fond of this poor old lady as you would be if she were your own mother. Well, now, just remember that these good people here seem to be prying into your affairs because they, too, are fond of her! . . .

PONZA. But they're killing her, I tell you, governor! They're killing her, and I warned them in advance.

PREFECT. Very well, Ponza, very well! Now we'll get through with this matter in no time. See here, it is all very simple. There is one way that you can convince these people without the least doubt in the world. Oh, not me—I don't need convincing. I believe *you*.

PONZA. But *they* won't believe me, no matter what I say.

AGAZZI. That's not so! When you came here after your mother-in-law's first visit and told us that she was mad, all of us . . . well, we were surprised, but we believed you. [*Turning to the* PREFECT.] But after he left, you understand, the old lady came back . . .

PREFECT. Yes, yes, I know. He told me. [*Turning to* PONZA *again.*] She came back here and said that she was trying to do with you exactly what you say you were trying to do with her. It's natural, isn't it, that people hearing both stories, should be somewhat confused. Now you see that these good people, in view of what your mother-in-law says, can't possibly be sure of what you say. So there you are. Now, such being the case, you and your mother-in-law—why, it's perfectly simple—you two just step aside. Now you know you're telling the truth, don't you? So do I! So you can't possibly object to their hearing the testimony of the only person who does know, aside from you two.

PONZA. And who may that be, pray?

PREFECT. Why, your wife!

PONZA. My wife! [*Decisively and angrily.*] Ah, no! I refuse! Never in the world! Never!

PREFECT. And why not, old man?

PONZA. Bring my wife here to satisfy the curiosity of these strangers?

PREFECT [*sharply*]. And my curiosity, too, if you don't mind! What objection can you have?

PONZA. Oh, but governor, no! My wife! Here? No! Why drag my wife in? These people ought to believe me!

PREFECT. But don't you see, my dear fellow, that the course you're taking now is just calculated to discredit what you say?

AGAZZI. His mistake in the first place, governor, was trying to prevent his mother-in-law from coming here and calling—a double discourtesy, mark you, to my wife and to my daughter!

PONZA. But what in the name of God do you people want of me? You've been nagging and nagging at that poor old woman next door; and now you want to get your clutches on my wife! No, governor! I refuse to submit to such an indignity! She owes nothing to anybody. My wife is not making visits in this town. You say you believe me, governor? That's enough for me! Here's my resignation! I'll go out and look for another job!

PREFECT. No, no, Ponza, I must speak plainly. In the first place I have always treated you on the square; and you have no right to speak in that tone of voice to me. In the second place you are beginning to make me doubt your word by refusing to furnish me—not other people—but me, the evidence that I have asked for in your interest, evidence, moreover, that so far as I can see, cannot possibly do you any harm. It seems to me that my colleague here, Signor Agazzi, can ask a lady to come to his house! But no, if you prefer, we'll go and see her.

PONZA. So you really insist, governor?

PREFECT. I insist, but as I told you, in your own interest. You realize, besides, that I might have the legal right to question her . . .

PONZA. I see, I see! So that's it! An official investigation! Well, why not, after all? I will bring my wife here, just to end the whole matter. But how can you guarantee me that this poor old lady next door will not catch sight of her?

PREFECT. Why, I hadn't thought of that! She does live right next door.

AGAZZI [speaking up]. We are perfectly willing to go to Signor Ponza's house.

PONZA. No, no, I was just thinking of you people. I don't want you to play any more tricks on me. Any mistakes might have the most frightful consequences, set her going again!

AGAZZI. You're not very fair to us, Ponza, it seems to me.

PREFECT. Or you might bring your wife to my office, rather . . .

PONZA. No, no! Since you're going to question her anyway, we might as well get through with it. We'll bring her here, right here. I'll keep an eye on my mother-in-law myself. We'll have her here right away, governor, and get an end of this nonsense once and for all, once and for all! [He hurries away through the rear exit.]

PREFECT. I confess I was not expecting so much opposition on his part.

AGAZZI. Ah, you'll see. He'll go and cook up with his wife just what she's to say!

PREFECT. Oh, don't worry as to that! I'll question the woman myself.

SIRELLI. But he's more excited than he's ever been before.

PREFECT. Well, I confess I never saw him just in this state of mind. Perhaps it is the sense of outrage he feels in having to bring his wife . . .

SIRELLI. In having to let her loose for once, you ought to say!

PREFECT. A man isn't necessarily mad because he wants to keep an eye on his wife.

AGAZZI. Of course he says it's to protect her from the mother-in-law.

PREFECT. I wasn't thinking of just that—he may be jealous of the woman!

SIRELLI. Jealous to the extent of refusing her a servant? For you know, don't you, he makes his wife do all the housework?

AGAZZI. And he does all the marketing himself every morning.

COMMISSIONER. That's right, governor! I've had him shadowed. An errand boy from the market carries the stuff as far as the door.

SIRELLI. But he never lets the boy inside.

PREFECT. Dear me, dear me! He excused himself for that servant business when I took the matter up with him.

LAUDISI. And that's information right from the source!

PREFECT. He says he does it to save money.

LAUDISI. He has to keep two establishments on one salary.

SIRELLI. Oh, we weren't criticizing how he runs his house; but I ask you as a matter of common sense: he is a man of some position, and do you think that this second wife of his, as he calls her, who ought to be a lady, would consent to do all the work about the house? . . .

AGAZZI. The hardest and most disagreeable work, you understand . . .

SIRELLI. . . . just out of consideration for the mother of her husband's first wife?

AGAZZI. Oh, I say, governor, be honest now! That doesn't seem probable, does it?

PREFECT. I confess it does seem queer . . .

LAUDISI. . . . in case this second woman is an ordinary woman!

PREFECT. Yes, but let's be frank. It doesn't seem reasonable. But yet, one might say—well, you could explain it as generosity on her part, and even better, as jealousy on his part. Mad or not mad, there is no denying that he's jealous!

[*A confused clamor of voices is heard from the next door.*]

AGAZZI. My, I wonder what's going on in there!

[AMALIA *enters from the door on the left in a state of great excitement.*]

AMALIA. Signora Frola is here!

AGAZZI. Impossible! How in the world did she get in? Who sent for her?

AMALIA. Nobody! She came of her own accord!

PREFECT. Oh, no, please—just a moment! No! Send her away, madam, please!

AGAZZI. We've got to get rid of her. Don't let her in here! We must absolutely keep her out!

[SIGNORA FROLA *appears at the door on the left, trembling, beseeching, weeping, a handkerchief in her hand. The people in the next room are crowding around behind her.*]

SIGNORA FROLA. Oh, please, please! You tell them, Signor Agazzi! Don't let them send me away!

AGAZZI. But you must go away, madam! We simply can't allow you to be here now!

SIGNORA FROLA [*desperately*]. Why? Why? [*Turning to* AMALIA.] I appeal to you, Signora Agazzi.

AMALIA. But don't you see? The prefect is there! They're having an important meeting.

SIGNORA FROLA. Oh, the prefect! Please, governor, please! I was intending to go and see you.

PREFECT. No, I am so sorry, madam. I can't see you just now! You must go away!

SIGNORA FROLA. Yes, I am going away. I am going to leave town this very day! I am going to leave town and never come back again!

AGAZZI. Oh, we didn't mean that, my dear Signora Frola. We meant that we couldn't see you here, just now, in this room. Do me a favor, please! You can see the governor by and by.

SIGNORA FROLA. But why? I don't understand! What's happened!

AGAZZI. Why, your son-in-law will soon be here! There, now do you see?

SIGNORA FROLA. Oh, he's coming here? Oh, yes, in that case . . . Yes, yes, . . . I'll go! But there was something I wanted to say to you people. You must stop all this. You must let us alone. You think you are helping me. You are trying to do me a favor; but really, what you're doing is working me a great wrong. I've got to leave town this very day because he must not be aroused. What do you want of him anyway? What are you trying to do to him? Why are you having him come here? Oh, Mr. Governor . . .

PREFECT. Come, Signora Frola, don't worry, don't worry. I'll see you by and by and explain everything. You just step out now, won't you?

AMALIA. Please, Signora Frola . . . yes, that's right! Come with me!

SIGNORA FROLA. Oh, my dear Signora Agazzi, you are trying to rob me of the one comfort I had in life, the chance of seeing my daughter once in a while, at least from a distance! [*She begins to weep.*]

PREFECT. What in the world are you thinking of? We are not asking you to leave town. We just want you to leave this room, for the time being. There, now do you understand?

SIGNORA FROLA. But it's on his account, governor . . . it's on his account I was coming to ask you to help him! It was on his account, not on mine!

PREFECT. There, there, everything will be all right. We'll take care of him. And we'll have this whole business settled in a jiffy.

SIGNORA FROLA. But how . . . how can I be sure? I can see that everybody here hates him. They are trying to do something to him.

PREFECT. No, no, not at all! And even if they were, I would look after him. There, there, don't worry, don't worry!

SIGNORA FROLA. Oh, so you believe him? Oh, thank you; thank you, sir! That means that at least *you* understand!

PREFECT. Yes, yes, madam, I understand, I understand! And I cautioned all these people here. It's a misfortune that came to him long, long ago. He's all right now! He's all right now!

SIGNORA FROLA. . . . Only he must not go back to all those things.

PREFECT. You're right, you're quite right, Signora Frola, but as I told you, I understand!

SIGNORA FROLA. Yes, governor, that's it! If he compels us to live this way—well, what does it matter. That doesn't do anybody any harm so long as we're satisfied, and my daughter is happy this way. That's enough for me, and for her! But you'll look after us, governor. They mustn't spoil anything. Otherwise there's nothing left for me except to leave town and never see her again—never, not even from a distance. You must not irritate him. You must leave him alone. Oh, please!

[*At this moment a wave of surprise, anxiety, dismay, sweeps over the company. Everybody falls silent and turns to the door. Suppressed exclamations are audible.*]

VOICES. Oh! Oh! Look! There she is! Oh! Oh!

SIGNORA FROLA [*noticing the change in people, and groaning, all of a tremble*]. What's the matter? What's the matter?

[*The COMPANY divides to either hand. A LADY has appeared at the door in back. She is dressed in deep mourning and her face is concealed with a thick, black, impenetrable veil.*]

SIGNORA FROLA [*uttering a piercing shriek of joy*]. Oh, Lena! Lena! Lena! Lena!

[*She dashes forward and throws her arms about the veiled woman with the passionate hysteria of a mother who has not embraced her daughter for years and years. But at the same time from beyond the door in the rear another piercing cry comes. PONZA dashes into the room.*]

PONZA. No! Julia! Julia! Julia!

[*At his voice SIGNORA PONZA draws up stiffly in the arms of SIGNORA FROLA who is clasping her tightly. PONZA notices that his mother-in-law is thus desperately entwined about his wife and he shrieks desperately.*]

PONZA. Cowards! Liars! I knew you would! I knew you would! It is just like the lot of you!

SIGNORA PONZA [*turning her veiled head with a certain austere solemnity toward her husband*]. Don't be afraid! Just take her away! Go!

[SIGNORA FROLA, *at these words, turns to her son-in-law and humbly, tremblingly, goes over and embraces him.*]

SIGNORA FROLA. Yes, yes, you poor boy, come with me, come with me!

[*Their arms about each other's waists, and holding each other up affectionately, PONZA and his mother-in-law withdraw through the rear door. They are both weeping. Profound silence in the company. ALL those present stand there with their eyes fixed upon the departing couple. As SIGNORA FROLA and PONZA are lost from view, all eyes turn expectantly upon the veiled lady. Some of the women are weeping.*]

SIGNORA PONZA [*having looked at them through her veil, speaking with dark solemnity*]. What else do you want of me, after this, ladies and gentlemen? There is a misfortune here, as you see, which must stay hidden: otherwise the remedy which our compassion has found cannot avail.

THE PREFECT [*moved*]. We want to respect your compassion, madam. It's only that we'd like you to tell us . . .

SIGNORA PONZA [*slowly, and with clear articulation*]. Tell you what? The truth? Simply this: I am the daughter of Signora Frola . . .

ALL [*with a happy intake of breath*]. Ah!

SIGNORA PONZA. . . . and the second wife of Signor Ponza . . .

ALL [*amazed and disenchanted, quietly*]. . . . What?

SIGNORA PONZA [*continuing*]. . . . and, for myself, I am nobody!

THE PREFECT. No, no, madam, for yourself you must be either one or the other!

SIGNORA PONZA. No! I am she whom you believe me to be. [*She looks at them all through her veil for a moment, then leaves. Silence.*]

LAUDISI. And there, my friends, you have the truth! [*With a look of derisive defiance at them all.*] Are you satisfied? [*He bursts out laughing.*]

# CHAPTER TWO

# Prostitution:
# Hustling to Make a Living

The problem of establishing the reality of a social scene is made vivid in the following excerpt from *One Hundred Dollar Misunderstanding*. The basic problem reflected in the reading is one of how societal members acquire an understanding of "what's really going on." The need to achieve a "reciprocity of standpoints and relevances,"[1] or the ability to appreciate the other person's perspective by "putting yourself in his shoes," is in the final analysis a precondition for understanding the social meaning of social actions.

In the following selection, a Northern, white, middle-class fraternity boy faces the problem in trying to understand and communicate with a Southern, black, lower-class prostitute. In a formal sense both share the same constraints. They are ethnic-bound, sex-bound, language-bound, class-bound, regionally-bound, and culture-bound, all of which lead to a "hundred dollar misunderstanding." The problems of the fraternity boy in understanding the prostitute are similar to those of the sociologist or anthropologist (particularly those of the participant-observation school) in trying to understand the social meanings of social actions. Indeed the fraternity boy, in anticipating the need to neutralize (for himself and others) his deviant behavior (patronizing a whore house in the black ghetto), provides himself with the moral justification of his

[1] Alfred Schutz, *Collected Papers*, vol. 1, *The Problem of Social Reality* (The Hague: Martinus Nijhoff, 1962), p. 11.

intended deviance by convincing himself that he is acting, not in the role of a white, middle-class college student, but rather as a "cultural anthropologist." This particular rationalization, while providing an amusing literary aside, is also, sociologically speaking, very apt. We are all cast into the role of cultural anthropologists when it comes to the crucial task of imputing social meanings to the social actions of others.

*One Hundred Dollar Misunderstanding* should be viewed not as one, but as a series, of misunderstandings, each of which was being evaluated by both parties as it occurred, and later reevaluated, retrospectively, in an ongoing fashion. What one "really means" by a particular act in a particular circumstance at a particular time, is interpreted by the second party, not only with reference to that isolated event, but with respect to the interpretation he has given to his preceding encounters with the individual in question (or others "like him"). Conversely, all preceding encounters are reflexively evaluated with respect to the meaning one imputes to the current situation, "Oh, now I see what he (or it) was all along."[2]

It is through this process of interpretation that the social meanings of social actions are established and reestablished by the individual. The virtue of the following reading is that it offers (from the perspective of the student and the prostitute) what each is thinking about the same situation and how the discrepancies in perception (stemming from the constraints outlined above) are resolved at any given point to the temporary satisfaction of both. One's ability to achieve in everyday life the state of affairs outlined above may be seen as a precondition for the establishment and maintenance of meaningful social relationships. Failure to achieve this condition would lead one to live in the fragmented, unpredictable, nonsensible world of madness.

It is also interesting to note how each deviant in the following readings works to neutralize his own deviance and at the same time establishes the deviant character of the other. This procedure is not peculiar to persons in deviant situations. Normal persons also "rationalize" their morally questionable behavior, often establishing their respectability with reference to someone who is "really deviant."[3] The reader is

---

[2] For a discussion of "Reflexivity," see Harold Garfinkel, *Studies in Ethnomethodology* (Englewood Cliffs, N.J.: Prentice-Hall, 1967), pp. 9–10.

[3] Emile Durkheim makes this point in his discussion of "normal crime" in *The Rules of Sociological Method* (New York: Free Press, 1964), pp. 64–73.

urged to appreciate the universality of the above process. It is to Gover's credit that he recognized it, for all good literature and sociology have recognized and incorporated in one form or another the interactional processes noted above. In sociology, it has been a central concern of what has come to be referred to as the interactionist perspective.


# ROBERT GOVER

## *One Hundred Dollar Misunderstanding*

Immediately, right off the bat, without further ado, here and now, I wish to say that much of what happened to me that fateful weekend is completely unprintable, since it happened with a lady (colored) of ill repute. So all pornography-seekers are warned to seek elsewhere. I wish to make that point quite clear before proceeding further.

(Especially since Dad is chairman of our town's obscenity board so is well acquainted with the general subject and has impressed upon me the immense harm obscenity might do this great nation.) (Not that I'm a prude. Far from it! But nor am I a conveyor of illicit images and user of four-letter words and the mails to defraud.)

I mean, I plan to keep the telling of these unlikely events on as high a literary *plain* as I'm able, fully aware of my own shortcomings as I attempt this. After all, I'm a college sophomore, not a paid professional writer. You may ask why I didn't tell my experience to a paid professional ghost writer and have him write it for me. Well, I have a very good reason for that. I mean, for why I didn't do that. You see, I wish to remain anonymous for reasons which may or may not become clear to the reader, but are indeed clear to me. Only my legal initials will be used, but lots of others go by the same initials, so you'll never track me down from them.

So, to begin at the beginning, as they say, let me say that. . . .

Well, first of all, on Friday, we got our mid-term grades and I found I was flunking three—repeat three—subjects (biology, psychology, French) and so the second half of that semester was going to be heck, sheer heck.

Second, Barbara, who is my steady girl friend, telephoned to tell me she received a telegram telling her to come home immediately, that her grandmother had died. Which proved coincidental.

You see, I also received a letter from my grandmother and found in it a check for $100—a little birthday present. A bit late, yes, but better late than never, as they say.

Third, Dad called to say he was unable to bring me the Chevy for the weekend as per our previous agreement, that he had been urged by the hospital administration to attend some convention or clinic or something in Cleveland or some god-forsaken place like that, and Mom needed the stationwagon, having planned for months to attend her annual bridge tournament in Boston, and that left the Caddy, which is only used for special occasions and which I couldn't get home to get anyway.

No car, no girl, and that second half semester staring me in the face! I was in poor condition, I can tell you. I mean, I was depressed— psychologically depressed!

You see—I've completely neglected to mention—it was the weekend of the big frat formal. It was *the* weekend of all weekends. And this year, Christmas! The formal was scheduled to be held at the Sheldon Country Club, no less—the swankiest place in town.

Some of the brothers tried to cheer me up by saying they could fix me up with a blind date, some freshman, and I could travel with my roommate, Hank, in his car, certainly. But . . . I was feeling just too too low. I mean! A man can weather a little ill fortune once in a while, but a triple whammy like that was too psychologically depressing. I was in *no mood!*

I mean, it was that psychological depression—that was the trouble. That's what led to all my difficulties. That and all the stuff I'd been hearing.

The thing is, I didn't have to flunk those subjects. I mean I'm not a stupe, by a long shot. As for the other two strokes of misfortune . . . Well, I was entirely a victim of circumstances.

Anyway, about nine o'clock that evening I found myself sitting there in that fraternity house completely by myself. Everyone else was either at the big dance or had gone home. There I was, in front of the TV in the livingroom, all alone. And that started me thinking, being alone.

It was probably Hank, who is always trying to fill my head with lewd thoughts, beating and beating his filthy obscenities into my mind. (I never asked to have him for a roommate. I barely knew him before I moved in. They just assigned me to a room and there he was.) He's constantly running off with a bunch of the brothers to some Negro house of ill repute, saying—and I repeat this one bit of smut only to show what sort of fellows I've been forced to live with—they're going to get their *ashes hauled!* That's a way of saying they're going to pay and then make love (or, I should say, fornicate) with some Negro. They think that little phrase they use is pretty funny. One night they sat around for over an hour and talked about nothing but. That phrase, I mean. One brother (he's a jerk) said he thought it was a sort of poetry. (Good grief!)

What I'm trying to say is I'm constantly subjected to this kind of talk. It's constantly being beaten and beaten into my ears. And Hank (who calls me Soph O'More, and thinks he's being funny because—so *he* says—sophomore once meant Wise Fool) (but he's never proven that statement with hard cold facts)—Hank is forever telling me I should go and have my ashes hauled.

Well, after making a great and sustained effort to respond as little as possible to that foul suggestion, I gave up and told him why I thought I shouldn't.

There are two very good reasons, too. Why I shouldn't, I mean. One, as I've already mentioned, is that Dad is a member of our town's obscenity board. Chairman, no less. And if word ever got back to him that I'd done, or even contemplated doing such a thing, well . . . I'm not sure exactly what would happen, but I am sure it wouldn't be good.

The other reason is that—contrary to what some of these brothers around here think—I'm no prude and have myself a couple of very good *un*professional ladies of ill repute (though that isn't really what they're called, ha ha) back home.

But when I finally did get around to telling Hank about them, he countered by laughing and saying I'd never be a man until— Well, I won't say it the way he did. What he meant was that I must miscegenate before I can consider myself much of anything. Which I know is entirely fantastic, a horrid idea and utterly ridiculous, unfounded on hard cold fact, unsubstantiated—an old wives' tale, for gosh sakes! No, I don't mean *wives* exactly. I mean it's just another obscenity like ashes hauled. And I, of course, realize this full well. As for my masculinity, I pointed out to Hank that my chest is very hairy and his hasn't a hair on it— not one! He tried to defend against this concrete evidence by laughing his same old deluded laugh, and also by sticking to his silly miscegenation as a criterion.

So please, Dear Reader, get this picture: Here I am sitting in front of this TV all alone in that empty frat house, left without a date, without a car, flunking at midterms three subjects—biology, psychology, French —stranded miles from home in this god-forsaken town with nothing but a little extra cash, feeling extremely psychologically depressed. I mean, this picture is important!

That and what Hank is always saying. I mean, he also talks as if the Negro is sexually superior to the Whiteman, for gosh sakes! *Then,* he tries to say *that* isn't what he *means!* I mean, when I point this out— when I tell him that, in effect, is what he is trying to tell me—he *denies* it. I keep trying to tell him how cockeyed his idea is, but he keeps insisting *superior* isn't what he means, and I keep trying to tell him superior is exactly the false conception he has, and he keeps trying to deny this, so I never do get my point across.

And to top things off, Hank, for gosh sakes, has amply demonstrated—though he won't admit this either—the extreme psychotic degree of confusion to which he and other brothers have gone by once saying that we live—and I now quote directly—in a state of whoredom—unquote. This, I was quick to mention, was an attempt to temper by rationalization the fact that he enters frequently into the sort of commerce transacted in non-white houses of ill repute.

But—like Max Shulman in those clever cigarette advertisements—I digress.

About nine o'clock, I thought: James Cartwright Holland, Holy Christmas! (An assumed name, as I mentioned earlier, though J. C. are, as a matter of hard cold fact, my initials.) (Sometimes I take an awful ribbing because of those two actual initials, as any quick-witted reader might readily guess, but I assure you they're actually legally mine.) I thought: Aren't things bad enough without sitting around thinking about them?

Then all the stories I'd been subjected to about this Negro house of ill repute (located in this red-light district with other houses, some of which have Whitegirls, for crying out loud!) all these stories got the best of me and I decided to take a look for myself.

I mean, I certainly never intended to go fornicate with some paid professional woman of either race, I just meant to take a look for myself. I thought: When I return, I'll have an even clearer idea of what I'm talking about, so that next time I find myself in a discussion with Hank, I'll be even better prepared.

(As it actually turned out, my knowledge certainly was intensely deepened.)

So I checked my wallet ($135 in all) and took off for a night on the town. What I had in mind was going to this one bar the brothers are always going to when they have nothing better to do, where they have this jazz combo everyone says is very good, and where they also have paid professional ladies of ill repute floating about, sort of, because it's right smack dab in the middle of this red-light district. So I did. I went there. I took a taxi and went.

This place—it's called the Black-n-Tan—was, well, I don't know how to describe it. I wish I was (were) a writer so I could do it justice. (I mean a paid professional writer, of course, ha ha.) To begin with, it was jam-packed. It took me half an hour to work my way to the bar and then I got lucky and jumped onto a stool the moment some fellow left it. There seemed to be a lot of students in that place, but I didn't see anyone I recognized, so after awhile I relaxed and inspected the place. I just sat and listened and looked around.

I don't know much about jazz. I'll admit it—I don't. All I could tell was that one minute it was very loud and the next it wasn't. And it wasn't the sort of jazz you hear played on the radio. Also, the musicians (colored) seemed completely lost in what they were playing, and I could see where they would be. I couldn't tell where what ended and what began.

The only thing I could conclude was that this type of jazz just wasn't *normal.*

But the people in that place! Wow! I'd never seen such a motley collection of people. In one place at one time, I mean. There was black and white and every shade in between. I even saw two Chinese students and a Chinese girl. And Christmas! At one end of the bar sat these two dolls—and I mean *dolls*—who were non-white, but pretty nevertheless. One had blonde hair for gosh sakes! No doubt she dyed it, of course. And there was this guy with these two girls (you could tell he was with them by the way he would lean over and talk to them) this big, very-Negro guy dressed in an Ivy League suit and sitting there looking around as if he were looking for someone, expecting to see someone he knew. As a matter of fact, our eyes happened to meet once, while I was giving those girls the once-over, and he stared me down. Not only that, but the next time I looked up, there he was staring at me again. Christmas! He gave me the creeps! I don't mean he gave me dirty looks; I mean he kept looking as if we'd met some place and he suddenly recognized me. *Me,* for gosh sakes!

I was forced to conclude the two colored girls were paid professionals and he was sort of their solicitor, so to speak. (I'm aware that there's another word for what he was, but I'm trying to keep this factual narrative on a high plain.)

Though it's difficult, because the very next thing I knew, I was being tapped on the shoulder and when I turned around, here was some beady-eyed character (colored) staring at me. He said (and you may not believe this, but he actually said it): 'Looking for a date?'

'Certainly not!' I quickly responded. (To tell the truth, I wasn't sure, at that moment, what he meant exactly, and was tempted to give him a taste of my knuckles, just in case.)

Then he said, 'Got some fine girls, right around the corner.'

Which clarified things. Somewhat.

But I said, 'No. No thank you.'

He said, 'Just looking around?'

And I said, 'Well . . . yes. As a matter of fact, I am just looking around.' Which, of course, was true.

'Okay,' he said, and moved on. He sort of shoved his way through the crowd along behind the stools. I watched him for a time, thinking: Well, James Cartwright Holland, you've seen yourself a real one for sure. It's official. (And I won't say what! But I became certain of my observations when he stopped a few stools from mine and tapped another fellow who looked like a university student.)

Well, that's the way it works. Enough said.

I went back to looking and listening, and hadn't been doing this long before the beady-eyed character returned. This time, all he did was tap and when I swung around, stared at me with this comical grin on his face. I thought: Well, after all, no one here knows me and I have yet to see the inside of a house of ill repute. What the heck! Question: Who would be the wiser? Answer: Me!

So I said, 'Where are your girls?'

And he started mumbling directions, which I didn't catch until I had him repeat them. I was to go out, turn left, walk to the corner and turn right, and the place was three doors down on the right.

The whole thing seemed just too fantastic. I mean, I know such things go on elsewhere. But America! I'd always thought America was such a decent country. But then, even in the most decent country, the danger of moral cancer, as Dad calls it, is ever present. And don't get me wrong. I was not, for gosh sakes, diseased! I was curious. I mean, I owed this little excursion to my education, so to speak.

So feeling very much like Dad must feel when he has to inspect things or places for indecency, I went. I mean, I felt like a detective. That's how I felt. I just adopted a very scientifically objective viewpoint on the entire matter and went. And my feeling of detecting increased handsomely when I discovered I was hot on the heels of two other university students.

But wow! What a neighborhood! I mean, I found myself deep in the heart of a slum area with inadequate housing and all that. I mean, they show pictures on TV of blighted areas and tell how they need more money for slum clearance and urban renewal, but gosh! They can't give you the sounds and smells on TV.

I'll try. (After adding that I walked slowly—past some pretty ugly-looking Negro men, just standing around doing nothing—walked slowly to let those other two students get ahead of me.) Right off the bat, as soon as I turned off the avenue onto the sidestreet—Bamb!

No lights!

In fact, there was only one streetlight the whole length of that block, for crying out loud! It shone down over a vacant lot right across the street from where I stood (on the corner).

Well, I was about to go back and catch a taxi and take off for the frat house again, when I saw a sudden ray of light, and then those two college guys going in through a doorway—from which came the light, of course. Then I thought: Come come, JC, you're not going to be frightened off by darkness, for gosh sakes! Are you?

And right about here, I almost had a heart attack! There, right in the middle of that vacant lot, was this figure of a man. It would lean down and stand up and walk a step or two, then lean down again. I hadn't noticed him before, but there he was, all right. A rag picker, or something like that. Certainly a person of which to be leery. And, I can tell you, that, in spite of my scientific viewpoint, I was just that—leery.

So leery, in fact, that I began to worry about which door was the correct one to the ill repute house. I thought: Christmas, JC! Suppose you knock on the wrong door. Good gosh, in this neighborhood, no tell-ing what might happen!

But I recovered from the sight of that dark and dismal figure of a bum picking about in that vacant lot (the police should have been noti-fied, I realize), and went bravely forward. I thought: JC my friend you'll see the inside of an ill repute house if it's the last thing you ever do. And since you've come this far, you might as well keep up your courage and go on.

I did. Listening, all the time I was going bravely onward, to the most eerie-sounding barking dogs I'd ever heard. I mean, dogs barking here, there, everywhere. Not right where I was, exactly. But not so far away either. I couldn't be sure exactly where, I mean.

And, also, as referred to above, there were smells. Smells which you don't even get on TV public service programs. And a good thing, too, because they weren't very pleasant smells. It smelled dank, sort of. Like a mixture of wet earth and rotting lumber. It made me shudder, I can tell you. The whole place—that entire neighborhood made me shudder.

Still, I continued forging ahead. I marched. I said to myself, *Hup* two three four, *Hup* two three four, and marched! So that I finally made it to the third door from the corner, walked (marched) up the rotting wooden steps, and—Bamb!

Here goes me, I'm in the big chair. In come this trick by hisself. College Joe. I kin tell them anywhere.

She-it! This one walk like he ain got no toes. Jittery? Kee-ryess is he jittery.

Jackie an Carmie upstairs wiff two tricks jes come in a minit fore this one. On'y hiyellas leff is Flow an Francine, so I spect this mothah gonna go up wiff Flow.

That godam Francine been botherin me agen, sittin on the arm o' the big chair an messin roun.

Madam tell this jittery Whiteboy we is all the cats they is jes now, an everybody waitin fer him t'pick one o'us. But he jes standin there, lookin roun the sittin room like he think more girls gonna come outta the walls.

I say t'myseff, Girl you gotta git yer Friday night cherry broke sometime, might jes's well try an hussle this jittery Joe. So I smile.

He lookin roun dum, my smile catch his eye an he smile back. Jes a lil ol bashful smile, like he fraid it gonna break his face, he smile fer real.

I smile agen an try lookin Pickaninny pritty, an he smile agen.

Madam see him smilin, she jes touch him on the back an send him on his way.

Nex, Gee-zuz! Francine stan up. She think alla time this daddio been smilin at her. She think he's fixin t'go up wiff her. Yeah! He so gee-gee jittery an all, she guess she gonna git his gun wiffout hardly no work. She likes them jittery tricks cause they pop fast, give her a chance t'jackoff an piss roun while us other cats go on workin.

But I stan up too. Yeah! An he nod t'me.

I say, Come on, pritty baby, we go upstairs.

He comin. He okay. Dress like he got loot. I sat t'myseff, Girl maybe this trick like you enuff t'give you a pers'nal tip. Yeah! He dress like he got the jack fer tippin..

I say, This way, prittyboy.

Fore I swing on up, I look back at Francine an she lookin mean. Piss on Francine! I say t'myseff, I say, Keep a pucker' pussy, Francine, you'll get yer ass upstairs okay. Don' worry, Friday's big night, lotta bizness fer everybody, Friday night.

She-it! That Francine, she ack like she wanna go wiff my trick jes cause he wanna go wiff me. How come she alla time buggin me?

Piss on Francine!

I swing ass upstairs an my trick come on along behind. Some College Joes grab ass when I swings it, but this mothah, he too jittery for grabbin. Bout all he kin do t'git up them stairs.

I take him on in this room Francine alla time callin her room. Yeah! Godam that Francine! Nobody give one fas' toot bout no room but her, an she gotta go callin this one room her room, counta the bed don' make's much noise.

I take me my jittery trick on the hell in that room anyhow! Yeah! Way that Francine ack, she ain gonna need her no room a-tall!

Them quiet jittery ones, they's trouble sometime. This mothah, I git him in that room, he jes stan there lookin dum.

I say, Well Hello, Sweet Baby. Wha's on yer mind?

He don' say nothing.

I say, Hey Lover, what're we gonna do?

An he jes look dum.

I say, Yoo-hoo, pritty baby, you wanna lil french? Haff an haff? How bout jest a straight? I say, Twenty berries an you all roun the mothahfuggin worl'.

An then he look at me like he is gonna pee his pants! Right now! Yeah! I say, Mothahfuggin worl', an he bout t'shout.

Madam alla time tellin us cats, Don' never say *mothahfug* roun them real fay tricks, but Kee-ryess! Least that git him woke up some. Fore, he jes standin there lookin all roun, dreamin. Jes dum an dreamy.

I say, Hey Baby, this a cathouse, you dig? This an no place t'do yer daydreamin at. I say, Cathouse fer funnin, Sweetheart. Yeah! How bout we do us some funnin?

And he still jes look dum. Gee-zuz! I don' know jes where the fug he think he is at. I can' be takin no all night fer one fast fiver, so I start in playin roun wiff his lil ol pecker. I'm playing, he's lookin roun real gone, an we jes gittin along like seven crabs in one big bumhole.

Nex, he look like he bout t'come alive, an he go t'say somethin, then he shut up agen.

Kee-ryess! Maybe he walk in here by mistake. What a muddlehead.

I start in all over agen. I say, Hey Baby, you feel like havin some fun?

He say, Yeah!

I say t'myseff, Well kiss my blackass! This mothah kin talk affer all!

Then I gotta tell him how much is what. Fack, I gotta tell him an tell him, an still he look dum. Yeah! I talkin, he standin there wiff a lil ol hardon, lookin roun real dum. Gee-zuz! How dum kin one Whiteboy git?

I say, Kee-ryess Sugar! I can' make it no plainer! Ain you got no jack?

He say, Huh?

I say, Ain you got no green? No loot?

He say, Huh?

I say, Ain you got no skins, no kale? No bread? No bones, no berries, no boys?

He say, Whaaa?

I say, Man yer in a cathouse. You come here, us cats figure you wanna do some screwin. Fore you do yer screwin, you gotta pay.

An kiss my lil ol blackass Pickaninny me, I say *that*, this daddio pull out the biggest fuggin wad o'green I ever in my everlovin born days ever-ever did see in this mothahless cathouse! Yeah! Ooh-ooh-ooh Skinny Minnie! That bundle cork my ass! Yeah! It knock me clean off my feet! He so fishfry flush he kin hardly git his mothah-humpin hands roun that wad! This baby lo-o-o-o-*did!* Ooh-wee!

I sit ass right down. I say t'myseff, Girl you jes let this sweet Whiteboy make up his own muddlehead what he wanna do. I say, Girl you jes be nice's ever you been. He got him enuff t'git him all the pussy he kin ever use!

Maybe, I oughtta tell him, Hold the phone, man, I knock off work, we do the town! Like, on that wad, we kin dam well flyfug our way from here t'the moon an back. Yeah!

Sep, he jes standin there wiff his fay face all wrinkle up like a granmothah twoit, and he jes a-fingerin that everlovin stuff so nice, *so* nice! Way he finger, I know, I jes dee-diddly-dam well *know* him an it ain strangers.

Ain no wonder he's dum. All that mazoola, he kin be jes's dum's dum kin be!

Nex, this whole fuggin worl' start goin backwar's. Yeah! This trick, he standin there messin roun wiff his green, he say, What *you* wanna do?

Yeah! He say that! He ask *me* what *I* wanna do.

I bout pee! Kee-ryess! I dam well near tell him, I dam near say, Sweet Lovin Baby Sugar Doll, what I wanna do, I wanna fly! I wanna blow this cathouse an fly! I wanna bring you home t'Momma. I wanna hide you unner my bed!

But I don' say nothin. I git so diddly dizzy lookin that wad in the eye, all I kin do is sit an look.

He say, What you think best? He say, Wha's that you say bout roun the wor'? He say, Wha's this roun the worl', anyhow?

Meantime, I been gittin all fuss up over his wad, I sayin t'myself, I sayin, Girl you got you some fast considerin t'do. This College Joe, he is loaded and he is jittery.

Jackie all time sayin, Girl one o'these days yer gonna bump int' some nice invessment.

Look like I bump! Now what the hell m'I gonna do?

Jackie say, Treat invessment real real fine, an he ask you yer phone, and then yer in bizness. Yeah!

On'y I know what *he* wanna do, I kin treat him real fine, but he ain sayin. He askin me what *I* wanna do. Kee-ryess! An then he askin bout roun the worl' an alla time so jimjam jittery he ain gonna make it t'the corner!

She-it!

Nex, I say, Baby you don' want you no roun the worl'. Right now, jes yet. What you wanna do, you wanna stay for the whole mothar—Eh, you wanna stay fer all night!

He say, No. He say, He don' wanna do that. He say, He don' like the looks o'this place.

What the fug the looks o'the place got t'do wiff it? Oooh-wee! I do me some more considerin.

Then I say, Tell you what, Sugar. How bout a lil ol haff an haff, jes fer now, like. See how you like that. Huh?

He say, I say so, tha's okay by him.

Gee-zuz!

I say, Okay man, I say so.

He say, Fine.

Bless my blackass Pickaninny me!

Nex, he say, How much?

Ooh-ooh-ooh Skinny Minnie! Might je's well git me a lil ol English tip right now!

I say, Ten.

He say, Ten dollah?

What the fug he think? Ten peenuts?

I say, Yeah man, ten dollah.

Counta my considerin tell me, invessment or no invessment, this sweet baby got so much I might jes's well git me three lil boys fer myseff.

See, haff and haff really on'y cost seven, but crap! He ain gonna miss him no three outta that wad. No-oh-oh! He give me a five and five ones. I'm gonna git me three. Yeah. Tha's English tip.

Sep, he go and give me a *spot*, I ain gonna git me no three. I gotta go an put three in the tipbox fer all them other cats t'share my three, he give me a spot. I don' mind sharin, but I kin always use me three o'my own. Yeah!

Se Kee-ryess! He do. He give me a shot, an that finish that.

I ask him, Ain you got no lil bills, man?

He say, No. He say, Sorry.

So I don' git no English tip. I stick that ten tween my titties an swing ass down the hall. I pay up seven an git back three and put them three in the tipbox, an then I go fer the soap an water.

At first I thought my ears were deceiving me. Such language! From a girl! I mean! Even if she was non-white, such profanity! (I certainly won't repeat what she said. You'll just have to take my word for it that it was foul, dirty, and in exceptionally poor taste.)

And that room! I was flabbergasted! (I mean, this room this woman of ill repute took me to. A description of which will follow.)

Also, the downstairs! (Of the ill repute house.) (Which, I fear, I'm unable to describe without jeopardizing the high literary plain I'm attempting to maintain.)

And the stairway! It was practically as wide as a linen dispenser and every bit as steep as a ladder. (I'll bet that house was a hundred years old if it was a single day!) And this girl (yes, as you may have surmised by now, I permitted myself to continue along with this misadventure) (or investigation, as I prefer to think of it.) (After all, I thought; JC, it's now or never!)—this girl (I mean, this professional prostitute) wasn't as bad looking as I'd expected. She was Negro, yes, and she had that tight kinky hair and—well, she wasn't at all white in any way. I mean, there was a partly white one sitting on the arm of the chair in which sat this one which I picked out, but I figured as long as I was where I was when I was, I might as well pick a dark one. She wore a black blouse an a tight red skirt and didn't look very old. Matter of fact, she appeared approximately my age. (Nineteen.) But Christmas! Going up those narrow stairs, I almost bumped into her rear end, it was so dark, I mean, it wasn't so dark I couldn't *see* her rear end (which certainly did stick out far enough) (for such a little person, I mean) (in that tight skirt and all) (presenting me with two shiny spots, for gosh sakes!) but it was about all I could do to keep from bumping into her. It's a good thing we had only one flight up to climb. The way she swayed her rear end, I might have ended up hypnotized. (I mean, like you can become hypnotized watching a pendulum swinging back and forth.)

And the second floor was just one long hallway with doors all along either side, and one bare lightbulb hanging up for light. (Of course.) (But it didn't throw much, is what I mean.) Then, right off the bat, the next thing I knew, we were in this tiny little room and she was talking. Which is where the big trouble really began. I mean, I couldn't understand a word she was saying. At first. Gradually, as I got acclimatized to her dialect, I began hearing the wildest, most unprintable obscenities I think I've ever heard—and I mean I've been around. Around women who swore, even, but not this way. Hence, Dear Reader, even though I quite possibly might, at this juncture, give a snatch or so of dialogue, the language she employed was so utterly indecent it would have to be thoroughly censored before it would be legally permissible. And I am strictly against censorship. Therefore, I refrain from direct quotations. I mean, even a writer of filth could never quote such a person verbatim and expect to get it past even the lower courts. Her entire vocabulary, such as it was, seemed composed of pornographic slang and insincere endearments.

But, finally, I got so I could understand her enough for us to conduct our business transaction, so to speak.

But that room threw me. I certainly wish I was a paid professional writer so I could describe it to you. I'll try.

There was a lightbulb. I mean, this one bare lightbulb, and that's all. And there was a bed. Or, almost a bed. Really, it was just an old bedframe with an old mattress on it and an old bedspread over the mattress. And when I say old, I mean old! And the walls—good gosh, the walls! The wallpaper looked like it held up the entire building. And you couldn't be certain how much longer the building was going to hold up! Because the wallpaper was just sort of . . . disintegrating. It was crumbling and peeling off and just coming off the walls right before your very eyes! Under the wallpaper there were strips of old broken wood, only. Flimsy? Wow! Then, beyond those strips—upon which the wallpaper was *supposed* to hang—there was nothing but a surface, very substandard, which I am forced to conclude was the inside of the outside of that clapboard building—if you can call it a building.

Anyway: this room. The excuse for a bed was just inside the door to the right, between the door and the right wall. The room was that small. The left wall was that crumbling wallpaper and the right wall was sort of a partition affair—very temporary looking, but like it might hold up longer than the other wall. Because it was newer, I mean. The far wall (also disintegrating) had a round hole in it, which I was forced to conclude was supposed to serve as a window. And in the far right corner stood this dresser. Or, what had been a dresser. It no longer had drawers, just openings where drawers were supposed to be. And on top of it, looking very very out of place, sat this vase! With flowers in it! Imagine! Flowers in that room!

The floor was old wood and bare. Just as bare as anything. Nothing could be bare-er than that wooden floor.

And, believe it or not, that was all there was to this tiny room. I know that sounds fantastic, but it's factually true. Just this bed, the skeleton of a dresser, and that's all.

But the girl (did I neglect to describe her?) wasn't bad. I mean, of course, bad *looking*. For a non-white. I mean, she was, as they say, ha, ha, stacked! Not at all what I'd expected. (Though don't get me wrong. I'm not prejudiced. Far from it.) She had a very childish face. Also very dark. And eyes which were large and watery looking, with drooping eyelids, which never seemed to look directly at you. (Me.) And her voice was tiny and high-pitched, like a young girl's. Though, of course, I realize she had to be at least my age—at least—in order to be there.

But she moved like she was 60. That was the thing. I mean, she moved slow and easy—very slow. (Coming up the stairs, she even swayed her rear end slow, unlike most girls whom I know of, who are white, of course, and wiggle—if they do—quickly and nervous like. Squirrelly, if you get what I mean.)

But I don't, for gosh sakes, wish to dwell unduly on physical detail. So I will skip recounting certain actions she went through, as well as certain phrases she used while going through these afore-mentioned actions.

And, until we got around to sealing the transaction (if you can call it that) she seemed utterly and completely detached. I mean! Talk about detached! As a matter of hard cold fact, it was her detachment which aggravated me. I don't know what I had expected, but I had not expected detachment, for gosh sakes!

Just one word about her lingo. Or, as much of it as I could catch. She muttered something, about, among other things, French. Which made me think of my flunking grades—biology, psychology, French—and for one fraction of a second, I thought she wanted to discuss grades and other aspects of university life, though I certainly had no idea how we might go about such a discussion. She and I, I mean. However, this proved an erroneous assumption on my part. (As I learned later. French, in her dialect, meant something entirely different and as unprintable as nine-tenths of her jargon.)

She finally sort of fell back down on the bed and sat there looking slightly shaken, though for the life of me I was unable to learn what had troubled her. I didn't wish to appear boorish (I try to treat all peoples as equals, regardless of race, color or creed) so I asked, in an attempt to snap her out of her sudden mysterious depression, how she would like to spend our time together. And I wish to make it quite clear that—at this point, at least—I certainly had not resorted to any rationalizing or anything like that. But, after all, I had never found myself in an ill repute house before, and was not, for gosh sakes, familiar with their customs.) (I mean, by asking, I wished to kill two birds with one stone. I wished to disrupt her detachment, engage her interest in me as a person, so to speak, and also —second—to show her that I was magnanimous enough to consider her feelings in the matter, even if she was a paid professional of another color.) And apparently I was successful in this double-barreled endeavor, for she looked up after a moment of depression with new interest. (No doubt such persons have their own brand of troubles.) And we completed our business. I mean, it turned out that one pays in advance, so I paid.

I must add here that I did feel a bit uneasy carrying my money into that place at that time, because of the sort of neighborhood I was in, and all that. I mean, you never can tell. So many people lived in that neck of the woods who don't seem to want to go out in the world and get themselves a good job and advance themselves—and that sort of attitude is communistic and breeds crime. But she paid absolutely no attention to my money (which I carried bare in my trouser pocket, having had the good sense to leave my wallet back at the frat house in view of the type of neighborhood I was entering.) (I mean, if somebody was going to rob me, they certainly wouldn't get my valuable papers.) So I concluded she was too distracted by some sort of personal problem to be concerned with my money. And as it turned out, this was the first of a series of miscalculations on my part, which later led to a larger misunderstanding.

But, like those clever cigarette advertisements again, I digress.

Eventually, during our little preliminary conversation (or unconversation) she became more friendly and began sounding not honestly insincere. I mean, she seemed to drop her false sincerity when I demonstrated that I wished to be anything but boorish, and became, well—her entire approach toward me changed.

I thought: After all, JC, you do have something about you which attracts the ladies. And even if she is a paid professional lady of ill repute, she, after all, is human. Mom says it's that you're a natural born salesman. Why fight it?

Then the next second, the very next thing I knew—Bamb!

Gone. She was gone out the door, leaving me in that dismal cell by myself. Didn't say a word about where she was going or when she'd get back, simply went!

Well, I don't mind admitting at this point that I was just a little shaken. I didn't know whether to go after her or wait patiently for whatever might happen next. But I kept my head and waited. (Which, it seems, is accepted procedure.) And as it turned out, what happened next was not on the menu.

Here goes me, I come back. He tell me this other cat been in. I say, Who?

He say, He don' know who. He say, Firs' time in any cathouse, how he sposed t'know who's who.

I dam near believe it's his firs' time in any cathouse. I bout ready t'believe he fresh off some lost boat someplace. I bout ready t'believe anythin this mothah wanna tell me.

He tell me this other cat wearin a blue dress. He say, *Cocktail* dress! Yeah! He say that! Hee hee!

On'y one Jane in this cathouse got her a blue dress on, and that's Francine. I tell him fergit it.

But I gotta laugh. Francine all cocktail set t'go up wiff this big fat old wad o'jack. She think he wanna go wiff her. Alla time he pick my lil ol blackass Pickaninny me. Yeah! He my trick. He gonna like me. He gonna like me so much, he gonna ask me my phone!

Piss on Francine!

Nex—I been so all fuss up bout that sweet wad—I ain even seen he still dress'. He standin there wiff all them clothes on. How come he don't take 'em off so's when I git back we is all set?

She-it! This speed, he gonna be all night fer one lil ol haff and haff.

Jackie alla time sayin, Invessment is give and git, give and git.

But madam all time sayin, You cats git an git. Git yer ass upstairs and git them tricks off an git yer ass back downstairs. Don't be no mothahless whole night for one dum five-bill College Joe. She say, They ain got no loot worff worryin bout.

Yeah! Madam say that!

Kee-ryess! I got news for Madam.

Sep, for she git her news, I gotta do right so's he ask me my phone, so's I kin git me my invessment. Oncet I git givin and gittin, and we goin along invessment-fine, then I kin tell Madam. First, fore I kin do nother blessed thing, I gotta College Joe undress' t'git.

I say, Sweet Baby, you ain undress'? How come?

He say, Huh?

Gee-zuz!

I say t'myseff, Girl he can' unnerstan what yer sayin, on'y one way t'do. Ack it out. So I do. I do this right unner the light so's he kin look me over real good. He look. He lookin real hard. Then I'm standin there waitin, an he is still lookin. He look dummer an dummer.

I say, Baby you wanna keep yer clothes on?

He say, No! He say, Course he don' wanna keep his clothes on.

Ooh-wee!

I say, Honey you don' wanna keep 'em on, thing t'do is take 'em off!

He say, Yeah sure yeah! An he start in.

An he got a long way t'go. Kee-ryess!

But I say t'myself, I say. Hol' yer ass, Girl. This mothah kin be jes's dum's he wanna be, he got him that much mazoola.

He fold his clothes over the chair real careful. I ack like I'm daydreamin, he do that. He so dum, he might git t'thinkin I wanna rob him. He act a wee bit mistrussful anyhow. He ack that way, I ack like I'm the dummes' lil Pickaninny livin.

I gotta long wait till he finish undressin, he got so much on.

I wash him real nice an soff, counta him bein so awful tickledingus, and then I gits t'work. Time I start in, I got me so many worryful considerins t'do. I can' hardly pay no mind t'techneek. Workin an considerin, and wonnerin does this dum Whiteboy know what t'd wiff that thing fer the other haff o'his haff and haff, I find I done me too dam much considerin.

Nex, I aim been at him a minit, an pop, off he go!

Kee-ryess!

An then—I git up and go on over t'the basin—this Whiteboy, he sit up like a mothahjumpin jack-in-a-box an he start lookin at me like I done somethin wrong.

Gee-zuz! All that Jack an I can' make nothin go right, he so fuggin dum. Come in here all loaded up like that and I don' even git a chance t'show him how good I kin do. Naecher done mess me up at the most baddest time.

An he still lookin, Gee-zuz!

Then he say, That all?

Yeah! He say that! He say that like he think I sposed t'do a lil dance fer him nex. Kee-ryess!

I say, Yeah Baby, tha's all. Dam shame, too.

He say, Yeah it's a shame. He say, One ain never enuff fer *him!*

I feel like sayin, Baby way you go off, you musta been savin that *one* fer a mothahlumpin lifetime. On'y you ask me my phone, I fix you up fer the rest o'yer lifetime, long's you want. You ask me my phone, you ain never gonna go so long without pussy you gits *that* trigger-happy agen.

But I don' say nothin and he don' ask me my phone. Can' blame him. I don' even git me a chance t'show my stuff. *Poof!* Invessment gone.

I start in t'git dress' agen, feelin real blue, an he jes still layin there lookin real surprise, like I ain doin right.

I say, Come on, Baby, we gotta git outta here.

He say, Le's go nother one.

I say, Can'. Ain allowed, man. You gotta—

An then I cork ass an start in considerin all over agen. Hell! He done pay ten for haff and haff an don' even git one haff. But Kee-ryess! We been up here so mothahfuggin long now, Madam gonna send for the firetruck, we don' git ass back downstairs. I say t'myself, Gee-zuz Girl! You jes can' go breakin rules for no trick too dum t'ask you yer phone and git him a lil o'yer ass on the side.

But I can' help tryin one more fishline. I say, Baby ain you got you no sweet lil chick fer that pritty cock?

An she-it! Seem like I jes can' say the right thing roun this dum mothah. He wrinkle up an he start in tryin t'tell me he got him plenty.

I bout t'give him up fer lost. I say t'myseff, This daddio so dum, he gonna end up comin backwar's. Yeah, he gonna end up backfirin. He soun like he is backfirin right now.

Then he quit jawin that crap an he say, Come on, le's go jes one more real quick.

Real quick, he say. Hee hee! His lil ol genrill still up an lookin peppy. Madam say, trick wanna go agen, he pay up right now, else he start in from downstairs all over agen. But this poor mothah done pay fer haff and haff and don' even git haff, and I is out one big fat invessment chance. Gee-zuz! This ain right!

So I say, Now?

He say, Yeah now. Real quick, real quick.

Las' trick say that make me break the rule too, an he pay agen an then he turn out so fuggin slow on the secen', he dam near wear my ass clean out. Course, that weren't the same. That one, he don' give me no insprashun. This one, he the biggest invessment chance I ever seen in this cathouse. He dum, yeah! But crap, he can' help *that!*

I say t'myself, I say, Ain no good leavin him go downstairs an pick him out some new cat an give her her chance t'make invessment when I got him up here wiff me right now.

Piss on Madam and her git and git!

I say, Baby you promise t'be real quick an don' never tell nobody I do it?

He say, Yeah yeah yeah!

I say, Sure you kin go agen so quick?

He say, Sure sure sure!

I tease a lil more. I say, An you ain gonna tell nobody?

He say, No no no, he ain gonna tell.

I say, But Sugar, I better not. I say, We been up here too long already. I say, Go on, git! Go git you nother girl.

He look real sad, I say that. He look like he gonna go and find him nother girl. Fer real!

Gee-zuz! Ain nothin gonna go right fer me t'night?

I say—real fast—I say, Whoa Baby! I laugh. I say, I'm on'y teasin.

An I outta my clothes agen an on that bed so fast he don' know which end is up. I say, Shove over, Lover. I say, Honeydripper, make room fer this Honeydripper!

He do.

Nex, he no sooner in the saddle and we is jes bout ready t'raise hell when—

Gee-zuz Kee-ryess! The godam Francine pop in. Yeah! Loud's a fart in a empty tincan.

She say, Kitten yer in *my* room.

I say, Francine godam yer crazy ass, git outta here!

I kin see my trick gittin all jittery all over agen.

Francine, she say, Don' you know by this time, this *my* room?

I kin feel his ol soljer jes- a-wiltin and wiltin.

I say, Come on Baby, don' pay no nevermind t'her.

But he jes too fuss up. Counta Francine bein there.

I say, Francine up yers wiff a lawnmower, you git yer greezy hair the hell outta here.

An she say, Girl who you think yer talkin to?

An I say, You you cottinpickin crab nabber.

An she say, Don you talk t'me like that, you lil bitch, or I'll ruin you.

An I say, Francine can' you see I'm busy jes now? Now how come you don' git?

An she say, No. She say I gotta git, go find nother room.

I say, Francine yer flippin yer lid! You git right now or I'm gonna call fer Madam.

She say, like hell I'm gonna call fer Madam. She tell me *she* is gonna call fer Madam, I don' git. She say, I goin right downstairs right now an tell Madam yer in my room and yer takin all fuggin night for one lousy trick.

So I say, Okay Francine, go on, tell Madam.

She ain gonna tell Madam nothin. She do, Madam kick her ass right out! Francine she don' belong in no cathouse nohow. She don' git along wiff nobody, hardly. She ack like hers don' stink. It do.

Time she git her crazy ass the hell outta there, my poor lil ol Joe College done wilt like somebody bust his balloon, and I gotta start in all the everlovin over agen. Kee-ryess!

I ain never been nobody fer fightin, but Gee-zuz! I fraid I was bigger, I'd lose by blackass Pickaninny head for considerin an jes take an kick livin hell outta that Francine.

I gotta work real fast now. We was late fore she come in an we ain gettin no sooner.

I start in playin nice's I kin unner the circumstances but I gotta start in from scratch. Kee-ryess! I'm talkin pritty's ever I kin, an playin nice's I know how, an he comin along okay.

An nex, Gee-zuz! I git me more trouble!

This muddlehead pull up an look down on me real sad—real real sad—an he start in talkin sad too. Steada hoppin back in the saddle an goin, he is gonna try some make believe sweet talkin. He start in ackin like he's playin him some dum movie scene. Yeah! He talk sad an then he look at me like I'm sposed t'talk sad back.

Ooh-wee! He lose me!

I don' know what t'do. I considerin that jack he got an I considerin how long we been up here an I hearin more tricks jes a-streamin in that mothahless front door downstairs, and I jes *know* Madam gonna wonner what the hell happen t'me.

I say, Sweetheart Lover, we ain got *time* for that *now!* I say, You tol' me you gonna be quick. Here you go pissin roun like you think I got all fuggin night! I say, Gee-zuz Baby, Madam gonna think yer eatin my ass, steada—

Now godam come on, Baby. Giddy up!

I say all that nice's I kin at that time, an I make him smile. He do that, I hope t'toot an back he git the idea t'ask me my phone, but he don' git that idea a-tall! No!

Nex thing I know—jes bout the time we startin t'go good and I gits movin okay an I goin fine's I ever do go, and I snappin the whip an punchin the apple, an I wonnerin is my invessment ever gonna come thru an ask me my phone—an I rollin ass eas' an rollin ass wes', an breakin my poor ol Pickaninny back for this dum mothah—nex thin I know, he git him one more dee-diddly-dum idea, an fore I know what he is tryin t'do, he got my ass hung up clear off that bed!

Yeah!

I say, Hol' it, Baby! What the fug you doin?

She-it! I open my big mouff and that son-a-bitch jes stop, plop, an lay deadweight. Seem every cottin-pickin thing I do jes backfire. I git me nothin but trouble trouble trouble.

He say, He don' know wha's the matter. He say, Seem like I is doin all the *work!*

Yeah! He say I is doin the work!

I bout flip my lid right here. I say, Gee-zuz, Sweetie! An I try best I kin t'talk nice. I say, Course I is doin the work. What the hell you think? I say, I is the *cat, you* is the *trick!* Unnerstan? I say, Now come on, Lover, giddy up oncet agen an le's git the hell outta here. I keep tryin t'tell you, we ain got no *time* right *now*—fer talkin.

I say—an alla time tryin t'soun nice—I say, Giddy the sweet ever-lovin horsey ass up oncet agen, please!

Well she-it! He start in goin, yeah! Sep, this time he got him nother fancy fug idea, an he start in wham jammin me like he's choppin rock. Yeah! He jes agruntin and rammin away like he's mad at the whole mothahhumpin worl'.

Course, I know better'n t'open my big mouff *this* time. I keep tryin t'do my stuff best I kin unner the new circumstances, but it ain easy.

Meantime, I'm thinkin we jes gotta  make it this time an he can' git him nohow no more new dum ideas—an he git him nother one. Yeah! He do!

Gee-zuz! I don' know how one dum Whiteboy kin behave so mean! This time, he curl my blackass right up double and he piledrive like he is tryin' t'stan me on my poor ol' Pickaninny head an bump me straight down t'hell!

Yeah! He do that! I don' know what he is tryin t'prove, but I ain bout t'ask no more queshuns.

On'y thing I try, I try a lil reverse English. I say. Tha's-a-way, Baby! Hit it, Sweetheart! Go go go!

He go! An he git him his dee-diddly-godam ten dollah gun. At las'!

I up outta that bed and doosh on the run and dress—right now! I even fergit all bout that invessment idea, I so scared my ass gonna be mud, time I git back downstairs.

I say, Hey Lover, how come you wanna ack like that? You think pussy made o'steel?

I laugh when I say that. It ain easy, but I do.
He laugh too, dum she-it.
Good thing I laugh.

Even though I am trying to keep this on a high literary plain, I feel
it is obligatory at this point that I go into the matter of my past experience with women. For reasons which will become clear to the intelligent
reader, I'm sure.

As a I formerly mentioned, there are these two *un*professional
ladies of ill repute I happen to know at home. One is Marge and the other
is Susie. Despite their already ruined reputations, I refuse to mention
their last names. I'm not a cad, for gosh sakes! On the other hand, I'm
not a prude either. What I mean to say is, I'm just a normal nineteen-
year-old fellow, with normal appetites and all that, and these girls (at
home) are always calling me up anyway. Don't get me wrong—I certainly don't go with either one of them. As previously mentioned, Barbara
is my girl, and she's a very high-minded girl too. I wouldn't *touch* Barbara. I'm not that type. As a matter of fact, we may marry some day. But
marriage, for me, and also for Barbara, is in the future, so as I've already
mentioned, there are these two girls at home, whom I occasionally date. I
mean, *go out with.* I can't really consider them *dates,* for gosh sakes!

What I'm driving at is this: Both of them consider me the best lover
in town. I don't mean to brag, but they do. They're constantly telling me
they do, and they've been telling me this for some time now. And I'm
fully aware that the reason they feel this way—even though they run
with any number of other fellows, being the sort they are—is that I'm far
from unendowed physically. Also, I know how to handle myself in the
backseat of our family Chevy. Though, again I must emphasize, I'm not
trying to brag. I'm only stating the facts, the hard cold facts. And as for
my being loose enough to run with these two, I must mention that I do
not wish to enter wedlock, especially with such a fine girl as Barbara,
completely naive about such important matters as the techniques of love-
making.

Enough said. About that aspect, I mean. I do not wish to dwell on
such matters incessantly. I point the above out only to emphasize the sort
of fellow I am.

And as a preliminary to a comment on my ill repute experience.
Which is, namely: Much to my surprise, I found that in certain respects
Hank was almost right. I mean, he doesn't really *know* it. He's half right
without knowing it. He's right in that colored girls are not the same. That
is, *this* colored girl I found myself with was not the same as either Marge
or Susie. In several regards.

Not that I'm ready to concede to Hank's idea that Negro girls are
somehow, in some mysterious way, *superior* (and I insist that, despite
his denials, superior is what he means) to white girls. No, he's wrong

about that, and I was forced to conclude I was even more right than I had realized.

But different—that's my point. For instance (and this will be diffi-cult to tell without becoming obscene) this colored professional prostitute had the same inclination that Margie has, except she went about it . . . Well, she went about it *more* so than Margie ever did. I mean, she just acted as if it was quite natural, as I suppose, in view of her status, it was. Though I found her manner of approach more than slightly disquieting. I mean it, it was so professional, so undramatic and lacking in the neces-sary preliminaries. It was startling, almost sickening, for gosh sakes!

I suppose, however, that never having been to a house of ill repute, I had acquired certain misconceptions about how such women behaved— based on my natural, normal experiences. Experiences unpaid for, is what I mean.

In fact, I was so surprised by her manner of approach (and also by a couple of unlikely intrusions by some other paid professional colored girl, who kept opening our door and sticking her head inside, first while mine was gone, and then later) that I reached my first (if you'll pardon the expression) climax a bit too hastily. (I should also add that the sur-roundings I found myself in had something to do with the above.)

I then learned that it's one climax per customer, for gosh sakes! One and you're out. Well, again I don't mean to brag, but when I go out with Margie or Susie, one is far from enough. For me, at any rate. So, when I learned I was considered finished by this colored girl after that one, I objected. She then told me that this was the rule and that I had to go.

But—unsatisfied with my unsatisfactory experience, and convinced that I had much to learn about this phase of life (paid prostitution) before I could consider myself really truly a man of the world, I turned on the old sales charm and convinced that professional she should break her rules, just this once. Which she did, making it more evident that she found me to her liking.

And, at this point, I might add that, having the sort of analytical mind I have, I'm prone to vary my intellectual approach from time to time, and at times I think in representations. In fact, I began thinking in representations when this girl first approached in the hitherto described manner. I thought: Poor thing! Offspring of Southern slavery. And here she is (to my representation thinking) a slave once more. (I mean when she was going about it in the perverted way.) Here I am, the white master, just laying back while she works with no compensation—much like some nasty white slaveholder might have sat on his veranda, sipping mint juleps, while a gang of slaves picked his cotton.

Then, that thinking was interrupted, and later, after I'd persuaded her to break that house rule, I returned to thinking in representations, and I thought: From slave to employee! Now, at last, emancipation! And

she now works under me as part of an actively engaged company team
—employer and employee. Compensation at last! But is her compensation
adequate?

(And it is about right here that we were interrupted by this other
prostitute, who stuck her head in through the door—a most perturbing
habit she had. There seemed to be absolutely no privacy in that place.
And she and my girl got into an argument about whose room it was we
were in, and both of them shouted the most vile profanities at each other,
until the other one left, and I went back to thinking):

Is she adequately compensated? After all, she likes me, and after all,
I'm here to find out, to learn about a phase of life I've never come into
contact with. Why don't you, thought I, JC my friend, be a good employer
and up her wages? (Representatively thinking, you understand.) Why
don't you—One, show her you are far from a prejudiced white person,
and Two, that you know how to handle yourself in bed with a woman, no
matter what the color of her skin.

What I mean is, even though she was (to my representative thinking) at that time my employee, she was doing all the work. I thought:
Good gracious, JC, this will never do. You, after all, are the one who
should carry the old football, so to speak. You are the male component.

So I did. I mean, I went about showing her that I could, after all,
handle myself with a woman. I thought: It's about time she found out
that even though she's the employee (representatively thinking) I'll let
her know I'm every bit as good at this sort of business as she is, and by
letting her know, I'll increase her wages and decrease her working effort,
causing a marked rise in plant efficiency.

I mean, ha ha, just a manner of thinking—in representations.

But, lo and behold, I had apparently broken some other house rule,
for I learned she had not expected me to take the initiative in our—well,
you know what I mean.

But, having broken one house rule to reach this stage, I decided to
ignore that second house rule as well, and to proceed as per my original
representation thinking, which I did. I let her have it. I mean, I showed
manly initiative—the way I do especially with Susie—and showed that
ill repute colored girl a thing or two. I mean, I let her know she had a
*man* with her. I left her with no doubts about that!

Then . . .

But I've neglected to mention an important aspect. Another house
rule, apparently, for she seemed in a terrific hurry to get back downstairs.
I mean, it seems she was supposed to spend only so much time with each
customer and then rush him out, and that she was already running over-
time with me. (Ha ha.) So she rushed about and hopped back into her
blouse and skirt (all she wore, for gosh sakes!) and was hurrying out the
door, when I conceived an idea I felt at the time was a brilliant one, but
which later turned out to be the beginning of my misadventure proper,

which, though it enriched me in experience, led to some rather startling digressions.

My thinking at this point was extremely involved, subtle, and also rapid. First, I was laughing to myself at how startled Hank would be if he ever found out how I had impressed a paid professional colored prostitute, right in her own house of ill repute, for gosh sakes! Second, I was thinking that if I could persuade her to this point, with further objective planning and action, I might continue the trend and further my extra-curricular education somewhat. I might learn ever more about paid professional colored ladies by persuading her to meet me at some other time and some other place.

I was laying there wondering just how I could go about this when my idea struck. And I mean *struck!* It came like a bolt from the devine blue—the way Prof. McGillicuty says highly intellectual poetical ideas come.

My idea was, namely, this: That, in view of—First, how unintelligent and uneducated she was, and Second, how profoundly impressed she was with yours truly, (ha ha) and Third, of how easily I had charmed her several moments ago, I decided—

To tell her I was a burglar and wanted by the police and desperate for a place to hide until the heat was off.

Fantastic, I know. But that was my idea. And, lo and behold, it worked. Honest! I told her that I had been burglarizing homes in the Mount Woodstock District, and that by tracing my fingerprints the police had found me out.

This had a remarkable effect on her. She not only believed me but apparently decided I was her kind—her own underworld kind, I mean, to her mind, now that she found I was an actual criminal, for gosh sakes, she considered me a sort of friend. Well, more than just a friend, as it turned out. She went to some lengths to make sure we would meet some place else, and meet soon, and also that I would have a place to hide out. She did, in fact, (and I know this will sound just too too fantastic, but it's hard cold fact nevertheless) give me the key to her apartment.

I tell him so long, an I'm on my blackass way flyin out the door, and he grab my arm!

Yeah! I dam near leave that mothahless arm behind fore I stop. Then I draw me one bigass breath and I bout t'let that dum daddio know jes wha's on my mind, as he up and say, Hol' it, hol' it jes a secen'.

An then he babble him off some dum bull-she-it bout bein a burgler, fer Kee-ryess sake!

First, I say, Okay yer a burgler, I'm a bumblebee, but I ain got nothin fer you t'take jes now, mister burgler. I ain even got me no more fuggin time. No time a-tall!

But he still hangin on my arm an talkin an sayin he need him someplace t'hide. Yeah! He say that!

Gee-zuz! I bout t'tell him *I* is gonna need me someplace t'hide, he don' let go my arm. But I do me some o'the fastes considerin I ever in my whole poor ol Pickaninny life ever done, an I say, Man you wanna hide?

An he say, Yeah! Tha's what he wanna do.

Considerin an considerin, I don't know why he jes don' ask me my phone, but he ain done that, an he ain bout to. On'y thing I know is he ain got him no *faith,* No faith a-tall! All that mothahless jack an no faith.

But ooh-wee! I gotta do somethin. Madam gonna kick my blackass over the moon, I don' git back downstairs right now!

I say t'myseff, I say, He wanna place t'hide, an he got what it take. Dum way a-goin bout linin up a weekend, but I ain never had me no weekend trick an he got enuff so's he kin be jes's dum's he wanna be. Yeah! He got him at least one hunner, look like, an him an it ain strangers, and he ain got no faith. Long on loot, short on faith!

I say t'myseff, Girl fer that kinda jack you kin godam well believe anythin this dum Whiteboy wanna tell you.

I say, Okay Burgler, down is up. Le's go t'the moon. You wanna place t'hide, you got it.

An I tell him where I live.

Kee-ryess! I say t'myself, Girl you in such a bigass hurry over Madam git an git, you dam near run right past one Big Money Honey. Gee-zuz! Yer fourteen already, you gotta slow down and start in givin some.

He say he don' know where is that place I live. I tell him the number an say, Take a cab, man, take a cab. I see you in the mornin. Yeah! I see you all weekend. I say, I go back downstairs, an then I'm gonna mess roun some till you finish dressin an come on down, then I'm gonna come up t'you and I'm gonna have my partmin key in my hand. I do this, you mess roun an you jes perten like you is nuts, and that ain gonna be too hard! You come up t'me from behind, see, an start in nuzzlin me. You jes lean over an put yer arms roun me and then I kin slip you my key. Unnerstan? Okay? You dig?

He look a lil dum, but he say, Okay.

I take off, leave him t'git back in all them clothes.

Ooh-wee! This better'n waitin fer him t'call. I kin work this big Friday night now and go on home in the mornin an this Big Money Honey invessment gonna be there.

Invessment? She-it! I ain got no invessment, I got me a whole crazy-ass bank! Yeah! No telling where I go from here, everythin go right.

I git downstairs, the sittin room jes fulla tricks but I can' go up now. No!

I scoot like somebody lit my tail, right on back t'the dressin room, an make s'if I is gonna powder up some more, Madam see me go but she too busy t'do anythin right now. Tricks jes a-streamin in.

I git my key outta my purse an start peekin out thru the curtin, waitin fer my Big Money Honey. He bout take all night.

But he make it. I see him standin there, lookin dum, an I scoot back out t'the sittin room an he do like I tol' him. He ack dum and start sayin he wanna go back upstairs wiff me and while we is funning like that, I slip him my key.

I say, Nex time, Lover.

He say, Okay, nex time.

An he take off out the door.

Phew! Invessment ain easy t'git.

Burgler? Kee-ryess!

Trouble! Gee-zuz! Course he got trouble. Wiff that wad, course he got nothin but trouble.

I on my swingin ass way back upstairs wiff another College Joe, I say t'myself, Burgler you jes go on home t'my place and hide yerself cozy. Don' you go nowhere else, man. I git home, we gonna talk some real sweet weekend bizness t'begin wiff, then we gonna settle down t'invessment. An who know what that gonna lead to!

Kee-ryess! How come one cat git her ass so lucky so fast? Way he finger that wad, I *know*, I jes dee-diddly-dam well *know* this invessment gonna be long an happy.

# CHAPTER THREE

# White-Collar Crime:
# Scheming to Make a Living

The formal features of the confidence game are perhaps best outlined by Erving Goffman in his insightful article entitled "On Cooling the Mark Out." Goffman notes that:

> In the argot of the criminal world, the term "mark" refers to any individual who is a victim or prospective victim of certain forms of planned illegal exploitation. The mark is the sucker—the person who is taken in. An instance of the operation of any particular racket, taken through the full cycle of its steps or phases, is sometimes called a play. The persons who operate the racket and "take" the mark are occasionally called operators.
>
> The confidence game—the con, as its practitioners call it—is a way of obtaining money under false pretenses by the exercise of fraud and deceit.[1]

Goffman differentiated between white-collar crime and the confidence game, but such a distinction is inapplicable in the following selection. In *The Autobiography of a Quack* the "good doctor" may be seen as simultaneously incorporating the features of both con man and white-collar criminal. Goffman presents two major distinctions in these deviant careers.

1. The con is practiced on private persons by talented actors who methodically and regularly build up informal social

[1] Erving Goffman, "On Cooling the Mark Out," *Psychiatry* (November 1952): 451.

91

relationships just for the purpose of abusing them; white-collar crime is practiced on organizations by persons who learn to abuse positions of trust which they once filled faithfully. The one exploits poise; the other, position.

2. Further, a con man is someone who accepts a social role in the underworld community; he is a part of a brother-hood whose members make no pretense to one another of being "legit." A white-collar criminal, on the other hand, has no colleagues, although he may have an associate with whom he plans his crime and a wife to whom he confesses it.[2]

Dr. Sandcraft, the antihero in the following piece, fulfills both of these conditions in that he 1) exploits poise and posi-tion and 2) becomes part of an underworld community in which neither he nor his accomplices make any pretense of being "legit."

In fact so skillful a practitioner is the "doctor" that he is rarely called upon to take the role of "cooler."

Sometimes, however, a mark is not quite prepared to accept his loss as a gain in experience and to say and do nothing about his venture. He may feel moved to complain to the police or to chase after the operators. In the terminology of the trade, the mark may squawk, beef, or come through. From the operators' point of view, this kind of behavior is bad for business. . . . In order to avoid this adverse publicity, an additional phase is sometimes added at the end of the play. It is called cooling the mark out. . . . The operator stays behind his team-mates in the capacity of what might be called a cooler and exercises upon the mark the art of consolation. An at-tempt is made to define the situation for the mark in a way that makes it easy for him to accept the inevitable and quietly go home. The mark is given instruction in the philosophy of taking a loss.[3]

Goffman has rightly noted that the case of con man can be seen as a specific example of the general case of conning and cooling—a widespread social phenomenon.

Many respectable occupations have built into them the practice of conning and cooling. Lawyers[4] and social workers[5] are frequently called upon to cool out unhappy clients, man-

2 Ibid., pp. 451–452.
3 Ibid., pp. 451–452.
4 Abraham S. Blumberg, "Lawyers with Convictions," *Trans-Action* (July/August 1952): 19.
5 Jerry Jacobs, "Symbolic Bureaucracy: A Case Study of a Social Wel-fare Agency," *Social Forces* 47, no. 4 (June 1969): 419.

agement is frequently called upon to cool out workers,[6] professors to cool out students, and so on. The act of cooling, then, can be seen as a general condition of both deviant and normal careers.

In a broad sense, the process of socialization requires that one be cooled into and out of a variety of changing and conflicting roles and role expectations. For example, we are expected to go from childhood to adolescence to adulthood. In the course of these transitions, it is further anticipated that we give up certain ways of life and accept others that may initially seem at odds with our prior mode of existence. As a result, the transition stages in this process do not always go smoothly. The mark may sometimes "squawk."

A popular slogan of the younger generation, "establishment hypocrisy," is viewed by today's youth as a specific instance of the general case of ". . . talented actors [their elders] who methodically and regularly build up informal social relationships just for the purpose of abusing them." The inability of establishment personnel to live up to their avowed values (values they have asked the younger generation to accept and internalize) is viewed by the latter as a "sell out" or a con. Today's campus and urban unrest may be seen in terms of the establishment's inability to cool out the righteous indignation of youth.

I believe upon reflection that we could all find in the arena of everyday life ways in which we scheme to make a living or more generally scheme to make a life and partake, to one extent or another, in reciprocal acts of conning and cooling.

[6] Melville Dalton, *Men Who Manage* (New York: John Wiley & Sons, 1966), pp. 65–68.

# SILAS WEIR MITCHELL

# The Autobiography of a Quack

At this present moment of time I am what the doctors call an interesting case, and am to be found in bed No. 10, Ward 11, Massachusetts General Hospital. I am told that I have what is called Addison's disease, and that it is this pleasing malady which causes me to be covered with large blotches of a dark mulatto tint. However, it is a rather grim subject to joke about, because, if I believed the doctor who comes around every day, and thumps me, and listens to my chest with as much pleasure as if I were music all through—I say, if I really believed him, I should suppose I was going to die. The fact is, I don't believe him at all. Some of these days I shall take a turn and get about again; but meanwhile it is rather dull for a stirring, active person like me to have to lie still and watch myself getting big brown and yellow spots all over me, like a map that has taken to growing.

The man on my right has consumption—smells of cod-liver oil, and coughs all night. The man on my left is a down-easter with a liver which has struck work; looks like a human pumpkin; and how he contrives to whittle jackstraws all day, and eat as he does, I can't understand. I have tried reading and tried whittling, but they don't either of them satisfy me, so that yesterday I concluded to ask the doctor if he couldn't suggest some other amusement.

I waited until he had gone through the ward, and then seized my chance, and asked him to stop a moment.

"Well, my man," said he, "what do you want?"

I thought him rather disrespectful, but I replied, "Something to do, doctor."

He thought a little, and then said: "I'll tell you what to do. I think if you were to write out a plain account of your life it would be pretty well worth reading. If half of what you told me last week be true, you must be about as clever a scamp as there is to be met with. I suppose you would just as lief put it on paper as talk it."

"Pretty nearly," said I. "I think I will try it, doctor."

After he left I lay awhile thinking over the matter. I knew well that I was what the world calls a scamp, and I knew also that I had got little good out of the fact. If a man is what people call virtuous, and fails in life, he gets credit at least for the virtue; but when a man is a— is—well, one of liberal views, and breaks down, somehow or other people don't credit him with even the intelligence he has put into the busi-

Abridged from *The Autobiography of a Quack* by Silas Weir Mitchell, M.D. Published by The Gregg Press.

ness. This I call hard. If I did not recall with satisfaction the energy and skill with which I did my work, I should be nothing but disgusted at the melancholy spectacle of my failure. I suppose that I shall at least find occupation in reviewing all this, and I think, therefore, for my own satisfaction, I shall try to amuse my convalescence by writing a plain, straightforward account of the life I have led, and the various devices by which I have sought to get my share of the money of my countrymen. It does appear to me that I have had no end of bad luck.

As no one will ever see these pages, I find it pleasant to recall for my own satisfaction the fact that I am really a very remarkable man. I am, or rather I was, very good-looking, five feet eleven, with a lot of curly red hair, and blue eyes. I am left-handed, which is another unusual thing. My hands have often been noticed. I get them from my mother, who was a Fishbourne, and a lady. As for my father, he was rather common. He was a little man, red and round like an apple, but very strong, for a reason I shall come to presently. The family must have had a pious liking for Bible names, because he was called Zebulon, my sister Peninnah, and I Ezra, which is not a name for a gentleman. At one time I thought of changing it, but I got over it by signing myself "E. Sandcraft."

Where my father was born I do not know, except that it was somewhere in New Jersey, for I remember that he was once angry because a man called him a Jersey Spaniard. I am not much concerned to write about my people, because I soon got above their level; and as to my mother, she died when I was an infant. I get my manners, which are rather remarkable, from her.

My aunt, Rachel Sandcraft, who kept house for us, was a queer character. She had a snug little property, about seven thousand dollars. An old aunt left her the money because she was stone-deaf. As this defect came upon her after she grew up, she still kept her voice. This woman was the cause of some of my ill luck in life, and I hope she is uncomfortable, wherever she is. I think with satisfaction that I helped to make her life uneasy when I was young, and worse later on. She gave away to the idle poor some of her small income, and hid the rest, like a magpie, in her Bible or rolled in her stockings, or in even queerer places. The worst of her was that she could tell what people said by looking at their lips; this I hated. But as I grew and became intelligent, her ways of hiding her money proved useful, to me at least. As to Peninnah, she was nothing special until she suddenly bloomed out into a rather stout, pretty girl, took to ribbons, and liked what she called "keeping company." She ran errands for every one, waited on my aunt, and thought I was a wonderful person—as indeed I was. I never could understand her fondness for helping everybody. A fellow has got himself to think about, and that is quite enough. I was told pretty often that I was the most selfish boy alive. But, then, I am an unusual person, and there are several names for things.

My father kept a small shop for the sale of legal stationery and the like, on Fifth street north of Chestnut. But his chief interest in life lay in the bell-ringing of Christ Church. He was leader, or No. 1, and the whole business was in the hands of a kind of guild which is nearly as old as the church. I used to hear more of it than I liked, because my father talked of nothing else. But I do not mean to bore myself writing of bells. I heard too much about "back shake," "raising in peal," "scales," and "touches," and the Lord knows what.

My earliest remembrance is of sitting on my father's shoulder when he led off the ringers. He was very strong, as I said, by reason of this exercise. With one foot caught in a loop of leather nailed to the floor, he would begin to pull No. 1, and by and by the whole peal would be swinging, and he going up and down, to my joy; I used to feel as if it was I that was making the great noise that rang out all over the town. My familiar acquaintance with the old church and its lumber-rooms, where were stored the dusty arms of William and Mary and George II., proved of use in my later days.

My father had a strong belief in my talents, and I do not think he was mistaken. As he was quite uneducated, he determined that I should not be. He had saved enough to send me to Princeton College, and when I was about fifteen I was set free from the public schools. I never liked them. The last I was at was the high school. As I had to come down-town to get home, we used to meet on Arch street the boys from the grammar-school of the university, and there were fights every week. In winter these were most frequent, because of the snowballing. A fellow had to take his share or be marked as a deserter. I never saw any personal good to be had out of a fight, but it was better to fight than to be cobbed. That means that two fellows hold you, and the other fellows kick you with their bent knees. It hurts.

I find just here that I am describing a thing as if I were writing for some other people to see. I may as well go on that way. After all, a man never can quite stand off and look at himself as if he was the only person concerned. He must have an audience, or make believe to have one, even if it is only himself. Nor, on the whole, should I be unwilling, if it were safe, to let people see how great ability may be defeated by the crankiness of fortune.

I may add here that a stone inside of a snowball discourages the fellow it hits. But neither our fellows nor the grammar-school used stones in snowballs. I rather liked it. If we had a row in the springtime we all threw stones, and here was one of those bits of stupid custom no man can understand; because really a stone outside of a snowball is much more serious than if it is mercifully padded with snow. I felt it to be a rise in life when I got out of the society of the common boys who attended the high school.

When I was there a man by the name of Dallas Bache was the head master. He had a way of letting the boys attend to what he called the character of the school. Once I had to lie to him about taking another boy's ball. He told my class that I had denied the charge, and that he always took it for granted that a boy spoke the truth. He knew well enough what would happen. It did. After that I was careful.

Princeton was then a little college, not expensive, which was very well, as my father had some difficulty to provide even the moderate amount needed.

I soon found that if I was to associate with the upper set of young men I needed money. For some time I waited in vain. But in my second year I discovered a small gold-mine, on which I drew with a moderation which shows even thus early the strength of my character.

I used to go home once a month for a Sunday visit, and on these occasions I was often able to remove from my aunt's big Bible a five- or ten-dollar note, which otherwise would have been long useless.

Now and then I utilized my opportunities at Princeton. I very much desired certain things like well-made clothes, and for these I had to run in debt to a tailor. When he wanted pay, and threatened to send the bill to my father, I borrowed from two or three young Southerners; but at last, when they became hard up, my aunt's uncounted hoard proved a last resource, or some rare chance in a neighboring room helped me out. I never did look on this method as of permanent usefulness, and it was only the temporary folly of youth.

Whatever else the pirate necessity appropriated, I took no large amount of education, although I was fond of reading, and especially of novels, which are, I think, very instructive to the young, especially the novels of Smollett and Fielding.

There is, however, little need to dwell on this part of my life. College students in those days were only boys, and boys are very strange animals. They have instincts. They somehow get to know if a fellow does not relate facts as they took place. I like to put it that way, because, after all, the mode of putting things is only one of the forms of self-defense, and is less silly than the ordinary wriggling methods which boys employ, and which are generally useless. I was rather given to telling large stories just for the fun of it, and, I think, told them well. But somehow I got the reputation of not being strictly definite, and when it was meant to indicate this belief they had an ill-mannered way of informing you. This consisted in two or three fellows standing up and shuffling noisily with their feet on the floor. When first I heard this I asked innocently what it meant, and was told it was the noise of the bearers' feet coming to take away Ananias. This was considered a fine joke.

During my junior year I became unpopular, and as I was very cautious, I cannot see why. At last, being hard up, I got to be foolishly reckless. But why dwell on the failures of immaturity?

The causes which led to my leaving Nassau Hall were not, after all, the mischievous outbreaks in which college lads indulge. Indeed, I have never been guilty of any of those pieces of wanton wickedness which

injure the feelings of others while they lead to no useful result. When I
left to return home, I set myself seriously to reflect upon the necessity
of greater care in following out my inclinations, and from that time
forward I have steadily avoided, whenever it was possible, the vulgar
vice of directly possessing myself of objects to which I could show no
legal title. My father was indignant at the results of my college career;
and, according to my aunt, his shame and sorrow had some effect in
shortening his life. My sister believed my account of the matter. It ended
in my being used for a year as an assistant in the shop, and in being
taught to ring bells—a fine exercise, but not proper work for a man of
refinement. My father died while training his bell-ringers in the Oxford
triple bob—broke a blood-vessel somewhere. How I could have caused
that I do not see.

I was now about nineteen years old, and, as I remember, a middle-
sized, well-built young fellow, with large eyes, a slight mustache, and, I
have been told, with very good manners and a somewhat humorous turn.
Besides these advantages, my guardian held in trust for me about two
thousand dollars. After some consultation between us, it was resolved
that I should study medicine. This conclusion was reached nine years
before the Rebellion broke out, and after we had settled, for the sake
of economy, in Woodbury, New Jersey. From this time I saw very little
of my deaf aunt or of Peninnah. I was resolute to rise in the world, and
not to be weighted by relatives who were without my tastes and my
manners.

I set out for Philadelphia, with many good counsels from my aunt
and guardian. I look back upon this period as a turning-point of my life.
I had seen enough of the world already to know that if you can succeed
without exciting suspicion, it is by far the pleasantest way; and I really
believe that if I had not been endowed with so fatal a liking for all the
good things of life I might have lived along as reputably as most men.
This, however, is, and always has been, my difficulty, and I suppose that
I am not responsible for the incidents to which it gave rise. Most men
have some ties in life, but I have said I had none which held me. Peninnah cried a good deal when we parted, and this, I think, as I was still
young, had a very good effect in strengthening my resolution to do
nothing which could get me into trouble. The janitor of the college to
which I went directed me to a boarding-house, where I engaged a small
third-story room, which I afterwards shared with Mr. Chaucer of Georgia.
He pronounced it, as I remember, "Jawjah."

In this very remarkable abode I spent the next two winters, and
finally graduated, along with two hundred more, at the close of my two
years of study. I should previously have been one year in a physician's
office as a student, but this regulation was very easily evaded. As to my
studies, the less said the better. I attended the quizzes, as they call them,
pretty closely, and, being of a quick and retentive memory, was thus
enabled to dispense with some of the six or seven lectures a day which
duller men found it necessary to follow.

Dissecting struck me as a rather nasty business for a gentleman, and on this account I did just as little as was absolutely essential. In fact, if a man took his tickets and paid the dissection fees, nobody troubled himself as to whether or not he did any more than this. A like evil existed at the graduation: whether you squeezed through or passed with credit was a thing which was not made public, so that I had absolutely nothing to stimulate my ambition. I am told that it is all very different to-day.

The astonishment with which I learned of my success was shared by the numerous Southern gentlemen who darkened the floors and perfumed with tobacco the rooms of our boarding-house. In my companions, during the time of my studies so called, as in other matters of life, I was somewhat unfortunate. All of them were Southern gentlemen, with more money than I had. Many of them carried great sticks, usually sword-canes, and some bowie-knives or pistols; also, they delighted in swallow-tailed coats, long hair, broad-brimmed felt hats, and very tight boots. I often think of these gentlemen with affectionate interest, and wonder how many are lying under the wheat-fields of Virginia. One could see them any day sauntering along with their arms over their companions' shoulders, splendidly indifferent to the ways of the people about them. They hated the "Nawth" and cursed the Yankees, and honestly believed that the leanest of them was a match for any half a dozen of the bulkiest of Northerners. I must also do them the justice to say that they were quite as ready to fight as to brag, which, by the way, is no meager statement. With these gentry—for whom I retain a respect which filled me with regret at the recent course of events—I spent a good deal of my large leisure. The more studious of both sections called us a hard crowd. What we did, or how we did it, little concerns me here, except that, owing to my esteem for chivalric blood and bleeding, I was led into many practices and excesses which cost my guardian and myself a good deal of money. At the close of my career as a student I found myself aged twenty-one years, and the owner of some seven hundred dollars—the rest of my small estate having disappeared variously within the last two years. After my friends had gone to their homes in the South I began to look about me for an office, and finally settled upon very good rooms in one of the downtown localities of the Quaker City. I am not specific as to the number and street, for reasons which may hereafter appear. I liked the situation on various accounts. It had been occupied by a doctor; the terms were reasonable; and it lay on the skirts of a good neighborhood, while below it lived a motley population, among which I expected to get my first patients and such fees as were to be had. Into this new home I moved my medical text-books, a few bones, and myself. Also, I displayed in the window a fresh sign, upon which was distinctly to be read:

DR. E. SANDCRAFT.
*Office hours,* 8 to 9 A.M., 7 to 9 P.M.

I felt now that I had done my fair share toward attaining a virtuous subsistence, and so I waited tranquilly, and without undue enthusiasm, to see the rest of the world do its part in the matter. Meanwhile I read up on all sorts of imaginable cases, stayed at home all through my office hours, and at intervals explored the strange section of the town which lay to the south of my office. I do not suppose there is anything like it elsewhere. It was then filled with grog-shops, brothels, slop-shops, and low lodging-houses. You could dine for a penny on soup made from the refuse meats of the rich, gathered at back gates by a horde of half-naked children, who all told varieties of one woeful tale. Here, too, you could be drunk for five cents, and be lodged for three, with men, women, and children of all colors lying about you. . . . All of this, as it came before me, I viewed with mingled disgust and philosophy. I hated filth, but I understood that society has to stand on somebody, and I was only glad that I was not one of the undermost and worst-squeezed bricks.

I can hardly believe that I waited a month without having been called upon by a single patient. At last a policeman on our beat brought me a fancy man with a dog-bite. This patient recommended me to his brother, the keeper of a small pawnbroking-shop, and by very slow degrees I began to get stray patients who were too poor to indulge in up-town doctors. I found the police very useful acquaintances; and, by a drink or a cigar now and then, I got most of the cases of cut heads and the like at the next station-house. These, however, were the aristocrats of my practice; the bulk of my patients were soap-fat men, rag-pickers, oystermen, hose-house bummers, and worse, with other and nameless trades, men and women, white, black, or mulatto. How they got the levies, fips, and quarters with which I was reluctantly paid, I do not know; that, indeed, was none of my business. They expected to pay, and they came to me in preference to the dispensary doctor, two or three squares away, who seemed to me to spend most of his days in the lanes and alleys about us. Of course he received no pay except experience, since the dispensaries in the Quaker City, as a rule, do not give salaries to their doctors; and the vilest of the poor prefer a "pay doctor" to one of these disinterested gentlemen, who cannot be expected to give their best brains for nothing, when at everybody's beck and call. I am told, indeed I know, that most young doctors do a large amount of poor practice, as it is called; but, for my own part, I think it better for both parties when the doctor insists upon some compensation being made to him. This has been usually my own custom, and I have not found reason to regret it.

Notwithstanding my strict attention to my own interests, I have been rather sorely dealt with by fate upon several occasions, where, so far as I could see, I was vigilantly doing everything in my power to keep myself out of trouble or danger. I may as well relate one of them, merely to illustrate of how little value a man's intellect may be when fate and the prejudices of the mass of men are against him.

One evening, late, I myself answered a ring at the bell, and found a small black boy on the steps, a shoeless, hatless little wretch, curled darkness for hair, and teeth like new tombstones. It was pretty cold and he was relieving his feet by standing first on one and then on the other. He did not wait for me to speak.

"Hi, sah, Missey Barker she say to come quick away, sah, to Numbah 709 Bedford street."

The locality did not look like pay, but it is hard to say in this quarter, because sometimes you found a well-to-do "brandy-snifter" (local for gin-shop) or a hard-working "leather-jeweler" (ditto for shoemaker), with next door, in a house better or worse, dozens of human rats for whom every police trap in the city was constantly set. . . .

I did not like its looks; but I blundered up an alley and into a back room, where I fell over somebody, and was cursed and told to lie down and keep easy, or somebody, meaning the man stumbled over, would make me. At last I lit on a staircase which led into the alley, and, after much useless inquiry, got as high as the garret. People hereabout did not know one another, or did not want to know, so that it was of little avail to ask questions. At length I saw a light through the cracks in the attic door, and walked in. To my amazement, the first person I saw was a woman of about thirty-five, in pearl-gray Quaker dress—one of your quiet, good-looking people. She was seated on a stool beside a straw mattress upon which lay a black woman. There were three others crowded close around a small stove, which was red-hot—an unusual spectacle in this street. Altogether a most nasty den.

As I came in, the little Quaker woman got up and said: "I took the liberty of sending for thee to look at this poor woman. I am afraid she has the smallpox. Will thee be so kind as to look at her?" And with this she held down the candle toward the bed.

"Good gracious!" I said hastily, seeing how the creature was speckled, "I didn't understand this, or I would not have come. I have important cases which I cannot subject to the risk of contagion. Best let her alone, miss," I added, "or send her to the smallpox hospital."

Upon my word, I was astonished at the little woman's indignation. She said just those things which make you feel as if somebody had been calling you names or kicking you—Was I really a doctor? and so on. It did not gain by being put in the ungrammatical tongue of Quakers. However, I never did fancy smallpox, and what could a fellow get by doctoring wretches like these? So I held my tongue and went away. About a week afterwards I met Evans, the dispensary man, a very common fellow, who was said to be frank.

"Helloa!" says he. "Doctor, you made a nice mistake about that darky at No. 709 Bedford street the other night. She had nothing but measles, after all."

"Of course I knew," said I, laughing; "but you don't think I was going in for dispensary trash, do you?"

"I should think not," said Evans.

I learned afterwards that this Miss Barker had taken an absurd fancy to the man because he had doctored the darky and would not let the Quakeress pay him. The end was, when I wanted to get a vacancy in the Southwark Dispensary, where they do pay the doctors, Miss Barker was malignant enough to take advantage of my oversight by telling the whole story to the board; so that Evans got in, and I was beaten.

You may be pretty sure that I found rather slow the kind of practice I have described, and began to look about for chances of bettering myself. In this sort of locality rather risky cases turned up now and then; and as soon as I got to be known as a reliable man, I began to get the peculiar sort of practice I wanted. Notwithstanding all my efforts, I found myself, at the close of three years, with all my means spent, and just able to live meagerly from hand to mouth, which by no means suited a man of my refined tastes.

Once or twice I paid a visit to my aunt, and was able to secure moderate aid by overhauling her concealed hoardings. But as to these changes of property I was careful, and did not venture to secure the large amount I needed. As to the Bible, it was at this time hidden, and I judged it, therefore, to be her chief place of deposit. Banks she utterly distrusted.

Six months went by, and I was worse off than ever—two months in arrears of rent, and numerous other debts to cigar-shops and liquor-dealers. Now and then some good job, such as a burglar with a cut head, helped me for a while; but, on the whole, I was like Slider Downeyhylle in Neal's "Charcoal Sketches," and kept going "downer and downer" the more I tried not to. Something had to be done.

It occurred to me, about this time, that if I moved into a more genteel locality I might get a better class of patients, and yet keep the best of those I now had. To do this it was necessary to pay my rent, and the more so because I was in a fair way to have no house at all over my head. But here fortune interposed. I was caught in a heavy rainstorm on Seventh street, and ran to catch an omnibus. As I pulled open the door I saw behind me the Quaker woman, Miss Barker. I laughed and jumped in. She had to run a little before the 'bus again stopped. She got pretty wet. An old man in the corner, who seemed in the way of taking charge of other people's manners, said to me: "Young man, you ought to be ashamed to get in before the lady, and in this pour, too!"

I said calmly, "But you got in before her."

He made no reply to this obvious fact, as he might have been in the 'bus a half-hour. A large, well-dressed man near by said, with a laugh, "Rather neat, that," and, turning, tried to pull up a window-sash. In the effort something happened, and he broke the glass, cutting his hand in half a dozen places. While he was using several quite profane phrases, I caught his hand and said, "I am a surgeon," and tied my handkerchief around the bleeding palm.

The guardian of manners said, "I hope you are not much hurt, but there was no reason why you should swear."

On this my patient said, "Go to ——," which silenced the monitor.

I explained to the wounded man that the cuts should be looked after at once. The matter was arranged by our leaving the 'bus, and, as the rain had let up, walking to his house. This was a large and quite luxurious dwelling on Fourth street. There I cared for his wounds, which, as I had informed him, required immediate attention. It was at this time summer, and his wife and niece, the only other members of his family, were absent. On my second visit I made believe to remove some splinters of glass which I brought with me. He said they showed how shamefully thin was that omnibus window-pane. To my surprise, my patient, at the end of the month,—for one wound was long in healing,—presented me with one hundred dollars. This paid my small rental, and as Mr. Poynter allowed me to refer to him, I was able to get a better office and bedroom on Spruce street. I saw no more of my patient until winter, although I learned that he was a stock-broker, not in the very best repute, but of a well-known family.

Meanwhile my move had been of small use. I was wise enough, however, to keep up my connection with my former clients, and contrived to live. It was no more than that. One day in December I was overjoyed to see Mr. Poynter enter. He was a fat man, very pale, and never, to my remembrance, without a permanent smile. He had very civil ways, and now at once I saw that he wanted something.

I hated the way that man saw through me. He went on without hesitation, taking me for granted. He began by saying he had confidence in my judgment, and when a man says that you had better look out. He said he had a niece who lived with him, a brother's child; that she was out of health and ought not to marry, which was what she meant to do. She was scared about her health, because she had a cough, and had lost a brother of consumption. I soon came to understand that, for reasons unknown to me, my friend did not wish his niece to marry. His wife, he also informed me, was troubled as to the niece's health. Now, he said, he wished to consult me as to what he should do. I suspected at once that he had not told me all.

I have often wondered at the skill with which I managed this rather delicate matter. I knew I was not well enough known to be of direct use, and was also too young to have much weight. I advised him to get Professor C.

Then my friend shook his head. He said in reply, "But suppose, doctor, he says there is nothing wrong with the girl?"

Then I began to understand him.

"Oh," I said, "you get a confidential written opinion from him. You can make it what you please when you tell her."

He said no. It would be best for me to ask the professor to see Miss Poynter; might mention my youth, and so on, as a reason. I was to get his opinion in writing.

"Well?" said I.

"After that I want you to write me a joint opinion to meet the case— all the needs of the case, you see."

I saw, but hesitated as to how much would make it worth while to pull his hot chestnuts out of the fire—one never knows how hot the chestnuts are.

Then he said, "Ever take a chance in stocks?"

I said, "No."

He said that he would lend me a little money and see what he could do with it. And here was his receipt from me for one thousand dollars, and here, too, was my order to buy shares of P. T. Y. Would I please to sign it? I did.

I was to call in two days at his house, and meantime I could think it over. It seemed to me a pretty weak plan. Suppose the young woman— well, supposing is awfully destructive of enterprise; and as for me, I had only to misunderstand the professor's opinion. I went to the house, and talked to Mr. Poynter about his gout. Then Mrs. Poynter came in, and began to lament her niece's declining health. After that I saw Miss Poynter. There is a kind of innocent-looking woman who knows no more of the world than a young chicken, and is choke-full of emotions. I saw it would be easy to frighten her. There are some instruments anybody can get any tune they like out of. I was very grave, and advised her to see the professor. And would I write to ask him, said Mr. Poynter. I said I would.

As I went out Mr. Poynter remarked: "You will clear some four hundred easy. Write to the professor. Bring my receipt to the office next week, and we will settle."

We settled. I tore up his receipt and gave him one for fifteen hundred dollars, and received in notes five hundred dollars.

In a day or so I had a note from the professor stating that Miss Poynter was in no peril; that she was, as he thought, worried, and had only a mild bronchial trouble. He advised me to do so-and-so, and had ventured to reassure my young patient. Now, this was a little more than I wanted. However, I wrote Mr. Poynter that the professor thought she had bronchitis, that in her case tubercle would be very apt to follow, and that at present, and until she was safe, we considered marriage undesirable.

Mr. Poynter said it might have been put stronger, but he would make it do. He made it. The first effect was an attack of hysterics. The final result was that she eloped with her lover, because if she was to die, as she wrote her aunt, she wished to die in her husband's arms. Human nature plus hysteria will defy all knowledge of character. This was what our old professor of practice used to say.

Mr. Poynter had now to account for a large trust estate which had somehow dwindled. Unhappily, princes are not the only people in whom you must not put your trust. As to myself, Professor C. somehow got to know the facts, and cut me dead. It was unpleasant, but I had my five hundred dollars, and—I needed them. I do not see how I could have been more careful.

After this things got worse. Mr. Poynter broke, and did not even pay my last bill. I had to accept several rather doubtful cases, and once a policeman I knew advised me that I had better be on my guard.

But, really, so long as I adhered to the common code of my profession I was in danger of going without my dinner. . . .

One night, as I was debating with myself as to how I was to improve my position, I heard a knock on my shutter, and, going to the door, let in a broad-shouldered man with a whisky face and a great hooked nose. He wore a heavy black beard and mustache, and looked like the wolf in the pictures of Red Riding-hood which I had seen as a child.

"Your name's Sandcraft?" said the man.

"Yes; that's my name—Dr. Sandcraft."

As he sat down he shook the snow over everything, and said coolly: "Set down, doc; I want to talk with you."

"What can I do for you?" said I.

The man looked around the room rather scornfully, at the same time throwing back his coat and displaying a red neckerchief and a huge garnet pin. "Guess you're not overly rich," he said.

"Not especially," said I. "What's that your business?"

He did not answer, but merely said, "Know Simon Stagers?"

"Can't say I do," said I, cautiously. Simon was a burglar who had blown off two fingers when mining a safe. I had attended him while he was hiding.

"Can't say you do. Well, you can lie, and no mistake. Come, now, doc. Simon says you're safe, and I want to have a leetle plain talk with you."

With this he laid ten gold eagles on the table. I put out my hand instinctively.

"Let 'em alone," cried the man, sharply. "They're easy earned, and ten more like 'em."

"For doing what?" I said.

The man paused a moment, and looked around him; next he stared at me, and loosened his cravat with a hasty pull. "You're the coroner," said he.

"I! What do you mean?"

"Yes you're the coroner; don't you understand?" and so saying, he shoved the gold pieces toward me.

"Very good," said I; "we will suppose I'm the coroner. What next?"

"And being the coroner," said he, "you get this note, which requests you call at No. 9 Blank street to examine the body of a young man which is supposed—only supposed, you see—to have—well, to have died under suspicious circumstances."

"Go on," said I.

"No," he returned; "not till I know how you like it. Stagers and another knows it; and it wouldn't be very safe for you to split, besides not making nothing out of it. But what I say is this, Do you like the business of coroner?"

I did not like it; but just then two hundred in gold was life to me, so I said: "Let me hear the whole of it first. I am safe."

"That's square enough," said the man. "My wife's got"—correcting himself with a shivery shrug—"my wife had a brother that took to cutting up rough because when I'd been up too late I handled her a leetle hard now and again.

"Luckily he fell sick with typhoid just then—you see, he lived with us. When he got better I guessed he'd drop all that; but somehow he was worse than ever—clean off his head, and strong as an ox. My wife said to put him away in an asylum. I didn't think that would do. At last he tried to get out. He was going to see the police about—well—the thing was awful serious, and my wife carrying on like mad, and wanting doctors. I had no mind to run, and something had got to be done. So Simon Stagers and I talked it over. The end of it was, he took worse of a sudden, and got so he didn't know nothing. Then I rushed for a doctor. He said it was a perforation, and there ought to have been a doctor when he was first took sick.

"Well, the man died, and as I kept about the house, my wife had no chance to talk. The doctor fussed a bit, but at last he gave a certificate. I thought we were done with it. But my wife writes a note and gives it to a boy in the alley to put in the post. We suspicioned her, and Stagers was on the watch. After the boy got away a bit, Simon bribed him with a quarter to give him the note, which wasn't no less than a request to the coroner to come to the house to-morrow and make an examination, as foul play was suspected—and poison."

When the man quit talking he glared at me. I sat still. I was cold all over. I was afraid to go on, and afraid to go back, besides which, I did not doubt that there was a good deal of money in the case.

"Of course," said I, "it's nonsense; only I suppose you don't want the officers about, and a fuss, and that sort of thing."

"Exactly," said my friend. "It's all bosh about poison. You're the coroner. You take this note and come to my house. Says you: 'Mrs. File, are you the woman that wrote this note? Because in that case I must examine the body.'"

"I see," said I; "she needn't know who I am, or anything else; but if I tell her it's all right, do you think she won't want to know why there isn't a jury, and so on?"

"Bless you," said the man, "the girl isn't over seventeen, and doesn't know no more than a baby. As we live up-town miles away, she won't know anything about you."

"I'll do it," said I, suddenly, for, as I saw, it involved no sort of risk; "but I must have three hundred dollars."

"And fifty," added the wolf, "if you do it well."

Then I knew it was serious.

With this the man buttoned about him a shaggy gray overcoat, and took his leave without a single word in addition.

A minute later he came back and said: "Stagers is in this business, and I was to remind you of Lou Wilson,—I forgot that,—the woman that died last year. That's all." Then he went away, leaving me in a cold sweat.

I knew now I had no choice. I understand why I had been selected.

For the first time in my life, that night I couldn't sleep. I thought to myself, at last, that I would get up early, pack a few clothes, and escape, leaving my books to pay as they might my arrears of rent. Looking out of the window, however, in the morning, I saw Stagers prowling about the opposite pavement; and as the only exit except the street door was an alleyway which opened alongside of the front of the house, I gave myself up for lost. About ten o'clock I took my case of instruments and started for File's house, followed, as I too well understood, by Stagers.

I knew the house, which was in a small uptown street, by its closed windows and the craped bell, which I shuddered as I touched. However, it was too late to draw back, and I therefore inquired for Mrs. File. A haggard-looking young woman came down, and led me into a small parlor, for whose darkened light I was thankful enough.

"Did you write this note?"

"I did," said the woman, "if you're the coroner. Joe File—he's my husband—he's gone out to see about the funeral. I wish it was his, I do."

"What do you suspect?" said I.

"I'll tell you," she returned in a whisper. "I think he was made away with. I think there was foul play. I think he was poisoned. That's what I think."

"I hope you may be mistaken," said I. "Suppose you let me see the body."

"You shall see it," she replied; and following her, I went up-stairs to a front chamber where I found the corpse.

"Get it over soon," said the woman, with strange firmness. "If there ain't no murder been done I shall have to run for it; if there was"—and her face set hard—"I guess I'll stay." With this she closed the door and left me with the dead.

If I had known what was before me I never could have gone into the thing at all. It looked a little better when I had opened a window and let in plenty of light; for although I was, on the whole, far less afraid of dead than living men, I had an absurd feeling that I was doing this dead man a distinct wrong—as if it mattered to the dead, after all! When the affair was over, I thought more of the possible consequences than of its relation to the dead man himself; but do as I would at the time, I was in a ridiculous funk, and especially when going through the forms of a post-mortem examination.

I am free to confess now that I was careful not to uncover the man's face, and that when it was over I backed to the door and hastily escaped from the room. On the stairs opposite to me Mrs. File was seated, with her bonnet on and a bundle in her hand.

"Well," said she, rising as she spoke, and with a certain eagerness in her tone, "what killed him? Was it poison?"

"Poison, my good woman!" said I "When a man has typhoid fever he don't need poison to kill him. He had a relapse, that's all."

"And do you mean to say he wasn't poisoned," said she, with

more than a trace of disappointment in her voice—"not poisoned at all?"

"No more than you are," said I. "If I had found any signs of foul play I should have had a regular inquest. As it is, the less said about it the better. The fact is, it would have been much wiser to have kept quiet at the beginning. I can't understand why you should have troubled me about it at all. The man had a perforation. It is common enough in typhoid."

"That's what the doctor said—I didn't believe him. I guess now the sooner I leave the better for me."

"As to that,"I returned, "it is none of my business; but you may rest certain about the cause of your brother's death."

My fears were somewhat quieted that evening when Stagers and the wolf appeared with the remainder of the money, and I learned that Mrs. File had fled from her home and, as File thought likely, from the city also. A few months later File himself disappeared, and Stagers found his way for the third time into the penitentiary. Then I felt at ease. I now see, for my own part, that I was guilty of more than one mistake, and that I displayed throughout a want of intelligence. I ought to have asked more, and also might have got a good fee from Mrs. File on account of my services as coroner. It served me, however, as a good lesson; but it was several months before I felt quite comfortable.

Meanwhile money became scarce once more, and I was driven to my wit's end to devise how I should continue to live as I had done. I tried, among other plans, that of keeping certain pills and other medicines, which I sold to my patients; but on the whole I found it better to send all my prescriptions to one druggist, who charged the patient ten or twenty cents over the correct price, and handed this amount to me.

In some cases I am told the percentage is supposed to be a donation on the part of the apothecary; but I rather fancy the patient pays for it in the end. It is one of the absurd vagaries of the profession to discountenance the practice I have described, but I wish, for my part, I had never done anything more foolish or more dangerous. Of course it inclines a doctor to change his medicines a good deal, and to order them in large quantities, which is occasionally annoying to the poor; yet, as I have always observed, there is no poverty as painful as your own, so that I prefer to distribute pecuniary suffering among many rather than to concentrate it on myself. That's a rather neat phrase.

About six months after the date of this annoying adventure, an incident occurred which altered somewhat, and for a time improved, my professional position. During my morning office-hour an old woman came in, and putting down a large basket, wiped her face with a yellow-cotton handkerchief, and afterwards with the corner of her apron. Then she looked around uneasily, got up, settled her basket on her arm with a jerk which may have decided the future of an egg or two, and remarked briskly: "Don't see no little bottles about; got the wrong stall, I guess. You ain't no homeopath doctor, are you?"

With great presence of mind, I replied: "Well, ma'am, that depends upon what you want. Some of my patients like one, and some like the other." I was about to add, "You pay your money and you take your choice," but thought better of it, and held my peace, refraining from classical quotation.

"Being as that's the case," said the old lady, "I'll just tell you my symptoms. You said you give either kind of medicine, didn't you?"

"Just so," replied I.

"Clams or oysters, whichever opens most lively, as my old Joe says —tends the oyster-stand at stall No. 9. Happen to know Joe?"

No, I did not know Joe; but what were the symptoms?

They proved to be numerous, and included a stunning in the head and a misery in the side, with bokin after victuals.

I proceeded, of course, to apply a stethoscope over her ample bosom, though what I heard on this and similar occasions I should find it rather difficult to state. I remember well my astonishment in one instance where, having unconsciously applied my instrument over a clamorous silver watch in the watchfob of a sea-captain, I concluded for a moment that he was suffering from a rather remarkable displacement of the heart. As to my old lady, whose name was Checkers, and who kept an apple-stand near by, I told her that I was out of pills just then, but would have plenty next day. Accordingly, I proceeded to invest a small amount at a place called a homeopathic pharmacy, which I remember amused me immensely.

A stout little German, with great silver spectacles, sat behind a counter containing numerous jars of white powders labeled concisely "Lac.," "Led.," "Onis.," "Op.," "Puls.," etc., while behind him were shelves filled with bottles of what looked like minute white shot.

"I want some homeopathic medicine," said I.

"Vat kindt?" said my friend. "Vat you vants to cure?"

I explained at random that I wished to treat diseases in general.

"Vell, ve gifs you a case, mit a pook," and thereon produced a large box containing bottles of small pills and powders, labeled variously with the names of the diseases, so that all you required was to use the headache or colic bottle in order to meet the needs of those particular maladies.

I was struck at first with the exquisite simplicity of this arrangement; but before purchasing, I happened luckily to turn over the leaves of a book, in two volumes, which lay on the counter; it was called "Jahr's Manual." Opening at page 310, vol. i, I lit upon "Lachesis," which proved to my amazement to be snake-venom. This Mr. Jahr stated to be indicated for use in upward of a hundred symptoms. At once it occured to me that "Lach." was the medicine for my money, and that it was quite needless to waste cash on the box. I therefore bought a small jar of "Lach." and a lot of little pills, and started for home.

My old woman proved a fast friend; and as she sent me numerous patients, I by and by altered my sign to "Homeopathic Physician and

Surgeon," whatever that may mean, and was regarded by my medical brothers as a lost sheep, and by the little-pill doctors as one who had seen the error of his ways.

In point of fact, my new practice had decided advantages. All pills looked and tasted alike, and the same might be said of the powders, so that I was never troubled by those absurd investigations into the nature of remedies which some patients are prone to make. Of course I desired to get business, and it was therefore obviously unwise to give little pills of "Lac.," or "Puls.," or "Sep.," when a man needed a dose of oil, or a white-faced girl iron, or the like. I soon made the useful discovery that it was only necessary to prescribe cod-liver oil, for instance, as a diet, in order to make use of it where required. When a man got impatient over an ancient ague, I usually found, too, that I could persuade him to let me try a good dose of quinine; while, on the other hand, there was a distinct pecuniary advantage on those cases of the shakes which could be made to believe that it "was best not to interfere with nature." I ought to add that this kind of faith is uncommon among folks who carry hods or build walls.

For women who are hysterical, and go heart and soul into the business of being sick, I have found the little pills a most charming resort, because you cannot carry the refinement of symptoms beyond what my friend Jahr has done in the way of fitting medicines to them, so that if I had taken seriously to practising this double form of therapeutics, it had, as I saw, certain conveniences.

Another year went by, and I was beginning to prosper in my new mode of life. My medicines (being chiefly milk-sugar, with variations as to the labels) cost next to nothing; and as I charged pretty well for both these and my advice, I was now able to start a gig.

I solemnly believe that I should have continued to succeed in the practice of my profession if it had not happened that fate was once more unkind to me, by throwing in my path one of my old acquaintances. I had a consultation one day with the famous homeopath Dr. Zwanzig. As we walked away we were busily discussing the case of a poor consumptive fellow who previously had lost a leg. In consequence of this defect, Dr. Zwanzig considered that the ten-thousandth of a grain of aurum would be an overdose, and that it must be fractioned so as to allow for the departed leg, otherwise the rest of the man would be getting a leg-dose too much. I was particularly struck with this view of the case, but I was still more, and less pleasingly, impressed at the sight of my former patient Stagers, who nodded to me familiarly from the opposite pavement.

I was not at all surprised when, that evening quite late, I found this worthy waiting in my office. I looked around uneasily, which was clearly understood by my friend, who retorted: "Ain't took nothin' of yours, doc. You don't seem right awful glad to see me. You needn't be afraid—I've only fetched you a job, and a right good one, too."

I replied that I had my regular business, that I preferred he should get some one else, and pretty generally made Mr. Stagers aware that I had had enough of him. I did not ask him to sit down, and, just as I supposed him about to leave, he seated himself with a grin, remarking, "No use, doc; got to go into it this one time."

At this I, naturally enough, grew angry and used several rather violent phrases.

"No use, doc," said Stagers.

Then I softened down, and laughed a little, and treated the thing as a joke, whatever it was, for I dreaded to hear.

But Stagers was fate. Stagers was inevitable. "Won't do, doc—not even money wouldn't get you off."

"No?" said I, interrogatively, and as coolly as I could, contriving at the same time to move toward the window. It was summer, the sashes were up, the shutters half drawn in, and a policeman whom I knew was lounging opposite, as I had noticed when I entered. I would give Stagers a scare, charge him with theft—anything but get mixed up with his kind again. It was the folly of a moment and I should have paid dear for it.

He must have understood me, the scoundrel, for in an instant I felt a cold ring of steel against my ear, and a tiger clutch on my cravat. "Sit down," he said. "What a fool you are! Guess you forgot that there coroner's business and the rest." Needless to say that I obeyed. "Best not try that again," continued my guest. "Wait a moment"; and rising, he closed the window.

There was no resource left but to listen; and what followed I shall condense rather than relate it in the language employed by Mr. Stagers.

It appeared that my other acquaintance Mr. File had been guilty of a cold-blooded and long-premeditated murder, for which he had been tried and convicted. He now lay in jail awaiting his execution, which was to take place at Carsonville, Ohio. It seemed that with Stagers and others he had formed a band of expert counterfeiters in the West. Their business lay in the manufacture of South American currencies. File had thus acquired a fortune so considerable that I was amazed at his having allowed his passion to seduce him into unprofitable crime. In his agony he unfortunately thought of me, and had bribed Stagers largely in order that he might be induced to find me. When the narration had reached this stage, and I had been made fully to understand that I was now and hereafter under the sharp eye of Stagers and his friends, that, in a word, escape was out of the question, I turned on my tormentor.

"What does all this mean?" I said. "What does File expect me to do?"

"Don't believe he exactly knows," said Stagers. "Something or other to get him clear of hemp."

"But what stuff!" I replied. "How can I help him? What possible influence could I exert?"

"Can't say," answered Stagers, imperturbably. "File has a notion you're 'most cunning enough for anything. Best try something, doc."

"And what if I won't do it?" said I. "What does it matter to me if the rascal swings or no?"

"Keep cool, doc," returned Stagers. "I'm only agent in this here business. My principal, that's File, he says: "Tell Sandcraft to find some way to get me clear. Once out, I give him ten thousand dollars. If he don't turn up something that will suit, I'll blow about that coroner business and Lou Wilson, and break him up generally.' "

"You don't mean," said I, in a cold sweat—"you don't mean that, if I can't do this impossible thing, he will inform on me?"

"Just so," returned Stagers. "Got a cigar, doc?"

I only half heard him. What a frightful position! I had been leading a happy and an increasingly profitable life—no scrapes and no dangers; and here, on a sudden, I had presented to me the alternative of saving a wretch from the gallows or of spending unlimited years in a State penitentiary. As for the money, it became as dead leaves for this once only in my life. My brain seemed to be spinning round. I grew weak all over.

"Cheer up a little," said Stagers. "Take a nip of whisky. Things ain't at the worst, by a good bit. You just get ready, and we'll start by the morning train. Guess you'll try out something smart enough as we travel along. Ain't got a heap of time to lose."

I was silent. A great anguish had me in its grip. I might squirm as I would, it was all in vain. Hideous plans rose to my mind, born of this agony of terror. I might murder Stagers, but what good would that do? As to File, he was safe from my hand. At last I became too confused to think any longer. "When do we leave?" I said feebly.

"At six to-morrow," he returned.

How I was watched and guarded, and how hurried over a thousand miles of rail to my fate, little concerns us now. I find it dreadful to recall it to memory. Above all, an aching eagerness for revenge upon the man who had caused me these sufferings was uppermost in my mind. Could I not fool the wretch and save myself? Of a sudden an idea came into my consciousness. Then it grew and formed itself, became possible, probable, seemed to me sure. "Ah," said I, "Stagers, give me something to eat and drink." I had not tasted food for two days.

Within a day or two after my arrival, I was enabled to see File in his cell, on the plea of being a clergyman from his native place.

I found that I had not miscalculated my danger. The man did not appear to have the least idea as to how I was to help him. He only knew that I was in his power, and he used his control to insure that something more potent than friendship should be enlisted in his behalf. As the days went by, his behavior grew to be a frightful thing to witness. He threatened, flattered, implored, offered to double the sum he had promised if I would save him. My really reasonable first thought was to see the governor of the State, and, as Stager's former physician, make oath to his having had many attacks of epilepsy followed by brief periods of homicidal mania. He had, in fact, had fits of alcoholic epilepsy. Unluckily, the governor was in a distant city. The time was short, and the case against my man too clear. Stagers said it would not do. I was at my wit's end. "Got to do something," said File, "or I'll attend to your case, doc."

"But," said I, "suppose there is really nothing?"

"Well," said Stagers to me when were were alone, "you get him satisfied, anyhow. He'll never let them hang him, and perhaps—well, I'm going to give him these pills when I get a chance. He asked to have them. But what's your other plan?"

Stagers knew as much about medicine as a pig knows about the opera. So I set to work to delude him, first asking if he could secure me, as a clergyman, an hour alone with File just before the execution. He said money would do it, and what was my plan?

"Well," said I, "there was once a man named Dr. Chovet. He lived in London. A gentleman who turned highwayman was to be hanged. You see," said I, "this was about 1760. Well, his friends bribed the jailer and the hangman. The doctor cut a hole in the man's windpipe, very low down where it could be partly hid by a loose cravat. So, as they hanged him only a little while, and the breath went in and out of the opening below the noose, he was only just insensible when his friends got him—"

"And he got well," cried Stagers, much pleased with my rather melodramatic tale.

"Yes," I said, "he got well, and lived to take purses, all dressed in white. People had known him well, and when he robbed his great-aunt, who was not in the secret, she swore she had seen his ghost."

Stagers said that was a fine story; guessed it would work; small town, new business, lots of money to use. In fact, the attempt thus to save a man is said to have been made, but, by ill luck, the man did not recover. It answered my purpose, but how any one, even such an ass as this fellow, could believe it could succeed puzzles me to this day.

File became enthusiastic over my scheme, and I cordially assisted his credulity. The thing was to keep the wretch quiet until the business blew up or—and I shuddered—until File, in despair, took his pill. I should in any case find it wise to leave in haste. . . .

I shall be doing injustice to my own intellect if I do not hasten to state again that I had not the remotest belief in the efficacy of my plan for any purpose except to get me out of a very uncomfortable position and give me, with time, a chance to escape.

Stagers and I were both disguised as clergymen, and were quite freely admitted to the condemned man's cell. In fact, there was in the little town a certain trustful simplicity about all their arrangements. The day but one before the execution Stagers informed me that File had the pills, which he, Stagers, had contrived to give him. Stagers seemed pleased with our plan. I was not. He was really getting uneasy and suspicious of me—as I was soon to find out.

So far our plans, or rather mine, had worked to a marvel. Certain of File's old accomplices succeeded in bribing the hangman to shorten the time of suspension. Arrangements were made to secure me two hours alone with the prisoner, so that nothing seemed to be wanting to this tomfool business. I had assured Stagers that I would not need to see File again previous to the operation; but in the forenoon of the day before that set for the execution I was seized with a feverish impatience, which luckily prompted me to visit him once more. As usual, I was admitted readily, and nearly reached his cell when I became aware, from the sound of voices heard through the grating in the door, that there was a visitor in the cell. "Who is with him?" I inquired of the turnkey.

"The doctor," he replied.

"Doctor?" I said, pausing. "What doctor?"

"Oh, the jail doctor. I was to come back in half an hour to let him out; but he's got a quarter to stay. Shall I let you in, or will you wait?"

"No," I replied; "it is hardly right to interrupt them. I will walk in the corridor for ten minutes or so, and then you can come back to let me into the cell."

"Very good," he returned, and left me.

As soon as I was alone, I cautiously advanced until I stood alongside of the door, through the barred grating of which I was able readily to hear what went on within. The first words I caught were these:

"And you tell me, doctor, that, even if a man's windpipe was open, the hanging would kill him—are you sure?"

"Yes, I believe there would be no doubt of it. I cannot see how escape would be possible. But let me ask you why you have sent for me to ask these singular questions. You cannot have the faintest hope of escape, and least of all in such a manner as this. I advise you to think about the fate which is inevitable. You must, I fear, have much to reflect upon."

"But," said File, "if I wanted to try this plan of mine, couldn't some one be found to help me, say if he was to make twenty thousand or so by it? I mean a really good doctor." Evidently File cruelly mistrusted my skill, and meant to get some one to aid me.

"If you mean me," answered the doctor, "some one cannot be found, neither for twenty nor fifty thousand dollars. Besides, if any one were wicked enough to venture on such an attempt, he would only be deceiving you with a hope which would be utterly vain. You must be off your head."

I understood all this with an increasing fear in my mind. I had meant to get away that night at all risks. I saw now that I must go at once.

After a pause he said: "Well, doctor, you know a poor devil in my fix will clutch at straws. Hope I have not offended you."

"Not in the least," returned the doctor. "Shall I send you Mr. Smith?" This was my present name; in fact, I was known as the Rev. Eliphalet Smith.

"I would like it," answered File; "but as you go out, tell the warden I want to see him immediately about a matter of great importance."

At this stage I began to apprehend very distinctly that the time had arrived when it would be wiser for me to delay escape no longer. Accordingly, I waited until I heard the doctor rise, and at once stepped quietly away to the far end of the corridor. I had scarcely reached it when the door which closed it was opened by a turnkey who had come to relieve the doctor and let me into the cell. Of course my peril was imminent. If the turnkey mentioned my near presence to the prisoner, immediate disclosure would follow. If some lapse of time were secured before the warden obeyed the request from File that he should visit him, I might gain thus a much-needed hour, but hardly more. I therefore said to the officer: "Tell the warden that the doctor wishes to remain an hour longer with the prisoner, and that I shall return myself at the end of that time."

"Very good, sir," said the turnkey, allowing me to pass out, and, as he followed me, relocking the door of the corridor. "I'll tell him," he said. It is needless to repeat that I never had the least idea of carrying out the ridiculous scheme with which I had deluded File and Stagers, but so far Stagers' watchfulness had given me no chance to escape.

In a few moments I was outside of the jail gate, and saw my fellow-clergyman, Mr. Stagers, in full broadcloth and white tie, coming down the street toward me. As usual, he was on his guard; but this time he had to deal with a man grown perfectly desperate, with everything to win and nothing to lose. My plans were made, and, wild as they were, I thought them worth the trying. I must evade this man's terrible watch. How keen it was, you cannot imagine; but it was aided by three of the infamous gang to which File had belonged, for without these spies no one person could possibly have sustained so perfect a system.

I took Stager's arm. "What time," said I, "does the first train start for Dayton?"

"At twelve. What do you want?"

"How far is it?"

"About fifteen miles," he replied.

"Good. I can get back by eight o'clock to-night."

"Easily," said Stagers, "if you go. What do you want?"

"I want a smaller tube to put in the windpipe—must have it, in fact."

"Well, I don't like it," said he, "but the thing's got to go through somehow. If you must go, I will go along myself. Can't lose sight of you, doc, just at present. You're monstrous precious. Did you tell File?"

"Yes," said I; "he's all right. Come. We've no time to lose."

Nor had we. Within twenty minutes we were seated in the last car of a long train, and running at the rate of twenty miles an hour toward Dayton. In about ten minutes I asked Stagers for a cigar.

"Can't smoke here," said he.

"No," I answered; "of course not. I'll go forward into the smoking-car."

"Come along," said he, and we went through the train.

I was not sorry he had gone with me when I found in the smoking-car one of the spies who had been watching me so constantly. Stagers nodded to him and grinned at me, and we sat down together.

"Chut!" said I, "left my cigar on the window-ledge in the hindmost car. Be back in a moment." . . .

As I wish rather to illustrate my very remarkable professional career than to amuse by describing its lesser incidents, I shall not linger to tell how I succeeded, at last, in reaching St. Louis. Fortunately, I had never ceased to anticipate the moment when escape from File and his friends would be possible, so that I always carried about with me the very small funds with which I had hastily provided myself upon leaving. The whole amount did not exceed sixty-five dollars, but with this, and a gold watch worth twice as much, I hoped to be able to subsist until my own ingenuity enabled me to provide more liberally for the future. Naturally enough, I scanned the papers closely to discover some account of File's death and of the disclosures concerning myself which he was only too likely to have made.

I came at last on an account of how he had poisoned himself, and so escaped the hangman. I never learned what he had said about me, but I was quite sure he had not let me off easy. I felt that this failure to announce his confessions was probably due to a desire on the part of the police to avoid alarming me. Be this as it may, I remained long ignorant as to whether or not the villain betrayed my part in that unusual coroner's inquest.

Before many days I had resolved to make another and a bold venture. Accordingly appeared in the St. Louis papers an advertisement to the effect that Dr. von Ingenhoff, the well-known German physician, who had spent two years on the Plains acquiring a knowledge of Indian medicine, was prepared to treat all diseases by vegetable remedies alone. Dr. von Ingenhoff would remain in St. Louis for two weeks, and was to be found at the Grayson House every day from ten until two o'clock.

To my delight, I got two patients the first day. The next I had twice as many, when at once I hired two connecting rooms, and made a very useful arrangement, which I may describe dramatically in the following way:

There being two or three patients waiting while I finished my cigar and morning julep, enters a respectable-looking old gentleman who inquires briskly of the patients if this is really Dr. von Ingenhoff's. He is told it is. My friend was apt to overact his part. I had often occasion to ask him to be less positive.

"Ah," says he, "I shall be delighted to see the doctor. Five years ago I was scalped on the Plains, and now"—exhibiting a well-covered head—"you see what the doctor did for me. 'T isn't any wonder I've come fifty miles to see him. Any of you been scalped, gentlemen?"

To none of them had this misfortune arrived as yet; but, like most folks in the lower ranks of life and some in the upper ones, it was pleasant to find a genial person who would listen to their account of their own symptoms.

Presently, after hearing enough, the old gentleman pulls out a large watch. "Bless me! it's late. I must call again. May I trouble you, sir, to say to the doctor that his old friend called to see him and will drop in again to-morrow? Don't forget: Governor Brown of Arkansas." A moment later the governor visited me by a side door, with his account of the symptoms of my patients.

Enter a tall Hoosier, the governor having retired. "Now, doc," says the Hoosier, "I've been handled awful these two years back." "Stop!" I exclaimed. "Open your eyes. There, now, let me see," taking his pulse as I speak. "Ah, you've a pain there, and there, and you can't sleep; cocktails don't agree any longer. Weren't you bit by a dog two years ago?" "I was," says the Hoosier, in amazement. "Sir," I reply, "you have chronic hydrophobia. It's the water in the cocktails that disagrees with you. My bitters will cure you in a week, sir. No more whisky—drink milk."

The astonishment of my patient at these accurate revelations may be imagined. He is allowed to wait for his medicine in the anteroom, where the chances are in favor of his relating how wonderfully I had told all his symptoms at a glance.

Governor Brown of Arkansas was a small but clever actor, whom I met in the billiard-room, and who day after day, in varying disguises and modes, played off the same tricks, to our great common advantage.

At my friend's suggestion, we very soon added to our resources by the purchase of two electromagnetic batteries. This special means of treating all classes of maladies has advantages which are altogether peculiar. In the first place, you instruct your patient that the treatment is of necessity a long one. A striking mode of putting it is to say, "Sir, you have been six months getting ill; it will require six months for a cure." There is a correct sound about such a phrase, and it is sure to satisfy. Two sittings a week, at two dollars a sitting, will pay. In many cases the patient gets well while you are electrifying him. Whether or not the electricity cured him is a thing I shall never know. If, however, he began to show signs of impatience, I advised him that he would require a year's treatment, and suggested that it would be economical for him to buy a battery and use it at home. Thus advised, he pays you twenty dollars for an instrument which cost you ten, and you are rid of a troublesome case.

If the reader has followed me closely, he will have learned that I am a man of large and liberal views in my profession, and of a very justifiable ambition. The idea has often occurred to me of combining in one establishment all the various modes of practice which are known as irregular. This, as will be understood, is really only a wider application of the idea which prompted me to unite in my own business homeopathy and the practice of medicine. I proposed to my partner, accordingly, to combine with our present business that of spiritualism, which I knew had been very profitably turned to account in connection with medical practice. As soon as he agreed to this plan, which, by the way, I hoped to enlarge so as to include all the available isms, I set about making such preparations as were necessary. I remembered having read somewhere that a Dr. Schiff had shown that he could produce remarkable "knockings," so called, by voluntarily dislocating the great toe and then forcibly drawing it back into its socket. A still better noise could be made by throwing the tendon of the peroneus longus muscle out of the hollow in which it lies, alongside of the ankle. After some effort I was able to accomplish both feats quite readily, and could occasion a remarkable variety of sounds, according to the power which I employed or the positions which I occupied at the time. As to all other matters, I trusted to the suggestions of my own ingenuity, which, as a rule, has rarely failed me.

The largest success attended the novel plan which my lucky genius had devised, so that soon we actually began to divide large profits and to lay by a portion of our savings. It is, of course, not to be supposed that this desirable result was attained without many annoyances and some positive danger. My spiritual revelations, medical and other, were, as may be supposed, only more or less happy guesses; but in this, as in predictions as to the weather and other events, the rare successes always get more prominence in the minds of men than the numerous failures. Moreover, whenever a person has been fool enough to resort to folks like myself, he is always glad to be able to defend his conduct by bringing forward every possible proof of skill on the part of the men he consulted. These considerations, and a certain love of mysterious or unusual means, I have commonly found sufficient to secure an ample share of gullible individuals. I may add, too, that those who would be shrewd enough to understand and expose us are wise enough to keep away altogether. Such as did come were, as a rule, easy enough to manage, but now and then we hit upon some utterly exceptional patient who was both foolish enough to consult us and sharp enough to know he had been swindled. When such a fellow made a fuss, it was occasionally necessary to return his money if it was found impossible to bully him into silence. In one or two instances, where I had promised a cure upon prepayment of two or three hundred dollars, I was either sued or threatened with suit, and had to refund a part or the whole of the amount; but must people preferred to hold their tongues rather than expose to the world the extent of their own folly.

In one most disastrous case I suffered personally to a degree which I never can recall without a distinct sense of annoyance, both at my own want of care and at the disgusting consequences which it brought upon me.

Early one morning an old gentleman called, in a state of the utmost agitation, and explained that he desired to consult the spirits as to a heavy loss which he had experienced the night before. He had left, he said, a sum of money in his pantaloons pocket upon going to bed. In the morning he had changed his clothes and gone out, forgetting to remove the notes. Returning in an hour in great haste, he discovered that the garment still lay upon the chair where he had thrown it, but that the money was missing. I at once desired him to be seated, and proceeded to ask him certain questions, in a chatty way, about the habits of his household, the amount lost, and the like, expecting thus to get some clue which would enable me to make my spirits display the requisite share of sagacity in pointing out the thief. I learned readily that he was an old and wealthy man, a little close, too, I suspected, and that he lived in a large house with but two servants, and an only son about twenty-one years old. . . . I sat down at a table, and, after a brief silence, demanded in a solemn voice if there were any spirits present. By industriously cracking my big toe joint I was enabled to represent at once the presence of a numerous assembly of these worthies. Then I inquired if any one of them had been present when the robbery was effected. A prompt double knock replied in the affirmative. I may say here, by the way, that the unanimity of the spirits as to their use of two knocks for "yes" and one for "no" is a very remarkable point, and shows, if it shows anything, how perfect and universal must be the social intercourse of the respected departed. It is worthy of note, also, that if the spirit—I will not say the medium—perceives after one knock that it were wiser to say yes, he can conveniently add the second tap. Some such arrangement in real life would, it appears to me, be highly desirable. . . .

As soon as I explained that the spirit who answered had been a witness of the theft, the old man became strangely agitated. "Who was it?" said he. At once the spirit indicated a desire to use the alphabet. As we went over the letters,—always a slow method, but useful when you want to observe excitable people,—my visitor kept saying, "Quicker—go quicker." At length the spirit spelled out the words, "I know not his name."

"Was it," said the gentleman—"was it a—was it one of my household?"

I knocked "yes" without hesitation; who else, indeed, could it have been?

"Excuse me," he went on, "if I ask you for a little whisky."

This I gave him. He continued: "Was it Susan or Ellen?"

"No, no!"

"Was it—" He paused. "If I ask a question mentally, will the spirits reply?" I knew what he meant. He wanted to ask if it was his son, but did not wish to speak openly.

"Ask," said I.

"I have," he returned.

I hesitated. It was rarely my policy to commit myself definitely, yet here I fancied, from the facts of the case and his own terrible anxiety, that he suspected, or more than suspected, his son as the guilty person. I became sure of this as I studied his face. At all events, it would be easy to deny or explain in case of trouble; and, after all, what slander was there in two knocks? I struck twice as usual.

Instantly the old gentleman rose up, very white, but quite firm. "There," he said, and cast a bank-note on the table, "I thank you," and bending his head on his breast, walked, as I thought, with great effort out of the room.

On the following morning, as I made my first appearance in my outer room, which contained at least a dozen persons awaiting advice, who should I see standing by the window but the old gentleman with sandy-gray hair? Along with him was a stout young man with a head as red as mine, and mustache and whiskers to match. Probably the son, I thought—ardent temperament, remorse, come to confess, etc. I was never more mistaken in my life. I was about to go regularly through my patients when the old gentleman began to speak.

"I called, doctor," said he, "to explain the little matter about which I—about which I—"

"Troubled your spirits yesterday," added the youth, jocosely, pulling his mustache.

"Beg pardon," I returned; "had we not better talk this over in private? Come into my office," I added, touching the younger man on the arm.

Would you believe it? he took out his handkerchief and dusted the place I had touched. "Better not," said he. "Go on, father; let us get done with this den."

"Gentlemen," said the elder person, addressing the patients, "I called here yesterday, like a fool, to ask who had stolen from me a sum of money which I believed I left in my room on going out in the morning. This doctor here and his spirits contrived to make me suspect my only son. Well, I charged him at once with the crime as soon as I got back home, and what do you think he did? He said, 'Father, let us go upstairs and look for it,' and—"

Here the young man broke in with: "Come, father; don't worry yourself for nothing"; and then turning, added: "To cut the thing short, he found the notes under his candlestick, where he left them on going to bed. This is all of it. We came here to stop this fellow" (by which he meant me) "from carrying a slander further. I advise you, good people, to profit by the matter, and to look up a more honest doctor, if doctoring be what you want."

As soon as he had ended, I remarked solemnly: "The words of the spirits are not my words. Who shall hold them accountable?"

"Nonsense," said the young man. "Come, father"; and they left the room.

Now was the time to retrieve my character. "Gentlemen," said I, "you have heard this very singular account. Trusting the spirits utterly and entirely as I do, it occurs to me that there is no reason why they may not, after all, have been right in their suspicions of this young person. Who can say that, overcome by remorse, he may not have seized the time of his father's absence to replace the money?"

To my amazment, up gets a little old man from the corner. "Well, you are a low cuss!" said he, and taking up a basket beside him, hobbled hastily out of the room. . . .

An hour later . . . I heard a rough knock at my door, and opening it hastily, saw my red-headed young man with the cripple.

"Now," said the former, taking me by the collar, and pulling me into the room among my patients, "I want to know, my man, if this doctor said that it was likely I was the thief after all?"

"That's what he said," replied the cripple; "just about that, sir."

I do not desire to dwell on the after conduct of this hot-headed young man. It was the more disgraceful as I offered but little resistance, and endured a beating such as I would have hesitated to inflict upon a dog. Nor was this all. He warned me that if I dared to remain in the city after a week he would shoot me. In the East I should have thought but little of such a threat, but here it was only too likely to be practically carried out. Accordingly, with my usual decision of character, but with much grief and reluctance, I collected my whole fortune, which now amounted to at least seven thousand dollars, and turned my back upon this ungrateful town. I am sorry to say that I also left behind me the last of my good luck.

I traveled in a leisurely way until I reached Boston. The country anywhere would have been safer, but I do not lean to agricultural pursuits. It seemed an agreeable city, and I decided to remain.

I took good rooms at Parker's, and concluding to enjoy life, amused myself in the company of certain, I may say uncertain, young women who danced at some of the theaters. I played billiards, drank rather too much, drove fast horses, and at the end of a delightful year was shocked to find myself in debt, and with only seven dollars and fifty-three cents left—I like to be accurate. I had only one resource: I determined to visit my deaf aunt and Peninnah, and to see what I could do in the role of the prodigal nephew. At all events, I should gain time to think of what new enterprise I could take up; but, above all, I needed a little capital and a house over my head. I had pawned nearly everything of any value which I possessed.

I left my debts to gather interest, and went away to Woodbury. It was the day before Christmas when I reached the little Jersey town, and it was also by good luck Sunday. I was hungry and quite penniless. I wandered about until church had begun, because I was sure then to find Aunt Rachel and Peninnah out at the service, and I desired to explore a little. The house was closed, and even the one servant absent. I got in with ease at the back through the kitchen, and having at least an hour and a half free from interruption, I made a leisurely search. The role of prodigal was well enough, but here was a better chance and an indulgent opportunity.

In a few moments I found the famous Bible hid away under Aunt Rachel's mattress. The Bible bank was fat with notes, but I intended to be moderate enough to escape suspicion. Here were quite two thousand dollars. I resolved to take, just now, only one hundred, so as to keep a good balance. Then, alas! I lit on a long envelop, my aunt's will. Every cent was left to Christ Church; not a dime to poor Pen or to me. I was in a rage. I tore up the will and replaced the envelop. To treat poor Pen that way—Pen of all people! There was a heap more will than testament, for all it was in the Bible. After that I thought it was right to punish the old witch, and so I took every note I could find. When I was through with this business, I put back the Bible under the mattress, and observing that I had been quite too long, I went downstairs with a keen desire to leave the town as early as possible. I was tempted, however, to look further, and was rewarded by finding in an old clock case a small reticule stuffed with bank-notes. This I appropriated, and made haste to go out. I was too late. As I went into the little entry to get my hat and coat, Aunt Rachel entered, followed by Peninnah.

At sight of me my aunt cried out that I was a monster and fit for the penitentiary. As she could not hear at all, she had the talk to herself, and went by me and up-stairs, rumbling abuse like distant thunder overhead.

Meanwhile I was taken up with Pen. The pretty fool was seated on a chair, all dressed up in her Sunday finery, and rocking backward and forward, crying, "Oh, oh, ah!" like a lamb saying, "Baa, baa, baa!" She never had much sense. I had to shake her to get a reasonable word. She mopped her eyes, and I heard her gasp out that my aunt had at last decided that I was the person who had thinned her hoards. This was bad, but involved less inconvenience than it might have done an hour earlier. Amid tears Pen told me that a detective had been at the house inquiring for me. When this happened it seems that the poor little goose had tried to fool deaf Aunt Rachel with some made-up story as to the man having come about taxes. I suppose the girl was not any too sharp, and the old woman, I guess, read enough from merely seeing the man's lips. You never could keep anything from her, and she was both curious and suspicious. She assured the officer that I was a thief, and hoped I might be caught. I could not learn whether the man told Pen any particulars, but as I was slowly getting at the facts we heard a loud scream and a heavy fall.

Pen said, "Oh, oh!" and we hurried up-stairs. There was the old woman on the floor, her face twitching to right, and her breathing a sort of hoarse croak. The big Bible lay open on the floor, and I knew what had happened. It was a fit of apoplexy.

At this very unpleasant sight Pen seemed to recover her wits, and said: "Go away, go away! Oh, brother, brother, now I know you have stolen her money and killed her, and—and I loved you, I was so proud of you! Oh, oh!"

This was all very fine, but the advice was good. I said: "Yes, I had better go. Run and get some one—a doctor. It is a fit of hysterics; there is no danger. I will write to you. You are quite mistaken."

This was too feeble even for Pen, and she cried:

"No, never; I never want to see you again. You would kill me next."

"Stuff!" said I, and ran down-stairs. I seized my coat and hat, and went to the tavern, where I got a man to drive me to Camden. I have never seen Pen since. As I crossed the ferry to Philadelphia I saw that I should have asked when the detective had been after me. I suspected from Pen's terror that it had been recently.

It was Sunday and, as I reminded myself, the day before Christmas. The ground was covered with snow, and as I walked up Market street my feet were soon soaked. In my haste I had left my overshoes. I was very cold, and, as I now see, foolishly fearful. I kept thinking of what a conspicuous thing a fire-red head, and of how many people knew me. As I reached Woodbury early and without a cent, I had eaten nothing all day. I relied on Pen. . . .

I decided to go back to Boston. I got to New York prudently in a roundabout way, and in two weeks' time was traveling east from Albany.

I felt well, and my spirits began at last to rise to their usual level. When I arrived in Boston I set myself to thinking how best I could contrive to enjoy life and at the same time to increase my means. I possessed sufficient capital, and was able and ready to embark in whatever promised the best returns with the smallest personal risks. I settled myself in a suburb, paid off a few pressing claims, and began to reflect with my ordinary sagacity.

We were now in the midst of a most absurd war with the South, and it was becoming difficult to escape the net of conscription. It might be wise to think of this in time. Europe seemed a desirable residence, but I needed more money to make this agreeable, and an investment for my brains was what I wanted most. Many schemes presented themselves as worthy the application of industry and talent, but none of them altogether suited my case. I thought at times of traveling as a physiological lecturer, combining with it the business of a practitioner: scare the audience at night with an enumeration of symptoms which belong to ten out of every dozen healthy people, and then doctor such of them as are gulls enough to consult me next day. The bigger the fright the better the pay. I was a little timid, however, about facing large audiences, as a man will be naturally if he has lived a life of adventure, so that upon due consideration I gave up the idea altogether.

The patent medicine business also looked well enough, but it is somewhat overdone at all times, and requires a heavy outlay, with the probable result of ill success. . . .

Lastly, I inclined for a while to undertake a private insane asylum, which appeared to me to offer facilities for money-making, as to which, however, I may have been deceived by the writings of certain popular novelists. I went so far, I may say, as actually to visit Concord for the purpose of finding a pleasant locality and a suitable atmosphere. Upon reflection I abandoned my plans, as involving too much personal labor to suit one of my easy frame of mind.

Tired at last of idleness and lounging on the Common, I engaged in two or three little ventures of a semi-professional character, such as an exhibition of laughing-gas, advertising to cure cancer,—"Send twenty-

five stamps by mail to J. B., and receive an infallible receipt,"—etc.
I did not find, however, that these little enterprises prospered well in
New England. . . .

I therefore set to work, with my accustomed energy, to utilize on
my own behalf the resources of my medical education, which so often
before had saved me from want. The war, then raging at its height, appeared to offer numerous opportunities to men of talent. The path which
I chose was apparently a humble one, but it enabled me to make very
practical use of my professional knowledge, and afforded for a time rapid
and secure returns, without any other investment than a little knowledge
cautiously employed. In the first place, I deposited my small remnant of
property in a safe bank. Then I went to Providence, where, as I had
heard, patriotic persons were giving very large bounties in order, I suppose, to insure the government the services of better men than themselves. On my arrival I lost no time in offering myself as a substitute, and
was readily accepted, and very soon mustered into the Twentieth Rhode
Island. Three months were passed in camp, during which period I received bounty to the extent of six hundred and fifty dollars, with which
I tranquilly deserted about two hours before the regiment left for the
field. With the product of my industry I returned to Boston, and deposited all but enough to carry me to New York, where within a month
I enlisted twice, earning on each occasion four hundred dollars.

After this I thought it wise to try the same game in some of the
smaller towns near to Philadelphia. I approached my birthplace with
a good deal of doubt; but I selected a regiment in camp at Norristown,
which is eighteen miles away. Here I got nearly seven hundred dollars
by entering the service as a substitute for an editor, whose pen, I pre-
sume, was mightier than his sword. I was, however, disagreeably surprised by being hastily forwarded to the front under a foxy young lieutenant, who brutally shot down a poor devil in the streets of Baltimore
for attempting to desert. At this point I began to make use of my medical
skill, for I did not in the least degree fancy being shot, either because
of deserting or of not deserting. It happened, therefore, that a day or
two later, while in Washington, I was seized in the street with a fit,
which perfectly imposed upon the officer in charge, and caused him to
leave me at the Douglas Hospital. Here I found it necessary to perform
fits about twice a week, and as there were several real epileptics in the
ward, I had a capital chance of studying their symptoms, which, finally,
I learned to imitate with the utmost cleverness.

I soon got to know three or four men who, like myself, were personally averse to bullets, and who were simulating other forms of disease
with more or less success. One of them suffered with rheumatism of
the back, and walked about like an old man; another, who had been
to the front, was palsied in the right arm. A third kept open an ulcer on
the leg, rubbing in a little antimonial ointment, which I bought at fifty
cents, and sold him at five dollars a box.

A change in the hospital staff brought all of us to grief. The new surgeon was a quiet, gentlemanly person, with pleasant blue eyes and clearly cut features, and a way of looking at you without saying much. I felt so safe myself that I watched his procedures with just that kind of enjoyment which one clever man takes in seeing another at work.

The first inspection settled two of us.

"Another back case," said the assistant surgeon to his senior.

"Back hurt you?" says the latter, mildly.

"Yes, sir; run over by a howitzer; ain't never been able to stand straight since."

"A howitzer!" says the surgeon. "Lean forward, my man, so as to touch the floor—so. That will do." Then turning to his aid, he said, "Prepare this man's discharge papers."

"His discharge, sir?"

"Yes; I said that. Who's next?"

"Thank you, sir," groaned the man with the back. "How soon, sir, do you think it will be?"

"Ah, not less than a month," replied the surgeon, and passed on.

Now, as it was unpleasant to be bent like the letter C, and as the patient presumed that his discharge was secure, he naturally allowed himself a little relaxation in the way of becoming straighter. Unluckily, those nice blue eyes were everywhere at all hours, and one fine morning Smithson was appalled at finding himself in a detachment bound for the field, and bearing on his descriptive list an ill-natured indorsement about his malady.

The surgeon came next on O'Callahan, standing, like each of us, at the foot of his own bed.

"I've paralytics in my arm," he said, with intention to explain his failure to salute his superior.

"Humph!" said the surgeon; "you have another hand."

"An' it's not the rigulation to saloot with yer left," said the Irishman, with a grin, while the patients around us began to smile.

"How did it happen?" said the surgeon.

"I was shot in the shoulder," answered the patient, "about three months ago, sir. I haven't stirred it since."

The surgeon looked at the scar.

"So recently?" said he. "The scar looks older; and, by the way, doctor,"—to his junior,—"it could not have gone near the nerves. Bring the battery, orderly."

In a few moments the surgeon was testing one after another, the various muscles. At last he stopped. "Send this man away with the next detachment. Not a word, my man. You are a rascal, and a disgrace to honest men who have been among bullets."

The man muttered something, I did not hear what.

"Put this man in the guard-house," cried the surgeon, and so passed on without smile or frown.

As to the ulcer case, to my amusement he was put in bed, and his leg locked up in a wooden splint, which effectually prevented him from touching the part diseased. It healed in ten days, and he too went as food for powder.

The surgeon asked me a few questions, and requesting to be sent for during my next fit, left me alone.

I was, of course, on my guard, and took care to have my attacks only during his absence, or to have them over before he arrived. At length, one morning, in spite of my care, he chanced to enter the ward as I fell on the floor. I was laid on the bed, apparently in strong convulsions. Presently I felt a finger on my eyelid, and as it was raised, saw the surgeon standing beside me. To escape his scrutiny I became more violent in my motions. He stopped a moment and looked at me steadily. "Poor fellow!" said he, to my great relief, as I felt at once that I had successfully deceived him. Then he turned to the ward doctor and remarked: "Take care he does not hurt his head against the bed; and, by the by, doctor, do you remember the test we applied in Carstairs's case? Just tickle the soles of his feet and see if it will cause those backward spasms of the head."

The aid obeyed him, and, very naturally, I jerked my head backward as hard as I could.

"That will answer," said the surgeon, to my horror. "A clever rogue. Send him to the guard-house."

Happy had I been had my ill luck ended here, but as I crossed the yard an officer stopped me. To my disgust, it was the captain of my old Rhode Island company.

"Hello!" said he; "keep that fellow safe. I know him."

To cut short a long story, I was tried, convicted, and forced to refund the Rhode Island bounty, for by ill luck they found my bankbook among my papers. I was finally sent to Fort Delaware and kept at hard labor, handling and carrying shot, policing the ground, picking up cigar-stumps, and other light, unpleasant occupations.

When the war was over I was released. I went at once to Boston, where I had about four hundred dollars in bank. I spent nearly all of this sum before I could satisfy the accumulated cravings of a year and a half without drink or tobacco, or a decent meal. I was about to engage in a little business as a vender of lottery policies when I first began to feel a strange sense of lassitude, which soon increased so as quite to disable me from work of any kind. Month after month passed away, while my money lessened, and this terrible sense of weariness went on from bad to worse. At last one day, after nearly a year had elapsed, I perceived on my face a large brown patch of color, in consequence of which I went in some alarm to consult a well-known physician. He asked me a multitude of tiresome questions, and at last wrote off a prescription, which I immediately read. It was a preparation of arsenic.

"What do you think," said I, "is the matter with me, doctor?"

"I am afraid," said he, "that you have a very serious trouble—what we call Addison's disease."

"What's that?" said I.

"I do not think you would comprehend it," he replied; "it is an affection of the suprarenal capsules."

I dimly remembered that there were such organs, and that nobody knew what they were meant for. It seemed that doctors had found a use for them at last.

"Is it a dangerous disease?" I said.

"I fear so," he answered.

"Don't you really know," I asked, "what's the truth about it?"

"Well," he returned gravely, "I'm sorry to tell you it is a very dangerous malady."

"Nonsense!" said I; "I don't believe it"; for I thought it was only a doctor's trick, and one I had tried often enough myself.

"Thank you," said he; "you are a very ill man, and a fool besides. Good morning." He forgot to ask for a fee, and I did not therefore find it necessary to escape payment by telling him I was a doctor.

Several weeks went by; my money was gone, my clothes were ragged, and, like my body, nearly worn out, and now I am an inmate of a hospital. To-day I feel weaker than when I first began to write. How it will end, I do not know. If I die, the doctor will get this pleasant history, and if I live, I shall burn it, and as soon as I get a little money I will set out to look for my sister. I dreamed about her last night. What I dreamed was not very agreeable. I thought it was night. I was walking up one of the vilest streets near my old office, and a girl spoke to me— a shameless, worn creature, with great sad eyes. Suddenly she screamed, "Brother, brother!" and then remembering what she had been, with her round, girlish, innocent face and fair hair, and seeing what she was now, I awoke and saw the dim light of the half-darkened ward.

I am better to-day. Writing all this stuff has amused me and, I think, done me good. That was a horrid dream I had. I suppose I must tear up all this biography.

"Hello, nurse! The little boy—boy—"

"GOOD HEAVENS!" said the nurse, "he is dead! Dr. Alston said it would happen this way. The screen, quick—the screen—and let the doctor know."

# CHAPTER FOUR

# Drug Use and Abuse:
# A Route to Marginal Employment

The following selection is a departure, since it is not strictly speaking a reading from belles lettres. It is rather a transcribed tape-recorded interview with a heroin addict. I have included it here for two reasons: 1) it is an honest, insightful, and eminently readable piece; and 2) its contents are (sociologically speaking) inherently interesting, particularly when viewed from an interactionist perspective.

Its strong attraction lies primarily in the fact that it outlines 1) a series of contingency circumstances that are responsible for Danny's "drift" into addiction; 2) the nature of his moral justification (to himself and others) for his addiction; 3) what he and others in like circumstances typically do to maintain "their habit"; and 4) how those responsible for the addict's rehabilitation may inadvertently and/or intentionally contribute to their real and potential adoption of other forms of deviance without contributing significantly to reducing the addict's level of addiction.

The reader should be particularly attuned to the rationalizations the addict invokes. Without first providing himself with a moral justification for his deviant behavior, the addict could not have initiated or perpetuated his addiction. For example, Danny's success at one point in "kicking the habit," although it was responsible for his temporarily abstaining from the use of heroin and the lowering of his consumption when he reverted to its use again, served on another level as a rationale for his continued heroin addiction. The addict relates:

129

But I found one thing. What that did [kicking the habit the first time] was open a door to me. You see, kicking the first time is the hard one. I didn't know what to expect; I heard so much about it. You die, you're in agony, you suffer, you carry on something terrible. I admit it: I carried on something terrible, I suffered, I vomited, I threw up, I sweated, I chilled—I did everything that all addicts do when they kick. And I had been on some strong narcotics at the time. . . . You say well, I got it beaten, I won, I'm not dead. I can take another beating, it won't kill me. And that's the way I looked at it.

I stayed off it approximately a month. And I was running around with the same boys. It was a test of will power to myself. I did this on my own. I hung out with my old cronies, I carried on all the scenes they made: I went to the dances— they blew pot, I refused; they shot up heroin, I refused. I refused everything for one month, and at the end of the month I said to myself, Danny, you have the will power. Now it's up to you. If you want to do it, go ahead. But in my heart I knew that anytime I wanted to, I could stop.[1]

Secure in the knowledge that he was able to refrain from heroin use, the addict felt that if things went badly for whatever reason, he could always kick it.

It is important for the reader to keep in mind the way in which even the most obvious "manifest function"[2] (kicking the heroin habit) may turn out to have "latent consequences," i.e., serve as a rationale for its continued use. The sociologist's success in recognizing and incorporating such inconsistencies will determine how well he is able to make sense out of many forms of social behavior that may otherwise seem "irrational" or without order.[3] In the final analysis his success in this undertaking will depend to a large extent upon how seriously the sociologist takes Weber's injunction to first understand the definition of the situation held by the actor (an understanding

[1] Jeremy Larner and Ralph Tefferteller, *The Addict in the Street* (New York: Grove Press, 1965), pp. 102–103.

[2] Robert K. Merton, *Social Theory and Social Structure* (New York: Free Press, 1957), pp. 19–82.

[3] The way in which kicking the habit may actually contribute to the perpetuation of heroin addiction was noted above. Another interesting example, of an "obvious" inconsistency taking the above form, is the way in which suicidal ideation may actually serve to prolong the life of the suicidal person. In this regard see Jerry Jacobs, "Harry Haller's Private Sky Hook: The Role of Suicidal Ideation in the Prolongation of Life," *Existential Psychiatry* (in press).

gained through empathy) before undertaking the reconstruc-
tion of the social meanings of social actions.[4]

The following selection has much to offer in this respect,
for it allows the reader to see through the addict's eyes how his
immersion in the drug culture led him into a "route to mar-
ginal employment." Notwithstanding its importance, the key
question is not why drug use and abuse frequently lead to
thievery, lying, and a reciprocal lack of trust between addicts
and/or others. Nondrug users may also exhibit these behaviors
and incorporate such feelings. What is important is how these
end results come about within the context of the situated actions found within drug cultures (in the case of the following
reading, heroin use) and how these processes differ from or
are similar to those found among nondrug using deviants
and/or "normal" persons. The selection offers many insights in
this regard, especially if we attend to the four features outlined
on page 129.

# JEREMY LARNER and RALPH TEFFERTELLER

## The Addict in the Street

I'm twenty-three years old and I've been on narcotics for about six
years. It was in vogue at the time; everybody was doing it. There were
four or five of us; one boy had been doing it for quite a while and said,
would you like to try? This was at a sweet sixteen party at the Clinton
Plaza. To prove a lot of fallacies wrong, it was heroin and it was a main-
line shot from the very first. The boy who'd been taking narcotics staked
everybody to a free shot, and administered it and made a big adventure
out of it. He said that we could try it once and not get addicted, which
I can say, so many years later, was the truth. He explained that you can
steal and carry on all kinds of perverted things to get it, but at the time
you're not concerned about what's going to happen later; it's what's

---

[4] H. H. Gerth and C. Wright Mills, trans. and ed., *From Max Weber:
Essays in Sociology* (New York: Oxford University Press, 1946), pp. 55–61.

---

going to happen now and the feeling you're going to achieve. And the feeling was so overpowering that it clouds your mind to any idea of going to jail, breaking society's rules, stealing or anything like it. You don't believe it.

Of the kids who took a shot at that party, all of us became addicts—only one didn't. He was what we considered a weekender. He partied and partied until he finally got married and settled down. Then he felt that it was passé; it was out of style, and he quit. Of the five who took shots, four of us are still addicts today, that still keep in touch and see each other, and try and play this big game of not getting caught by the police.

I just came back last November from doing a hitch at Elmira. It was June 26, 1957; I was out with a boy and we decided to buy some narcotics up in Harlem. We took a fix, I was feeling kind of good, there was nothing to do, we were just walking around enjoying the sensation, and we decided to take a taxi ride home, all the way back to Queens. We took the taxi without the driver. We took people around, and we pretended that we were hacking this cab. We didn't take any of the money—just a weekend prank. I was sent to Elmira for zip-five and I did forty-eight months. And upon my getting out, the first thing I did, the first day, was look to secure some narcotics. To see if, was this forty-eight months worth it? And now that I took that fix, I feel that no amount of keeping anyone incapacitated will cure it—if you want to do it you will do it.

I wouldn't consider myself honestly a criminal. This was done in a clouded mind, as a prank. It was an out-and-out robbery, grand larceny, but I don't think that I'm a criminal at heart. I'm disturbed to a degree, because I like narcotics and I wouldn't want anyone to sway me from the thought of narcotics. But I was subjected to perverts, wise guys, guys that had much more time than me. They send a guy that has zip-five—that's a maximum of five years—in with a guy that has twenty to life. And that boy who has twenty to life, he's lost hope to a certain degree. He doesn't care how much aggravation he causes you while you're there. You run into so much difficulty; you have to be a fighter and you have to fight back. And it makes you hard. You come out, you resent people, and you just want to go into a shell. And that's only another reason I went back to narcotics. I forget the past. I don't want to remember that forty-eight months; it was the most horrible forty-eight months in my life. I don't think anything could have done as much harm as Elmira. I don't feel narcotics has done any greater harm to me.

It taught me things that I didn't have any need to learn, like how to steal a car. It graduated me into the higher crime bracket. It gave me telephone numbers of people to look up when I got out, more connections, more criminal activity. Narcotics is very easy to get, once you're in Elmira. You can get synthetic drugs. It's very easy to go to the hospital and get seconal or miltown or tranquilizers of all sorts. Dorazine, paraldehyde, achloral hydrate . . . I could go on and name more. Heroin, I will concede, is very hard to get in, but there have been cases where it has been gotten in. It's rough treatment; you're not treated like a human being, you're treated like an animal. And the only thing that you can do when you're treated like an animal is fight back. And there's no weapon. There's no weapon that a young boy that wants to help himself can fight back with other than his hands and his feet. They say, and I believe this, that the only person you hurt when you fight is yourself. But you're too blind to it, you can't see it.

The whole subject of narcotics has been gone at the wrong way. Everybody says you're a criminal. Basically I think that a narcotics addict, if he's under the influence of narcotics, will not bother anyone. If he's not under the influence of narcotics, and he's trying to secure his fix, he *will* bother you, to a certain degree. But it's not because he wants to bother you; he's not a violent individual. It isn't as bad as this gang warfare, believe me. They're out there causing trouble just for the sake of trouble. For the sole enjoyment of aggravating people, picking on somebody. We're doing it for a reason. We need narcotics, that's all.

After speaking to numerous addicts in the jail at Elmira, in The Tombs, and in the street, I find this: that when the dope addict needs money, he doesn't want to hurt anybody; he just wants the money. He will take your money and run. He's meek. He's the meekest of all people there is, because he's sick. Everybody says he's a killer, but he won't kill you. He's afraid. If you scare him, he might do it out of fear and not even know what he's doing. But that's not his goal. I've went on numerous things to get money, and I knew in my heart I didn't want to hurt anybody. And thank God, to this day I haven't hurt anybody.

An addict is very yellow. Once he's hooked, he's very afraid of withdrawal. So what he does, he steals from people he knows will not send him to jail. That takes in your own immediate family, your mom and pop's friends. People that like you, that you know will try and help you and say, well, it was a mistake. That is the first step in stealing for a narcotics addict.

Second step is boosting. That's going into a department store and walking out with two pair of pants. It's easy, it's tempting, and you learn very easy. Once you do it and get away with it, there's no stopping you from coming back and doing it a second or third time.

The third way is selling fake narcotics to other addicts, to fool them. In other words, you take a cellophane bag and fill it up with any white powder that looks like heroin. And when you see a sick addict that comes strutting down pounding the pavement begging for a fix, you sell him this. It's very cutthroat, you rob from one another. There's no honor among dope addicts.

Or you tell a fellow you're a gopher. You know the pusher and you'll gopher narcotics. The addict is from another neighborhood, but he knows you and he doesn't know the pusher. So you promise him: give me your ten-fifteen-twenty and I'll go look for the pusher for you. As soon as I score the dope, I'll bring it back to you. What happens then is you take his money and you buy the dope, but you never bring it back to him. You take it yourself. It's too overpowering. It's like being very sick, and a doctor says one shot of penicillin cures you. It's the same thing. Narcotics is mental; it's physical. One shot cures you.

You see, it works like this. Every boy in his teens, in his growing years, idolizes somebody—usually a tough guy. It's like the kids today watching TV—they idolize the Capones, and the Roaring Twenties, and the Untouchables. They're all glorious, picturesque characters. In my stages of growing up, there were certain boys in the neighborhood that were the big shots, the strong arm; everybody respected them. Now, we realize it's a false respect. At the time, I wanted to be so much like him. And when I realized he was taking dope, I said, well, if it's good for him it's good for me; he's the big shot. Now, today, when I see this boy, I know he's not a big shot.

But what I try and do is, being I'm taking narcotics, I try to keep it to a minimum, where I can control it. I don't ever want narcotics to control me again. And I feel that if it's done rationally, with a realistic mind, to a certain degree you can control it. Unless it takes over your body. Mentally, if you're strong and have a good will power, you can control it to a degree.

When it really comes down to it basically, everybody wants to be recognized. Everybody. Now these boys that stick with it—the reason they stick with it is narcotics brought them a new way of life. It's an adventure. Let's face it: if narcotics was easy to come by, there wouldn't be half as many addicts. To take narcotics right now, it is cloak-and-dagger, it's spy work, it's something out of television, believe me. You have to walk the street, you have to secure a pusher, you have to locate the money to buy this narcotics, you have to check in dark hallways, on roofs, go through cellars, all this running about, all the time keeping one eye out for the police.

All this. This is an adventure for a young man. And when you finally get your narcotics back to your pad where you can use it, you say to yourself: man, I did it, I beat the fuzz. I made the scene. And you feel relieved.

Then the second stage is to take it. And that clouds your mind. You feel content just to sit there and not be annoyed and let the world go by. Just leave me alone, I'm happy the way I am.

When people see these glorious characters like Buggsy Siegel walking around with Rolls Royces and diamond stickpins and bodyguards and throwing money around with all these fine-looking broads on their arm, it gets you wondering. I know myself, I'm from a pretty well-to-do family, I have never been in want of anything in my whole life, except narcotics. Anything I asked for, I got. I had broken rules—when I was sixteen, I had secured an automobile. Through a forged birth certificate. It wasn't completely legal, but I drove around. I was a big shot in the neighborhood. Everybody looked up to me. There goes Danny in his big Buick convertible!

Everybody wants to be recognized. And to be recognized as an Al Capone, it's a great thing for these people. It gives them a chance. I have a cousin who's been to college six years; he's gonna be a psychiatrist. I talk to him; I think I'm of an intelligence to understand some of the things he tries to explain to me. And right now I'm a common laborer— I'm a painter by trade, I paint apartments in housing projects. And I make $127 a week, union scale. I'm bringing home more money right now than my cousin who works for the Board of Education as a clinical psychologist! Those are the things that warp the youth today; that's what's warping me. This false sense of values—everybody has a price. That's what children are taught today.

Recently in the papers there's seventeen boys from well-to-do families in Queens arrested for 500 burglaries and fencing. Now these boys were offered help by a psychiatrist. Now I know this case personally; I know all the defendants in this case. I know all the parents. To my knowledge, this is a shyster move on the part of the families, pooling their funds to secure this psychiatrist, who's head of a clinic in Forest Hills. He is probably going to say all these boys are mentally disturbed, and offer for a dismissal of the case, pending that they have psychiatric treatment. Which will last for approximately a week. I have had the same circumstances for myself. I've had a shyster psychiatrist say that I was not well, and after everything was dropped he declared me sane again. And the probation officer dropped the case. That's what the youth today learns. How do they expect them, when they send them to institutions to be helped for narcotics, to be helped?

When you get in the hospital the first thing they do is give you sedation, they put you to sleep, they keep you in a state of complete obliviousness for a week. And then they tell you you're cured of your narcotics habit, go home. When you go home you're not really cured; all you do is tell all the boys in the neighborhood about, man, what a hospital this hospital was! I went up there and ate steak, and lamb chops, and milk! Which some of these boys don't eat when they're home. They're getting it the first time in the hospital, and talking about, man, free dope! This isn't solving the problem. There has to be another way to do it.

It got to the point once where I wanted to quit. I'd gotten to the stage where I felt I would go out and commit a robbery of some type. I knew I was on the verge of violating a law. So I went to my parents and asked help. I explained the situation, I was a dope addict. At first everybody got excited and nobody knew how to handle it, so I tried to help. I explained to them that there's only one right way to do it, and that's cold turkey. I explained that I would like everything removed from my bedroom. My father and my uncle and two cousins much older than I came in a bare room—all it was was a nine by twelve room, with nothing in it, a bare floor. I was told I could secrete on the floor, I could vomit— anything I wanted to do. Just stay in here. And I asked them to please not let me out for at least four days, and if possible to keep me there a week. This went on for five days. They stayed there around the clock. They changed shifts like changing of the guard at Buckingham Palace. And I kicked my habit.

But I found one thing. What that did was open a door to me. You see, kicking the first time is the hard one. I didn't know what to expect; I heard so much about it. You die, you're in agony, you suffer, you carry on something terrible. I admit it: I carried on something terrible, I suffered, I vomited, I threw up, I sweated, I chilled—I did everything that all addicts do when they kick. And I had been on some strong narcotics at the time.

But—it's like a kid. When you take a kid, and he beats you up all your life, you're afraid of him. And when you beat up this kid, you flex your muscles every time you see him. Because finally you beat him. And it's the same thing. I had feared withdrawal so bad that when I finally accomplished complete withdrawal—conquered the physical aspects of it—I felt very good and I was flexing my muscles. I was ripe right then to get addicted again. Because I knew, well, I know what it is to kick now, and I think it's possible. The human mind is an irrational mind at times like that. You say well, I got it beaten. I won, I'm not dead. I can take another beating, it won't kill me. And that's the way I looked at it.

I stayed off it approximately a month. And I was running around with the same boys. It was a test of will power to myself. I did this on my own. I hung out with my old cronies, I carried on all the scenes they made: I went to the dances—they blew pot, I refused; they shot up heroin, I refused. I refused everything for one month, and at the end of the month I said to myself, Danny, you have the will power. Now it's up to you. If you want to do it, go ahead. But in my heart I knew that anytime I wanted to, I could stop.

Physically, I find now that it's impossible. Eventually, you do get hooked. You get hooked physically. Mentally, the aspect may take twenty-thirty years; you may never get cured. The mental outlook is a very hard subject to go into. But to institutionalize people is very wrong in a narcotics problem. It won't help them. It only makes them bitter.

I don't want to condemn Riverside, I've never been there. I have been to Lexington, Kentucky, at the federal hospital. And I found that, speaking to people about Riverside, it's a home away from home. The boys say, look, man, let me get high. Let me catch a habit. Who cares? What's the consequences? If worst comes to worst, they send me up to North Brother Island, I kick my habit, I eat good, I come out sixty-five pounds heavier, I look like a million dollars with a sun tan, and everything is great. I'm healthy again, and I'm ripe to start again. This is what it is: it's a big merry-go-round.

The boys don't want to get off. It's like a child with sex. You ask a little boy what he's gonna do. Go out and play with the girls? No no no, I wanna play with the boys, I don't want to be with the girls. But when he comes into his teens and he finally has an experience with a girl, sexually, all he does now when he sees girls with big fannies, he's out after girls and running after girls. He's had his taste. It's the same thing with narcotics. Once you have your taste, you just keep running and running and running.

I have a cousin that had been an addict since 1949. He got out of Lexington, Kentucky, in February. He got married. He died two months later, in April, in Miami Beach, Florida, of an overdose of narcotics. Now this is in my own family. I should sit down and feel terrible about it, because we were very close. We were more or less junkies-under-the-skin, so to speak. But I know that he played the game, and he paid. Because he played wrong. The idea is to be careful. I'm careful now. I don't want to hurt anybody; I don't want to hurt myself. I just want to achieve the better things I can out of life.

Today, the world is in such a turmoil that the pressure on youth, and the people not understanding us, it's just terrible. The boys have nothing to do; they're bored with themselves. You take a boy nineteen years old. His friend has a car so he buys a car. And the first thing you know the car gets him in trouble. He's joy-riding all hours of the night, drinking beer. It's the same thing. Some boys find that narcotics is a lot cleaner and easier than alcohol, because if you take whisky you have to drink for hours. Whereas if you take narcotics you feel the effect within a few seconds. That's the easy way.

I've taken about six overdoses. One overdose I've taken was on Rivington and Avenue D. I was out for thirteen hours; I thought I died. But when I woke up, came to, and all these boys was there, I really felt indebted to these fellows for not leaving, for sticking to me for thirteen hours. Now thirteen hours when you say it in numbers is nothing. But in reality, when you're unconscious from an overdose of narcotics, it's a lifetime. I died and was born again in that time. And I feel that I owe these boys something.

I was on a landing in a hallway, one landing down from the roof. I was injected with salt into my veins—I don't know if that has any effect at all, to be honest—and rubbing and massaging, trying to keep the blood circulating through my body. They inject the salt water with the same needle they use the heroin with. It's just that to call up an ambulance and to say there's somebody up here took an overdose of narcotics, we know the treatment that's gonna happen. The ambulance takes three hours to get there. The police come, they'll beat your brains in. They're liable to find you and say they found dope in your pocket. Which we know isn't true. If a dope addict is unconscious from an overdose, there's nothing in his pockets. Because addicts today do not take off by themselves. Everybody wants somebody there, just in case, because there's been an epidemic of bad narcotics. And everybody's afraid.

I took an overdose, and upon being out and coming to, I felt that this was it. I was quitting. But when you go out, everything is so white and pure. The world goes by. You don't care about anything, you have no worries. You're not thinking about Mom paying the telephone bill or your wife being sick. Everything is so great. I want to do everything for everybody. I may act a little spooky and groggy, and appear to be not in my senses, but really I'm in my senses, more so than a lot of people believe. Nothing goes past your hearing; everything is extra-sensitive as far as your hearing goes. The only thing that's numb is your thinking mind. You can't think abstractly, you can't think of the future. You just think for now.

About cops and bribery, I wouldn't like to talk about what other boys tell me, because I don't hold too much to a narcotic addict's word; a lot of it is fantasy. I will say this has happened to me. There is a neighborhood cop, he knows what I'm up to, he knows I'm an addict, he knows that I do things in the neighborhood concerning drugs. He watches me every time he sees me; he'll tail me for hours. Twice he stopped me. And I was sick both times, in dire need of a fix. And he looked in my pocket, and there, sure enough, he found an eighth of heroin. Which I know was not there, because I know at the time he "found" it, my goal was to secure narcotics. The agent had put it there, and he threatened me.

Another time I was stopped in a brand-new car. It was my own, I had bought it from my hard-earned money. It had nothing to do with narcotics; I have never peddled narcotics to that extent. I have peddled narcotics among my own friends, in my immediate club. If I had bought $40 worth, I could afford to sell $20 to my friends, and save them a trip up to Harlem. But what happened was I got stopped, and at this time I had about $300 in my pocket. A narcotics agent took the $300 and said it was money I had earned pushing dope. He refused to give it back, and said if I put up a big stink I'd find myself in the seventh precinct. So, of course, being a narcotic addict and not wanting to be arrested, I gave him the money and never said anything about it. Because my word is nothing. I'm the bad guy.

This one policeman told me, he said, look, Danny, you just come home. I have this circular, I got the wire on you, you're here, I know what you're up to. You're still an addict, you're still associating with the same people. I'm gonna catch you. It'll take me a week or two, and you bastard, if I don't catch you, I'm gonna frame you. You're going back anyway. So get out of the neighborhood; don't get into trouble.

Now things like that, where there were no grounds for it. . . . All right, I admit, I might have had narcotics hidden on me. But he didn't find them. That does not give him the grounds to call me guilty. He's supposed to call me innocent till I'm proven guilty.

This Harry Anslinger, the head of the Federal Narcotics Commission. I had two of his agents come down to the precinct and question me when I was arrested. They offered me a deal: they told me if I gave names and places, I would go home on a *state* robbery charge. It just shows you how the two agencies work hand in hand. The federal agent promised that if they had the names, he could sway the state into dropping the robbery charges. It doesn't give a guy the sense of values that he's supposed to have. It shows you that there's graft and corruption.

Two fellows get arrested; one fellow has $800 in his pocket. Who goes away? Of course, the boy that had no money. The boy that had the $800, he doesn't go to jail; he gets a boot in the pants and get home, and don't let me see you in the neighborhood. This has been going on, but nobody believes it. It's the same cry all the time: aah, he's a junkie! He's looking for a way out, so he's making the police a patsy. But it isn't so.

The police, they're undermanned. They're going about apprehending narcotics addicts. They should leave the darn addict alone. Don't get the addict, he's helpless. Get the pusher. Not the pusher that's selling it so he could get a fix. He's not really a pusher. He buys ten dollars' worth of narcotics and takes an eighth and cuts it into two sixteenths. He sells you a sixteenth for ten dollars, so he gets his fix free. He's not a pusher; it's the guy dealing in the ounces—$350 an ounce, $475 an ounce— these are the businessmen. They don't take narcotics themselves, but they sell it. They beg you to sell it for them.

It's not like it used to be. They give drugs on consignment these days. It's been offered to me on numerous occasions—take three ounces of pure heroin. It's not pure—it would come out about eighty-six per cent on a police meter. Anyway, I could get a good grade of heroin— three ounces for $750. That's the bargain for buying the three ounces in a batch. Now I can bag this up into five-dollar bags, and I can turn over exactly 340 per cent over the price I pay. So even a small nobody, a nothing like me, a street dope addict, if I had the initial money, I can have that big car and those three-hundred-dollar suits and all those pretty girls and the money to burn. But the consequences are great.

You're working with neighborhood police, who know who's doing what, but don't say anything because it's bigger than them. They can't fight it. They're joining it. They'd rather accept the fifty dollars under the table to forget this bar and forget that there's junkies hanging out in the bar. They're not in there to arrest them. They know where they hang out; they're there all the time. We're not stupid, we know their cars. We know twenty minutes before they're in the neighborhood that they're coming, so when they get there they don't find anything. But I give them credit for the arrests they do make, if they're honest arrests. Because the dope addict will fight back; he fears going to the city jail, because that means kicking cold turkey right there.

From meeting them and seeing them, I'd say that out of every ten dope addicts, three are girls. Girls are a big factor in making boys dope addicts, believe it or not. Let's face it. You take a quiet guy, a little backward and shy, the potential raper, the guy that has trouble getting a girlfriend. He's slow and awkward with girls; he doesn't know the female sex. He's the type of fellow that will snatch a little girl in the street and rape her. Or force a lady to do things that are perverted. You take a guy like that, and you get one of these real, so-called "hip chicks," a swinger that knows the score. She's a hustler, she's been around, she turns tricks. She'll do anything for a buck to secure her fix. She has an outlet. It's easier for a girl to secure a habit and to keep it under control, because all she has to do is lay down on the bed and there's ten dollars. She can put any price she wants on that, see? Because she's a woman, and men will buy women. Those girls take a plain ordinary joe that doesn't know too much, and they say, look honey, you can sleep with me and live with me and I'll take care of you. They give this guy his first taste of sex. And believe me, he's at their beck and call. They'll make him anything they want to make him. They'll make him a dope addict, eventually. Girls are the biggest factor in making dope addicts.

My sex drive, before narcotics, was so great that upon having intercourse with a girl, I would achieve my climax almost immediately. And I noticed something. That upon taking narcotics, it killed my sex drive. But on drugs, I was able to have sex for three-four hours at a time. Which made me feel superior over the girl. The girl was always begging me to stop, she couldn't take it, when it used to be the other way around, when I used to tell this girl, you're wearing me out, honey. I never reach a climax when I'm under the influence of narcotics, but mentally, I feel that I can satisfy the woman I'm with.

Any girl that has sexual intercourse with a dope addict will never be satisfied by a normal person. Because there are very few normal human beings on this earth that can have a sexual intercourse for three-four hours, without achieving a climax. It's almost an impossibility. Heroin will help you achieve that effect. And you'd be surprised the effects when you have a few girls running after you, talking about your powers as a lady's man. It does something to your ego, and your super-ego, and you get all excited and you go out and you do sillier things to prove it.

I don't know the figures on narcotics addiction in New York City, but I will say that of the narcotic addicts that I know personally, I found that eight out of ten have never been arrested and are not known addicts. So therefore, whatever figures the state and the federal might have, the number of addicts is actually five times larger than that. You have a minority who get the blame for everything.

My parents were very hurt by my addiction, because I never asked for anything in my life that I didn't get it. They're trying to trust me now, 'cause I'm fresh home from Elmira Reformatory, but other than that. . . . There's the sneaky look at my armpit, to see if I have any new marks. It's where ya goin?—it's eleven o'clock! I'm a boy of twenty-four and that bothers me, that annoys me. I'm not a baby, I want to be a man. I feel I'm strong enough to take care of myself right now, even though I use narcotics. I use narcotics that I feel I have control over. I've proved it to myself on numerous occasions. When narcotics have gotten the best of me, I went into seclusion for a few weeks, staying away from the neighborhood and my old friends.

But it's not that taking a boy out of his environment will keep him from using narcotics. That's wrong. I lived on the East Side all my life. While using narcotics I have met boys from Queens, Brooklyn, Bronx. . . . Now, no matter where I go, I can pick out a dope addict. You can take me to a strange neighborhood where I've never been, with people I don't even know, put one dope addict in the crowd, give me twenty minutes and I'll pick him out. It's like a brother club. One junkie knows another junkie. You smell each other.

It's not a matter of take him away. I was taken away. They moved me to Queens, in one of the most exclusive parts of Jamaica, Long Island. And I find narcotics addicts. I might not find the type of narcotic addict I find on the East Side now, because of the big migration of Puerto Rican and Negro into the neighborhood. The older addicts are Irish, Jewish and Italian. But I find dope addicts. If I don't find a C.P.A. that's a dope addict, I find a lawyer, I find a sculptor, I find them all over. These are the lucky few. They have never been to court, so they're not considered addicts, they're not statistics. But they do exist.

Living out in Jamaica Estates, I migrate to Harlem to get my narcotics. Harlem is the center-point for narcotics in the New York area. From 100th Street to 140th Street is narcotics row. Narcotics can be got very easy, it's not too much trouble, most of the policemen are paid off, and the ones that aren't—they're not out for the big people. The big people pay too much. The big people are covered. When they do a business that turns in twenty thousand dollars a week, they're not letting a little patrolman—a nothing that makes $5,800 a year—arrest them. They pay him. They give him a thousand dollars. A thousand dollars is gold to this officer, I don't care who he is. It's very tempting.

I have worked for this lady up in Harlem, around the corner from the Park Palace. I have been there one night when there was a raid. I was up there for the purpose of securing one-quarter of an ounce of heroin. I wasn't up there to buy weight, so-called, ounces. As a personal favor from this girl to me, she was giving me a quarter of pure heroin. It was a raid. The cops came in, money was passed, the cops walked out. Nobody was arrested. When I came down-stairs I seen what they did. They had arrested two junkies on the street—street junkies. Poor, helpless creatures. They didn't arrest her. She's probably still in circulation to this day. Because she pays, and she pays big and to the right people.

I feel that if they legalized narcotics to a certain degree, that would kill half of the narcotics problem. If you look at the crime statistics in New York City, they say that crime is up 50 per cent. And the crimes are committed by dope addicts. We don't have a big crime rate in New York City, we definitely do not—it's the dope addict, the guy who boosts a pocketbook from an open car, he takes a camera or he goes in a candy store and boosts a box of candy—or something. This is what makes a big crime rate. Of every five thousand burglaries, all but three hundred are by dope addicts that couldn't help themselves.

If they had some sort of system where narcotics could be administered free of charge, or for costs, it would kill the black market trade. We're not strong enough to kill it otherwise; it's run by a lot of people with a lot of money that runs into millions and billions, and they're not letting anybody push them out. They like money. They smuggle in dope on planes and on boats—with their merchant marine friends that I know bring stuff in.

Now you open up a clinic and you take away the main incentives of a dope addict. You take away the adventure in it. There's no more adventure; it becomes hospitalization. Dope addicts thrive on this adventure of running around and going to buy it and getting off without getting caught. And then sitting and being with all the boys and *talking* about how it felt. That would be taken away. There wouldn't be all this scariness, and all the worries. It wouldn't get to the point where you would get addicted—and even if you did get addicted, it could be controlled to a degree. If a dope addict can be maintained so that he will not get sick, he will not commit a crime. He will be content not to be sick.

What they do is they make it hard for the dope addict to get dope, they make the prices go up and the business illicit, and the addict has to steal. He has to do something to keep up with it.

So I feel they should have some sort of a clinic, where you can come in and get fingerprinted if you want to be a known addict. Let it be known! If you want to be an addict, don't be ashamed of it. Take your card, go in, get your thing to keep you happy. It would kill the crime and they'd live a happy life.

There would be a few that would want more than whatever the clinic would be administering. If the clinic was giving just enough to keep them satisfied and not on cloud nine, they'd want a little extra so they could get up to cloud nine. That kind of illicit drug trade you can't stop. But taking the adventure away would kill a lot of the drugs. It would stop a lot of these young schoolboys that are ripe for picking. There wouldn't be anything interesting to them; it would be just a bore.

Take any kid. You just walk up and say, you want to be a junkie? I'll get you a fix. But you gotta go down to Joe's Hospital with me. He wouldn't want it. What is it to walk into a hospital? It's a cold institution where somebody sticks a needle in your arm, you get a fix and you go back. They don't want that.

The teenagers today are standing on the street corners and sitting in the luncheonettes. They're talking baloney. *Nothing* to talk about—they're beat for conversation. They're not intellectuals. They ain't even pseudo-intellectuals. They just stand there. And when somebody offers them a cloak-and-dagger game, it's like taking a kid and giving him cowboys-and-Indians, or let's play-soldier. They enjoy it. It gives them something to do, it keeps their mind occupied.

How to beat the cop on the beat? How to beat the narcotic agent who's sneaking up on you in the hallway? You think at the time that your mind is working. Your mind isn't working—I know that now. But I feel that I can't be helped, because I have found in drugs something to keep me calm, collected. I'm happy with the knowledge I have; I think I can make my way in the world. But I want to be an honest citizen. I don't want to hurt people, I don't want to bother anybody. I'm just content—like somebody comes home and has his five beers, I want to come home and be able to smoke marijuana, take a shot of dope.

I find marijuana never to be habit-forming. I feel that the only reason they don't legalize marijuana is that the liquor industry and the A.B.C. [Alcoholic Beverage Control Board] would go crazy. Let's figure it out. Take a couple, they go into a bar. It takes eight dollars to drink before they feel a little giddy. Where marijuana, with sixteen cents for one stick, puts you in the same state as twenty dollars' worth of liquor. And it has no after effects. I've had two occasions to drink—once I drank rye and once I drank scotch. And I had some head in the morning; I had a hangover, I was sick, I was nauseous—all the works. I smoked three sticks of marijuana, I was loaded all night, I woke up in the morning and never even knew I did it. Everything was good.

Marijuana made my senses more alert—more so than heroin. Heroin calms me down, more like a tranquilizer. Whereas marijuana made me lively, like whisky. It made me a little boisterous. Everything is funny, whole world is a big joke.

And I feel the only reason they never make it legal is the A.B.C. My ideas may be warped, I grant you that. I need help, I know I need help. I want to help myself; I eventually will, in time. But fighting people with a lot of money, you can't.

# CHAPTER FIVE

# The Mentally Ill:
# Alienation and the Loss of Self

Awakening one morning to find one's self physically transformed into a giant beetle would be disconcerting at best. However, one's *total* transformation would present less of a dilemma than awakening with the physiognomy of a beetle and the understanding of a human. Living the life of a human beetle (where "human beetle" is taken literally and not allegorically) would present one with a myriad of problems. What's more, these problems would not be obvious at the outset. With the unfolding of each new and unanticipated set of events, one would experience a "culture shock," much as a stranger experiences upon first trying to interact appropriately with others in a foreign country.[1] Apart from a stigmatized appearance, such a creature, although capable of understanding, could not be understood and as a consequence would be unable to establish or maintain meaningful forms of interaction with humans. Inasmuch as man's humanity results from and is contingent upon his ability to establish and perpetuate meaningful forms of interaction with "significant others," the perpetuation of this condition would ultimately result in the total transformation of such a human-insect from a partial to a total beetle. The beginning and end points of this process may be delineated by contrasting Gregor's sister's attitude and

[1] Alfred Schutz, "The Stranger: An Essay in Social Psychology," *American Journal of Sociology* 44 (1944): 499–507.

behavior toward him in the earlier and later phases of his completed metamorphosis, the latter corresponding to the time when Gregor not only looked, but had begun to think and behave, as a "dung beetle."

> Very early in the morning, it was still almost night, Gregor had the chance to test the strength of his new resolutions, for his sister, nearly fully dressed, opened the door from the hall and peered in. She did not see him at once, yet when she caught sight of him under the sofa—well, he had to be somewhere, he couldn't have flown away, could he?—she was so startled that without being able to help it she slammed the door shut again. But as if regretting her behavior she opened the door again immediately and came in on tiptoe, as if she were visiting an invalid or even a stranger. Gregor had pushed his head forward to the very edge of the sofa and watched her. Would she notice that he had left the milk standing, and not for lack of hunger, and would she bring in some other kind of food more to his taste? If she did not do it of her own accord, he would rather starve than draw her attention to the fact, although he felt a wild impulse to dart out from under the sofa, throw himself at her feet and beg her for something to eat. But his sister at once noticed, with surprise, that the basin was still full, except for a little milk that had been spilt all around it, she lifted it immediately, not with her bare hands, true, but with a cloth and carried it away. Gregor was wildly curious to know what she would bring instead, and made various speculations about it. Yet what she actually did next, in the goodness of her heart, he could never have guessed at. To find out what he liked she brought him a whole selection of food, all set out on an old newspaper. . . . Besides all that, she set down again the same basin, into which she had poured some water, and which was apparently to be reserved for his exclusive use. And with fine tact, knowing that Gregor would not eat in her presence, she withdrew quickly and even turned the key, to let him understand that he could take his ease as much as he liked.[2]

Such acts of understanding and compassion are usually reserved for and associated with one's interactions with other humans. Although they characterized Grete's attitudes and behavior toward Gregor in the earlier stages of his transformation, they are completely absent in the later stages.

[2] Franz Kafka, "The Metamorphosis," in *The Penal Colony,* trans. Willa and Edwin Muir (New York: Schocken Books, 1948), pp. 90–91.

"My dear parents," said his sister, slapping her hand on the table by way of introduction, "things can't go on like this. Perhaps you don't realize that, but I do. I won't utter my brother's name in the presence of this creature, and so all I say is: we must try to get rid of it. We've tried to look after it and to put up with it as far as is humanly possible, and I don't think anyone could reproach us in the slightest." . . .

"If he could understand us," said her father, half questioningly; Grete, still sobbing, vehemently waved a hand to show how unthinkable that was.

"If he could understand us," repeated the old man, shutting his eyes to consider his daughter's conviction that understanding was impossible, "then perhaps we might come to some agreement with him. But as it is—"

"He must go," cried Gregor's sister, "that's the only solution, Father. You must just try to get rid of the idea that this is Gregor. The fact that we've believed it for so long is the root of all our trouble. But how can it be Gregor? If this were Gregor, he would have realized long ago that human beings can't live with such a creature, and he'd have gone away on his own accord."[3]

The expanding state of Gregor's social isolation took the form of a self-fulfilling prophesy, for Gregor grew less and less human and more and more beetlelike as his family and others grew more and more convinced that he was a beetle and reacted accordingly. Lemert, in an insightful article on paranoia, notes a similar process at work.[4] It has also been found to occur between parents and their retarded children,[5] between the physically-handicapped and the "normal" public,[6] and between mothers and their drug-addicted children.[7] In fact, whenever "significant others" become convinced that the "deviant" is somehow less than human, e.g., lacking in intelligence, responsibility, will, soul, understanding, or sanity, this process may be initiated and result in the untoward consequences noted above.

The following selection may be seen as a description of

---

[3] Ibid., pp. 124–125.

[4] Edwin M. Lemert, "Paranoia and the Dynamics of Exclusion," *Sociometry* 25, no. 1 (March 1962): 1–20.

[5] Jerry Jacobs, *The Search for Help* (New York: Brunner/Mazel, 1969), pp. 101–102.

[6] Fred Davis, "Deviance Disavowal: The Management of Strained Interaction by the Visibly Handicapped," in *The Other Side: Perspectives on Deviance*, ed. Howard Becker (Glencoe: Free Press, 1964), pp. 119–130.

[7] Jeremy Larner and Ralph Tefferteller, *The Addict in the Street* (New York: Grove Press, 1965), pp. 169–186.

the progressive separation of a human being from his humanness.[8] The end point in this process may be viewed as Gregor's total loss of self, i.e., the end of his existence as a human being and his total transformation to a "dung beetle." The annihilation of self is presented allegorically as the death of the beetle and the end of Gregor.

From an interactionist perspective, it is less important to deal with the psychological questions of Gregor's "split personality" or the "dynamics" of his localized thought disorders (e.g., he is oblivious to the fact that beetles do not catch commuter trains to the office in the morning) than to follow the changing forms of his interactions with others that result from his new state of being and the reciprocal consequences of these new forms of interaction for everyone concerned. The reader is asked to pay particular attention to the disruptive encounters that may result from communication problems, and how they may unwittingly contribute to the individual's progressive isolation from meaningful social relationships and his progressive loss of self.

[8] The use of the word "alienation" in reference to the following selection may be viewed from a Marxian perspective, where man's relationship to the means of production serves to alienate him from his "true species nature," so that the more one works the more one is alienated from himself. Or one can see Gregor's growing alienation in terms of Melvin Seeman's subjective classifications, i.e., Gregor's growing feeling of "meaninglessness," "normlessness," "powerlessness," "isolation," and "self-estrangement." (See Melvin Seeman, "On the Meaning of Alienation," *American Sociological Review* XXVI (1961): 753–758.) Whether one becomes increasingly alienated without being aware of the "true" social-historical roots of his alienation, i.e., suffers "false consciousness," or whether the subjective states of mind themselves constitute the alienation, both conceptual frameworks seek to explain what their advocates see as a growing trend toward insectlike behavior on the part of the humans resulting from a progressive loss of self.

# FRANZ KAFKA

## *The Metamorphosis*

I

As Gregor Samsa awoke one morning from uneasy dreams he found himself transformed in his bed into a gigantic insect. He was lying on his hard, as it were armor-plated, back and when he lifted his head a little he could see his dome-like brown belly divided into stiff arched segments on top of which the bed quilt could hardly keep in position and was about to slide off completely. His numerous legs, which were pitifully thin compared to the rest of his bulk, waved helplessly before his eyes.

What has happened to me? he thought. It was no dream. His room, a regular human bedroom, only rather too small, lay quiet between the four familiar walls. Above the table on which a collection of cloth samples was unpacked and spread out—Samsa was a commercial traveler—hung the picture which he had recently cut out of an illustrated magazine and put into a pretty gilt frame. It showed a lady, with a fur cap on and a fur stole, sitting upright and holding out to the spectator a huge fur muff into which the whole of her forearm had vanished!

Gregor's eyes turned next to the window, and the overcast sky—one could hear rain drops beating on the window gutter—made him quite melancholy. What about sleeping a little longer and forgetting all this nonsense, he thought, but it could not be done, for he was accustomed to sleep on his right side and in his present condition he could not turn himself over. However violently he forced himself towards his right side he always rolled on to his back again. He tried it at least a hundred times, shutting his eyes to keep from seeing his struggling legs, and only desisted when he began to feel in his side a faint dull ache he had never experienced before.

Oh God, he thought, what an exhausting job I've picked on! Traveling about day in, day out. It's much more irritating work than doing the actual business in the office, and on top of that there's the trouble of constant traveling, of worrying about train connections, the bed and irregular meals, casual acquaintances that are always new and never become intimate friends. The devil take it all! He felt a slight itching up on his belly; slowly pushed himself on his back nearer to the top of the bed so that he could lift his head more easily; identified the itching place which was surrounded by many small white spots the nature of which he could

Reprinted by permission of Schocken Books Inc. from *The Penal Colony* by Franz Kafka, Copyright © 1948 by Schocken Books Inc.

149

not understand and made to touch it with a leg, but drew the leg back immediately, for the contact made a cold shiver run through him.

He slid down again into his former position. This getting up early, he thought, makes one quite stupid. A man needs his sleep. Other commercials live like harem women. For instance, when I come back to the hotel of a morning to write up the orders I've got, these others are only sitting down to breakfast. Let me just try that with my chief; I'd be sacked on the spot. Anyhow, that might be quite a good thing for me, who can tell? If I didn't have to hold my hand because of my parents I'd have given notice long ago, I'd have gone to the chief and told him exactly what I think of him. That would knock him endways from his desk! It's a queer way of doing, too, this sitting on high at a desk and talking down to employees, especially when they have to come quite near because the chief is hard of hearing. Well, there's still hope; once I've saved enough money to pay back my parents' debts to him—that should take another five or six years—I'll do it without fail. I'll cut myself completely loose then. For the moment, though, I'd better get up, since my train goes at five.

He looked at the alarm clock ticking on the chest. Heavenly Father! he thought. It was half-past six o'clock and the hands were quietly moving on, it was even past the half-hour, it was getting on toward a quarter to seven. Had the alarm clock not gone off? From the bed one could see that it had been properly set for four o'clock; of course it must have gone off. Yes, but was it possible to sleep quietly through that ear-splitting noise? Well, he had not slept quietly, yet apparently all the more soundly for that. But what was he to do now? The next train went at seven o'clock; to catch that he would need to hurry like mad and his samples weren't even packed up, and he himself wasn't feeling particularly fresh and active. And even if he did catch the train he wouldn't avoid a row with the chief, since the firm's porter would have been waiting for the five o'clock train and would have long since reported his failure to turn up. The porter was a creature of the chief's, spineless and stupid. Well, supposing he were to say he was sick? But that would be most unpleasant and would look suspicious, since during his five years' employment he had not been ill once. The chief himself would be sure to come with the sick-insurance doctor, would reproach his parents with their son's laziness and would cut all excuses short by referring to the insurance doctor, who of course regarded all mankind as perfectly healthy malingerers. And would he be so far wrong on this occasion? Gregor really felt quite well, apart from a drowsiness that was utterly superfluous after such a long sleep, and he was even unusually hungry.

As all this was running through his mind at top speed without his being able to decide to leave his bed—the alarm clock had just struck a quarter to seven—there came a cautious tap at the door behind the head of his bed. "Gregor," said a voice—it was his mother's—"it's a quarter to seven. Hadn't you a train to catch?" That gentle voice! Gregor had a shock as he heard his own voice answering hers, unmistakably his own voice, it was true, but with a persistent horrible twittering squeak behind it like an undertone, that left the words in their clear shape only for the first moment and then rose up reverberating round them to destroy their sense, so that one could not be sure one had heard them rightly. Gregor wanted to answer at length and explain everything, but in the circumstances he confined himself to saying: "Yes, yes, thank you, Mother, I'm getting up now." The wooden door between them must have kept the change in his voice from being noticeable outside, for his mother contented herself with this statement and shuffled away. Yet this brief exchange of words had made the other members of the family aware that Gregor was still in the house, as they had not expected, and at one of the side doors his father was already knocking, gently, yet with his fist. "Gregor, Gregor," he called, "what's the matter with you?" And after a little while he called again in a deeper voice: "Gregor! Gregor!" At the other side door his sister was saying in a low, plaintive tone: "Gregor? Aren't you well? Are you needing anything?" He answered them both at once: "I'm just ready," and did his best to make his voice sound as normal as possible by enunciating the words very clearly and leaving long pauses between them. So his father went back to his breakfast, but his sister whispered: "Gregor, open the door, do." However, he was not thinking of opening the door, and felt thankful for the prudent habit he had acquired in traveling of locking all doors during the night, even at home.

His immediate intention was to get up quietly without being disturbed, to put on his clothes and above all eat his breakfast, and only then to consider what else was to be done, since in bed, he was well aware, his meditations would come to no sensible conclusion. He remembered that often enough in bed he had felt small aches and pains, probably caused by awkward postures, which had proved purely imaginary once he got up, and he looked forward eagerly to seeing this morning's delusions gradually fall away. That the change in his voice was nothing but the precursor of a severe chill, a standing ailment of commercial travelers, he had not the least possible doubt.

To get rid of the quilt was quite easy; he had only to inflate himself a little and it fell off by itself. But the next move was difficult, especially because he was so uncommonly broad. He would have needed arms and hands to hoist himself up; instead he had only the numerous little legs which never stopped waving in all directions and which he could not control in the least. When he tried to bend one of them it was the first to stretch itself straight; and did he succeed at last in making it do what he wanted, all the other legs meanwhile waved the more wildly in a high degree of unpleasant agitation. "But what's the use of lying idle in bed," said Gregor to himself.

He thought that he might get out of bed with the lower part of his body first, but this lower part, which he had not yet seen and of which he could form no clear conception, proved too difficult to move; it shifted so slowly; and when finally, almost wild with annoyance, he gathered his forces together and thrust out recklessly, he had miscalculated the direc-

tion and bumped heavily against the lower end of the bed, and the sting-
ing pain he felt informed him that precisely this lower part of his body
was at the moment probably the most sensitive.

So he tried to get the top part of himself out first, and cautiously
moved his head towards the edge of the bed. That proved easy enough,
and despite its breadth and mass the bulk of his body at last slowly followed the movement of his head. Still, when he finally got his head free
over the edge of the bed he felt too scared to go on advancing, for after
all if he let himself fall in this way it would take a miracle to keep his
head from being injured. And at all costs he most not lose consciousness
now, precisely now; he would rather stay in bed.

But when after a repetition of the same efforts he lay in his former
position again, sighing, and watched his little legs struggling against each
other more wildly than ever, if that were possible, and saw no way of
bringing any order into this arbitrary confusion, he told himself again
that it was impossible to stay in bed and that the more sensible course
was to risk everything for the smallest hope of getting away from it. At
the same time he did not forget meanwhile to remind himself that cool
reflection, the coolest possible, was much better than desperate resolves.
In such moments he focused his eyes as sharply as possible on the window, but, unfortunately, the prospect of the morning fog, which muffled
even the other side of the narrow street, brought him little encouragement
and comfort. "Seven o'clock already," he said to himself when the alarm
clock chimed again, "seven o'clock already and still such a thick fog." And
for a little while he lay quiet, breathing lightly, as if perhaps expecting
such complete repose to restore all things to their real and normal condition.

But then he said to himself: "Before it strikes a quarter past seven
I must be quite out of this bed, without fail. Anyhow, by that time someone will have come from the office to ask for me, since it opens before
seven." And he set himself to rocking his whole body at once in a regular
rhythm, with the idea of swinging it out of the bed. If he tipped himself
out in that way he could keep his head from injury by lifting it at an
acute angle when he fell. His back seemed to be hard and was not likely
to suffer from a fall on the carpet. His biggest worry was the loud crash
he would not be able to help making, which would probably cause anxiety,
if not terror, behind all the doors. Still, he must take the risk.

When he was already half out of the bed—the new method was
more a game than an effort, for he needed only to hitch himself across
by rocking to and fro—it struck him how simple it would be if he could
get help. Two strong people—he thought of his father and the servant
girl—would be amply sufficient; they would only have to thrust their
arms under his convex back, lever him out of the bed, bend down with
their burden and then be patient enough to let him turn himself right
over on to the floor, where it was to be hoped his legs would then find their
proper function. Well, ignoring the fact that the doors were all locked,

ought he really to call for help? In spite of his misery he could not suppress a smile at the very idea of it.

He had got so far that he could barely keep his equilibrium when he rocked himself strongly, and he would have to nerve himself very soon for the final decision since in five minutes' time it would be a quarter past seven—when the front door bell rang. "That's someone from the office," he said to himself, and grew almost rigid, while his little legs only jigged about all the faster. For a moment everything stayed quiet. "They're not going to open the door," said Gregor to himself, catching at some kind of irrational hope. But then of course the servant girl went as usual to the door with her heavy tread and opened it. Gregor needed only to hear the first good morning of the visitor to know immediately who it was—the chief clerk himself. What a fate, to be condemned to work for a firm where the smallest omission at once gave rise to the gravest suspicion! Were all employees in a body nothing but scoundrels, was there not among them one single loyal devoted man who, had he wasted only an hour or so of the firm's time in a morning, was so tormented by conscience as to be driven out of his mind and actually incapable of leaving his bed? Wouldn't it really have been sufficient to send an apprentice to inquire—if any inquiry was necessary at all—did the chief clerk himself have to come and thus indicate to the entire family, an innocent family, that this suspicious circumstance could be investigated by no one less versed in affairs than himself? And more through the agitation caused by these reflections than through any act of will Gregor swung himself out of bed with all his strength. There was a loud thump, but it was not really a crash. His fall was broken to some extent by the carpet, his back, too, was less stiff than he thought, and so there was merely a dull thud, not so very startling. Only he had not lifted his head carefully enough and had hit it; he turned it and rubbed it on the carpet in pain and irritation.

"That was something falling down in there," said the chief clerk in the next room to the left. Gregor tried to suppose to himself that something like what had happened to him today might some day happen to the chief clerk; one really could not deny that it was possible. But as if in brusque reply to this supposition the chief clerk took a couple of firm steps in the next-door room and his patent leather boots creaked. From the right-hand room his sister was whispering to inform him of the situation: "Gregor, the chief clerk's here." "I know," muttered Gregor to himself; but he didn't dare to make his voice loud enough for his sister to hear it.

"Gregor," said his father now from the left-hand room, "the chief clerk has come and wants to know why you didn't catch the early train. We don't know what to say to him. Besides, he wants to talk to you in person. So open the door, please. He will be good enough to excuse the untidiness of your room." "Good morning, Mr. Samsa," the chief clerk was calling amiably meanwhile. "He's not well," said his mother to the visitor, while his father was still speaking through the door, "he's not well, sir, believe me. What else would make him miss a train! The boy thinks about nothing but his work. It makes me almost cross the way he never goes out in the evenings; he's been here the last eight days and has stayed at home every single evening. He just sits there quietly at the table reading a newspaper or looking through railway timetables. The only amusement he gets is doing fretwork. For instance, he spent two or three evenings cutting out a little picture frame; you would be surprised to see how pretty it is; it's hanging in his room; you'll see it in a minute when Gregor opens the door. I must say I'm glad you've come, sir; we should never have got him to unlock the door by ourselves; he's so obstinate; and I'm sure he's unwell, though he wouldn't have it to be so this morning." "I'm just coming," said Gregor slowly and carefully, not moving an inch for fear of losing one word of the conversation. "I can't think of any other explanation, madam," said the chief clerk, "I hope it's nothing serious. Although on the other hand I must say that we men of business—fortunately or unfortunately—very often simply have to ignore any slight indisposition, since business must be attended to." "Well, can the chief clerk come in now?" asked Gregor's father impatiently, again knocking on the door. "No," said Gregor. In the left-hand room a painful silence followed this refusal, in the right-hand room his sister began to sob.

Why didn't his sister join the others? She was probably newly out of bed and hadn't even begun to put on her clothes yet. Well, why was she crying? Because he wouldn't get up and let the chief clerk in, because he was in danger of losing his job, and because the chief would begin dunning his parents again for the old debts? Surely these were things one didn't need to worry about for the present. Gregor was still at home and not in the least thinking of deserting the family. At the moment, true, he was lying on the carpet and no one who knew the condition he was in could seriously expect him to admit the chief clerk. But for such a small discourtesy, which could plausibly be explained away somehow later on, Gregor could hardly be dismissed on the spot. And it seemed to Gregor that it would be much more sensible to leave him in peace for the present than to trouble him with tears and entreaties. Still, of course, their uncertainty bewildered them all and excused their behavior.

"Mr. Samsa," the chief clerk called now in a louder voice, "what's the matter with you? Here you are, barricading yourself in your room, giving only 'yes' and 'no' for answers, causing your parents a lot of unnecessary trouble and neglecting—I mention this only in passing—neglecting your business duties in an incredible fashion. I am speaking here in the name of your parents and of your chief, and I beg you quite seriously to give me an immediate and precise explanation. You amaze me, you amaze me. I thought you were a quiet, dependable person, and now all at once you seem bent on making a disgraceful exhibition of yourself. The chief did hint to me early this morning a possible explanation for your disappearance—with reference to the cash payments that were entrusted to you recently—but I almost pledged my solemn word of honor that this could not be so. But now that I see how incredibly obstinate you are, I no longer have the slightest desire to take your part at all. And your position in the firm is not so unassailable. I came with the intention of telling you all this in private, but since you are wasting my time so needlessly I don't see why your parents shouldn't hear it too. For some time past your work has been most unsatisfactory; this is not the season of the year for a business boom, of course, we admit that, but a season of the year for doing no business at all, that does not exist, Mr. Samsa, must not exist."

"But, sir," cried Gregor, beside himself and in his agitation forgetting everything else, "I'm just going to open the door this very minute. A slight illness, an attack of giddiness, has kept me from getting up. I'm still lying in bed. But I feel all right again. I'm getting out of bed now. Just give me a moment or two longer! I'm not quite so well as I thought. But I'm all right, really. How a thing like that can suddenly strike one down! Only last night I was quite well, my parents can tell you, or rather I did have a slight presentiment. I must have showed some sign of it. Why didn't I report it at the office! But one always thinks that an indisposition can be got over without staying in the house. Oh sir, do spare my parents! All that you're reproaching me with now has no foundation; no one has ever said a word to me about it. Perhaps you haven't looked at the last orders I sent in. Anyhow, I can still catch the eight o'clock train, I'm much the better for my few hours' rest. Don't let me detain you here, sir; I'll be attending to business very soon, and do be good enough to tell the chief so and to make my excuses to him!"

And while all this was tumbling out pell-mell and Gregor hardly knew what he was saying, he had reached the chest quite easily, perhaps because of the practice he had had in bed, and was now trying to lever himself upright by means of it. He meant actually to open the door, actually to show himself and speak to the chief clerk; he was eager to find out what the others, after all their insistence, would say at the sight of him. If they were horrified then the responsibility was no longer his and he could stay quiet. But if they took it calmly, then he had no reason either to be upset, and could really get to the station for the eight o'clock train if he hurried. At first he slipped down a few times from the polished surface of the chest, but at length and with a last heave he stood upright; he paid no more attention to the pains in the lower part of his body, however they smarted. Then he let himself fall against the back of a near-by chair, and clung with his little legs to the edges of it. That brought him into control of himself again and he stopped speaking, for now he could listen to what the chief clerk was saying.

"Did you understand a word of it?" the chief clerk was asking; "surely he can't be trying to make fools of us?" "Oh dear," cried his mother, in tears, "perhaps he's terribly ill and we're tormenting him. Grete! Grete!" she called out then. "Yes Mother?" called his sister from the other side. They were calling to each other across Gregor's room. "You must go this minute for the doctor. Gregor is ill. Go for the doctor, quick. Did you hear how he was speaking?" "That was no human voice," said the chief clerk in a voice noticeably low beside the shrillness of the mother's. "Anna! Anna!" his father was calling through the hall to the kitchen, clapping his hands, "get a locksmith at once!" And the two girls were already running through the hall with a swish of skirts—how could his sister have got dressed so quickly?—and were tearing the front door open. There was no sound of its closing again; they had evidently left it open, as one does in houses where some great misfortune has happened.

But Gregor was now much calmer. The words he uttered were no longer understandable, apparently, although they seemed clear enough to him, even clearer than before, perhaps because his ear had grown accustomed to the sound of them. Yet at any rate people now believed that something was wrong with him, and were ready to help him. The positive certainty with which these first measures had been taken comforted him. He felt himself drawn once more into the human circle and hoped for great and remarkable results from both the doctor and the locksmith, without really distinguishing precisely between them. To make his voice as clear as possible for the decisive conversation that was now imminent he coughed a little, as quietly as he could, of course, since this noise too might not sound like a human cough for all he was able to judge. In the next room meanwhile there was complete silence. Perhaps his parents were sitting at the table with the chief clerk, whispering, perhaps they were all leaning against the door and listening.

Slowly Gregor pushed the chair towards the door, then let go of it, caught hold of the door for support—the soles at the end of his little legs were somewhat sticky—and rested against it for a moment after his efforts. Then he set himself to turning the key in the lock with his mouth. It seemed, unhappily, that he hadn't really any teeth—what could he grip the key with?—but on the other hand his jaws were certainly very strong; with their help he did manage to set the key in motion, heedless of the fact that he was undoubtedly damaging them somewhere, since a brown fluid issued from his mouth, flowed over the key and dripped on the floor. "Just listen to that," said the chief clerk next door; "he's turning the key." That was a great encouragement to Gregor; but they should all have shouted encouragement to him, his father and mother too: "Go on, Gregor," they should have called out, "keep going, hold on to that key!" And in the belief that they were all following his efforts intently, he clenched his jaws recklessly on the key with all the force at his command. As the turning of the key progressed he circled round the lock, holding on now only with his mouth, pushing on the key, as required, or pulling it down again with all the weight of his body. The louder click of the finally yielding lock literally quickened Gregor. With a deep breath of relief he said to himself: "So I didn't need the locksmith," and laid his head on the handle to open the door wide.

Since he had to pull the door towards him, he was still invisible when it was really wide open. He had to edge himself slowly round the near half of the double door, and to do it very carefully if he was not to fall plump upon his back just on the threshold. He was still carrying out this difficult manoeuvre, with no time to observe anything else, when he

heard the chief clerk utter a loud "Oh!"—it sounded like a gust of wind—
and now he could see the man, standing as he was nearest to the door,
clapping one hand before his open mouth and slowly backing away as if
driven by some invisible steady pressure. His mother—in spite of the
chief clerk's being there her hair was still undone and sticking up in all
directions—first clasped her hands and looked at his father, then took
two steps towards Gregor and fell on the floor among her outspread skirts,
her face quite hidden on her breast. His father knotted his fist with a
fierce expression on his face as if he meant to knock Gregor back into
his room, then looked uncertainly round the living room, covered his eyes
with his hands and wept till his great chest heaved.

Gregor did not go now into the living room, but leaned against the
inside of the firmly shut wing of the door, so that only half his body was
visible and his head above it bending sideways to look at the others. The
light had meanwhile strengthened; on the other side of the street one
could see clearly a section of the endlessly long, dark gray building opposite—it was a hospital—abruptly punctuated by its row of regular windows; the rain was still falling, but only in large singly discernible and
literally singly splashing drops. The breakfast dishes were set out on the
table lavishly, for breakfast was the most important meal of the day to
Gregor's father, who lingered it out for hours over various newspapers.
Right opposite Gregor on the wall hung a photograph of himself in military service, as a lieutenant, hand on sword, a carefree smile on his face,
inviting one to respect his uniform and military bearing. The door leading to the hall was open, and one could see that the front door stood open
too, showing the landing beyond and the beginning of the stairs going
down.

"Well," said Gregor, knowing perfectly that he was the only one who
had retained any composure, "I'll put my clothes on at once, pack up my
samples and start off. Will you only let me go? You see, sir, I'm not obstinate, and I'm willing to work; traveling is a hard life, but I couldn't live
without it. Where are you going, sir? To the office? Yes? Will you give a
true account of all this? One can be temporarily incapacitated, but that's
just the moment for remembering former services and bearing in mind
that later on, when the incapacity has been got over, one will certainly
work with all the more industry and concentration. I'm loyally bound to
serve the chief, you know that very well. Besides, I have to provide for
my parents and my sister. I'm in great difficulties, but I'll get out of them
again. Don't make things any worse for me than they are. Stand up for
me in the firm. Travelers are not popular there, I know. People think
they earn sacks of money and just have a good time. A prejudice there's
no particular reason for revising. But you, sir, have a more comprehensive view of the affairs than the rest of the staff, yes, let me tell you in
confidence, a more comprehensive view than the chief himself, who,
being the owner, lets his judgment easily be swayed against one of his
employees. And you know very well that the traveler, who is never seen
in the office almost the whole year round, can so easily fall a victim to

gossip and ill luck and unfounded complaints, which he mostly knows nothing about, except when he comes back exhausted from his rounds, and only then suffers in person from their evil consequences, which he can no longer trace back to the original causes. Sir, sir, don't go away without a word to me to show that you think me in the right at least to some extent!"

But at Gregor's very first words the chief clerk had already backed away and only stared at him with parted lips over one twitching shoulder. And while Gregor was speaking he did not stand still one moment but stole away towards the door, without taking his eyes off Gregor, yet only an inch at a time, as if obeying some secret injunction to leave the room. He was already at the hall, and the suddenness with which he took his last step out of the living room would have made one believe he had burned the sole of his foot. Once in the hall he stretched his right arm before him towards the staircase, as if some supernatural power were waiting there to deliver him.

Gregor perceived that the chief clerk must on no account be allowed to go away in this frame of mind if his position in the firm were not to be endangered to the utmost. His parents did not understand this so well; they had convinced themselves in the course of years that Gregor was settled for life in this firm, and besides they were so preoccupied with their immediate troubles that all foresight had forsaken them. Yet Gregor had this foresight. The chief clerk must be detained, soothed, persuaded and finally won over; the whole future of Gregor and his family depended on it! If only his sister had been there! She was intelligent; she had begun to cry while Gregor was still lying quietly on his back. And no doubt the chief clerk, so partial to ladies, would have been guided by her; she would have shut the door of the flat and in the hall talked him out of his horror. But she was not there, and Gregor would have to handle the situation himself. And without remembering that he was still unaware what powers of movement he possessed, without even remembering that his words in all possibility, indeed in all likelihood, would again be unintelligible, he let go the wing of the door, pushed himself through the opening, started to walk towards the chief clerk, who was already ridiculously clinging with both hands to the railing on the landing; but immediately, as he was feeling for a support, he fell down with a little cry upon all his numerous legs. Hardly was he down when he experienced for the first time this morning a sense of physical comfort; his legs had firm ground under them; they were completely obedient, as he noted with joy; they even strove to carry him forward in whatever direction he chose; and he was inclined to believe that a final relief from all his sufferings was at hand. But in the same moment as he found himself on the floor, rocking with suppressed eagerness to move, not far from his mother, indeed just in front of her, she, who had seemed so completely crushed, sprang all at once to her feet, her arms and fingers outspread, cried: "Help, for God's sake, help!" bent her head down as if to see Gregor better, yet on the contrary kept backing senselessly away; had quite forgotten that the laden table stood behind her; sat upon it hastily, as if in absence of mind, when she bumped into it; and seemed altogether unaware that the big coffee pot beside her was upset and pouring coffee in a flood over the carpet.

"Mother, Mother," said Gregor in a low voice, and looked up at her. The chief clerk, for the moment, had quite slipped from his mind; instead, he could not resist snapping his jaws together at the sight of the streaming coffee. That made his mother scream again, she fled from the table and fell into the arms of his father, who hastened to catch her. But Gregor had now no time to spare for his parents; the chief clerk was already on the stairs; with his chin on the banisters he was taking one last backward look. Gregor made a spring, to be as sure as possible of overtaking him; the chief clerk must have divined his intention, for he leaped down several steps and vanished; he was still yelling "Ugh!" and it echoed through the whole staircase.

Unfortunately, the flight of the chief clerk seemed completely to upset Gregor's father, who had remained relatively calm until now, for instead of running after the man himself, or at least not hindering Gregor in his pursuit, he seized in his right hand the walking stick which the chief clerk had left behind on a chair, together with a hat and greatcoat, snatched in his left hand a large newspaper from the table and began stamping his feet and flourishing the stick and the newspaper to drive Gregor back into his room. No entreaty of Gregor's availed, indeed no entreaty was even understood, however humbly he bent his head his father only stamped on the floor the more loudly. Behind his father his mother had torn open a window, despite the cold weather, and was leaning far out of it with her face in her hands. A strong draught set in from the street to the staircase, the window curtains blew in, the newspapers on the table fluttered, stray pages whisked over the floor. Pitilessly Gregor's father drove him back, hissing and crying "Shoo!" like a savage. But Gregor was quite unpracticed in walking backwards, it really was a slow business. If he only had a chance to turn round he could get back to his room at once, but he was afraid of exasperating his father by the slowness of such a rotation and at any moment the stick in his father's hand might hit him a fatal blow on the back or on the head. In the end, however, nothing else was left for him to do since to his horror he observed that in moving backwards he could not even control the direction he took; and so, keeping an anxious eye on his father all the time over his shoulder, he began to turn round as quickly as he could, which was in reality very slowly. Perhaps his father noted his good intentions, for he did not interfere except every now and then to help him in the manoeuvre from a distance with the point of the stick. If only he would have stopped making that unbearable hissing noise! It made Gregor quite lose his head. He had turned almost completely round when the hissing noise so distracted him that he even turned a little the wrong way again. But when at last his head was fortunately right in front of the doorway, it appeared that his body was too broad simply to get through the opening. His father, of course, in his present mood was far from thinking of such a thing as opening the other half of the door, to let Gregor have enough space. He had merely the fixed idea of driving Gregor back into his room as quickly as possible. He would never have suffered Gregor to make the circumstantial preparations for standing up on end and perhaps slipping his way through the door. Maybe he was now making more noise than ever to urge Gregor forward, as if no obstacle impeded him; to Gregor, anyhow, the noise in his rear sounded no longer like the voice of one single father; this was really no joke, and Gregor thrust himself—come what might—into the doorway. One side of his body rose up, he was tilted at an angle in the doorway, his flank was quite bruised, horrid blotches stained the white door, soon he was stuck fast and, left to himself, could not have moved at all, his legs on one side fluttered trembling in the air, those on the other were crushed painfully to the floor—when from behind his father gave him a strong push which was literally a deliverance and he flew far into the room, bleeding freely. The door was slammed behind him with the stick, and then at last there was silence.

## II

Not until it was twilight did Gregor awake out of a deep sleep, more like a swoon than a sleep. He would certainly have waked up of his own accord not much later, for he felt himself sufficiently rested and well-slept, but it seemed to him as if a fleeting step and a cautious shutting of the door leading into the hall had aroused him. The electric lights in the street cast a pale sheen here and there on the ceiling and the upper surfaces of the furniture, but down below, where he lay, it was dark. Slowly, awkwardly trying out his feelers, which he now first learned to appreciate, he pushed his way to the door to see what had been happening there. His left side felt like one single long, unpleasantly tense scar, and he had actually to limp on his two rows of legs. One little leg, moreover, had been severely damaged in the course of that morning's events—it was almost a miracle that only one had been damaged—and trailed uselessly behind him.

He had reached the door before he discovered what had really drawn him to it: the smell of food. For there stood a basin filled with fresh milk in which floated little sops of white bread. He could almost have laughed with joy, since he was now still hungrier than in the morning, and he dipped his head almost over the eyes straight into the milk. But soon in disappointment he withdrew it again; not only did he find it difficult to feed because of his tender left side—and he could only feed with the palpitating collaboration of his whole body—he did not like the milk either, although milk had been his favorite drink and that was certainly why his sister had set it there for him, indeed it was almost with repulsion that he turned away from the basin and crawled back to the middle of the room.

He could see through the crack of the door that the gas was turned on in the living room, but while usually at this time his father made a habit of reading the afternoon newspaper in a loud voice to his mother and occasionally to his sister as well, not a sound was now to be heard. Well, perhaps his father had recently given up this habit of reading aloud, which his sister had mentioned so often in conversation and in her letters. But there was the same silence all around, although the flat was certainly not empty of occupants. "What a quiet life our family has been leading," said Gregor to himself, and as he sat there motionless staring into the darkness he felt great pride in the fact that he had been able to provide such a life for his parents and sister in such a fine flat. But what if all the quiet, the comfort, the contentment were now to end in horror? To keep himself from being lost in such thoughts Gregor took refuge in movement and crawled up and down the room.

Once during the long evening one of the side doors was opened a little and quickly shut again, later the other side door too; someone had apparently wanted to come in and then thought better of it. Gregor now stationed himself immediately before the living room door, determined to persuade any hesitating visitor to come in or at least to discover who it might be; but the door was not opened again and he waited in vain. In the early morning, when the doors were locked, they had all wanted to come in, now that he had opened one door and the other had apparently been opened during the day, no one came in and even the keys were on the other side of the doors.

It was late at night before the gas went out in the living room, and Gregor could easily tell that his parents and his sister had all stayed awake until then, for he could clearly hear the three of them stealing away on tiptoe. No one was likely to visit him, not until the morning, that was certain; so he had plenty of time to meditate at his leisure on how he was to arrange his life afresh. But the lofty, empty room in which he had to lie flat on the floor filled him with an apprehension he could not account for, since it had been his very own room for the past five years—and with a half-unconscious action, not without a slight feeling of shame, he scuttled under the sofa, where he felt comfortable at once, although his back was a little cramped and he could not lift his head up, and his only regret was that his body was too broad to get the whole of it under the sofa.

He stayed there all night, spending the time partly in a light slumber, from which his hunger kept waking him up with a start, and partly in worrying and sketching vague hopes, which all led to the same conclusion, that he must lie low for the present and, by exercising patience and the utmost consideration, help the family to bear the inconvenience he was bound to cause them in his present condition.

Very early in the morning, it was still almost night, Gregor had the chance to test the strength of his new resolutions, for his sister, nearly fully dressed, opened the door from the hall and peered in. She did not see him at once, yet when she caught sight of him under the sofa— well, he had to be somewhere, he couldn't have flown away, could he?—

she was so startled that without being able to help it she slammed the
door shut again. But as if regretting her behavior she opened the door
again immediately and came in on tiptoe, as if she were visiting an invalid or even a stranger. Gregor had pushed his head forward to the very
edge of the sofa and watched her. Would she notice that he had left the
milk standing, and not for lack of hunger, and would she bring in some
other kind of food more to his taste? If she did not do it of her own
accord, he would rather starve than draw her attention to the fact, although he felt a wild impulse to dart out from under the sofa, throw
himself at her feet and beg her for something to eat. But his sister at
once noticed, with surprise, that the basin was still full, except for a
little milk that had been spilt all around it, she lifted it immediately,
not with her bare hands, true, but with a cloth and carried it away.
Gregor was wildly curious to know what she would bring instead, and
made various speculations about it. Yet what she actually did next, in
the goodness of her heart, he could never have guessed at. To find out
what he liked she brought him a whole selection of food, all set out on
an old newspaper. There were old, half-decayed vegetables, bones from
last night's supper covered with a white sauce that had thickened; some
raisins and almonds; a piece of cheese that Gregor would have called
uneatable two days ago; a dry roll of bread, a buttered roll, and a roll
both buttered and salted. Besides all that, she set down again the same
basin, into which she had poured some water, and which was apparently to be reserved for his exclusive use. And with fine tact, knowing
that Gregor would not eat in her presence, she withdrew quickly and
even turned the key, to let him understand that he could take his ease
as much as he liked. Gregor's legs all whizzed towards the food. His
wounds must have healed completely, moreover, for he felt no disability,
which amazed him and made him reflect how more than a month ago
he had cut one finger a little with a knife and had still suffered pain
from the wound only the day before yesterday. Am I less sensitive now?
he thought, and sucked greedily at the cheese, which above all the other
edibles attracted him at once and strongly. One after another and with
tears of satisfaction in his eyes he quickly devoured the cheese, the
vegetables and the sauce; the fresh food, on the other hand, had no
charms for him, he could not even stand the smell of it and actually
dragged away to some little distance the things he could eat. He had
long finished his meal and was only lying lazily on the same spot when
his sister turned the key slowly as a sign for him to retreat. That aroused
him at once, although he was nearly asleep, and he hurried under the
sofa again. But it took considerable self-control for him to stay under
the sofa, even for the short time his sister was in the room, since the
large meal had swollen his body somewhat and he was so cramped he
could hardly breathe. Slight attacks of breathlessness afflicted him and
his eyes were starting a little out of his head as he watched his unsus-
pecting sister sweeping together with a broom not only the remains of

what he had eaten but even the things he had not touched, as if these were now of no use to anyone, and hastily shoveling it all into a bucket, which she covered with a wooden lid and carried away. Hardly had she turned her back when Gregor came from under the sofa and stretched and puffed himself out.

In this manner Gregor was fed, once in the early morning while his parents and the servant girl were still asleep, and a second time after they had all had their midday dinner, for then his parents took a short nap and the servant girl could be sent out on some errand or other by his sister. Not that they would have wanted him to starve, of course, but perhaps they could not have borne to know more about his feeding than from hearsay, perhaps too his sister wanted to spare them such little anxieties wherever possible, since they had quite enough to bear as it was.

Under what pretext the doctor and the locksmith had been got rid of on that first morning Gregor could not discover, for since what he said was not understood by the others it never struck any of them, not even his sister, that he could understand what they said, and so whenever his sister came into his room he had to content himself with hearing her utter only a sigh now and then and an occasional appeal to the saints. Later on, when she had got a little used to the situation—of course she could never get completely used to it—she sometimes threw out a remark which was kindly meant or could be so interpreted. "Well, he liked his dinner today," she would say when Gregor had made a good clearance of his food; and when he had not eaten, which gradually happened more and more often, she would say almost sadly: "Everything's been left standing again."

But although Gregor could get no news directly, he overheard a lot from the neighboring rooms, and as soon as voices were audible, he would run to the door of the room concerned and press his whole body against it. In the first few days especially there was no conversation that did not refer to him somehow, even if only indirectly. For two whole days there were family consultations at every mealtime about what should be done; but also between meals the same subject was discussed, for there were always at least two members of the family at home, since no one wanted to be alone in the flat and to leave it quite empty was unthinkable. And on the very first of these days the household cook—it was not quite clear what and how much she knew of the situation—went down on her knees to his mother and begged leave to go, and when she departed, a quarter of an hour later, gave thanks for her dismissal with tears in her eyes as if for the greatest benefit that could have been conferred on her, and without any prompting swore a solemn oath that she would never say a single word to anyone about what had happened.

Now Gregor's sister had to cook too, helping her mother; true, the cooking did not amount to much, for they ate scarcely anything. Gregor was always hearing one of the family vainly urging another to eat and

getting no answer but: "Thanks, I've had all I want," or something similar. Perhaps they drank nothing either. Time and again his  sister kept
asking his father if he wouldn't like some beer and offered kindly to go
and fetch it herself, and when he made no answer suggested that she
could ask the concierge to fetch it, so that he need feel no sense of obligation, but then a round "No" came from his father and no more was said
about it.

In the course of that very first day Gregor's father explained the
family's financial position and prospects to both his mother and his sister.
Now and then he rose from the table to get some voucher or memoran-
dum out of the small safe he had rescued from the collapse of his business five years earlier. One could hear him opening the complicated lock
and rustling papers out and shutting it again. This statement made by his
father was the first cheerful information Gregor had heard since his im-
prisonment. He had been of the opinion that nothing at all was left over
from his father's business, at least his father had never said anything
to the contrary, and of course he had not asked him directly. At that time
Gregor's sole desire was to do his utmost to help the family to forget
as soon as possible the catastrophe which had overwhelmed the business
and thrown them all into a state of complete despair. And so he had
set to work with unusual ardor and almost overnight had become a
commercial traveler instead of a little clerk, with of course much greater
chances of earning money, and his success was immediately translated
into good round coin which he could lay on the table for his amazed
and happy family. These had been fine times, and they had never re-
curred, at least not with the same sense of glory, although later on
Gregor had earned so much money that he was able to meet the expenses
of the whole household and did so. They had simply got used to it, both
the family and Gregor; the money was gratefully accepted and gladly
given, but there was no special uprush of warm feeling. With his sister
alone had he remained intimate, and it was a secret plan of his that she,
who loved music, unlike himself, and could play movingly on the violin,
should be sent next year to study at the Conservatorium, despite the
great expense that would entail, which must be made up in some other
way. During his brief visits home the Conservatorium was often mentioned in the talks he had with his sister, but always merely as a beautiful
dream which could never come true, and his parents discouraged even
these innocent references to it; yet Gregor had made up his mind firmly
about it and meant to announce the fact with due solemnity on Christmas
Day.

Such were the thoughts, completely futile in his present condition,
that went through his head as he stood clinging upright to the door and
listening. Sometimes out of sheer weariness he had to give up listening
and let his head fall negligently against the door, but he always had to
pull himself together again at once, for even the slight sound his head
made was audible next door and brought all conversation to a stop.

"What can he be doing now?" his father would say after a while, obviously turning towards the door, and only then would the interrupted conversation gradually be set going again.

Gregor was now informed as amply as he could wish—for his father tended to repeat himself in his explanations, partly because it was a long time since he had handled such matters and partly because his mother could not always grasp things at once—that a certain amount of investments, a very small amount it was true, had survived the wreck of their fortunes and had even increased a little because the dividends had not been touched meanwhile. And besides that, the money Gregor brought home every month—he had kept only a few dollars for himself— had never been quite used up and now amounted to a small capital sum. Behind the door Gregor nodded his head eagerly, rejoiced at this evidence of unexpected thrift and foresight. True, he could really have paid off some more of his father's debts to the chief with this extra money, and so brought much nearer the day on which he could quit his job, but doubtless it was better the way his father had arranged it.

Yet this capital was by no means sufficient to let the family live on the interest of it; for one year, perhaps, or at the most two, they could live on the principal, that was all. It was simply a sum that ought not to be touched and should be kept for a rainy day; money for living expenses would have to be earned. Now his father was still hale enough but an old man, and he had done no work for the past five years and could not be expected to do much; during these five years, the first years of leisure in his laborious though unsuccessful life, he had grown rather fat and become sluggish. And Gregor's old mother, how was she to earn a living with her asthma, which troubled her even when she walked through the flat and kept her lying on a sofa every other day panting for breath beside an open window? And was his sister to earn her bread, she who was still a child of seventeen and whose life hitherto had been so pleasant, consisting as it did in dressing herself nicely, sleeping long, helping in the housekeeping, going out to a few modest entertainments and above all playing the violin? At first whenever the need for earning money was mentioned Gregor let go his hold on the door and threw himself down on the cool leather sofa beside it, he felt so hot with shame and grief.

Often he just lay there the long nights through without sleeping at all, scrabbling for hours on the leather. Or he nerved himself to the great effort of pushing an armchair to the window, then crawled up over the window sill and, braced against the chair, leaned against the window panes, obviously in some recollection of the sense of freedom that looking out of a window always used to give him. For in reality day by day things that were even a little way off were growing dimmer to his sight; the hospital across the street, which he used to execrate for being all too often before his eyes, was now quite beyond his range of vision, and if he had not known that he lived in Charlotte Street, a quiet street but still a city street, he might have believed that his window gave on a desert waste where gray sky and gray land blended indistinguishably into each other. His quick-witted sister only needed to observe twice that the armchair stood by the window; after that whenever she had tidied the room she always pushed the chair back to the same place at the window and even left the inner casements open.

If he could have spoken to her and thanked her for all she had to do for him, he could have borne her ministrations better; as it was, they oppressed him. She certainly tried to make as light as possible of whatever was disagreeable in her task, and as time went on she succeeded, of course, more and more, but time brought more enlightenment to Gregor too. The very way she came in distressed him. Hardly was she in the room when she rushed to the window, without even taking time to shut the door, careful as she was usually to shield the sight of Gregor's room from the others, and as if she were almost suffocating tore the casements open with hasty fingers, standing then in the open draught for a while even in the bitterest cold and drawing deep breaths. This noisy scurry of hers upset Gregor twice a day; he would crouch trembling under the sofa all the time, knowing quite well that she would certainly have spared him such a disturbance had she found it at all possible to stay in his presence without opening the window.

On one occasion, about a month after Gregor's metamorphosis, when there was surely no reason for her to be still startled at his appearance, she came a little earlier than usual and found him gazing out of the window, quite motionless, and thus well placed to look like a bogey. Gregor would not have been surprised had she not come in at all, for she could not immediately open the window while he was there, but not only did she retreat, she jumped back as if in alarm and banged the door shut; a stranger might well have thought that he had been lying in wait for her there meaning to bite her. Of course he hid himself under the sofa at once, but he had to wait until midday before she came again, and she seemed more ill at ease than usual. This made him realized how repulsive the sight of him still was to her, and that it was bound to go on being repulsive, and what an effort it must cost her not to run away even from the sight of the small portion of his body that stuck out from under the sofa. In order to spare her that, therefore, one day he carried a sheet on his back to the sofa—it cost him four hours' labor—and arranged it there in such a way as to hide him completely, so that even if she were to bend down she could not see him. Had she considered the sheet unnecessary, she would certainly have stripped it off the sofa again, for it was clear enough that this curtaining and confining of himself was not likely to conduce to Gregor's comfort, but she left it where it was, and Gregor even fancied that he caught a thankful glance from her eye when he lifted the sheet carefully a very little with his head to see how she was taking the new arrangement.

For the first fortnight his parents could not bring themselves to the point of entering his room, and he often heard them expressing their

appreciation of his sister's activities, whereas formerly they had frequently scolded her for being as they thought a somewhat useless daughter. But now, both of them often waited outside the door, his father and
his mother, while his sister tidied his room, and as soon as she came out
she had to tell them exactly how things were in the room, what Gregor
had eaten, how he had conducted himself this time and whether there
was not perhaps some slight improvement in his condition. His mother,
moreover, began relatively soon to want to visit him, but his father and
sister dissuaded her at first with arguments which Gregor listened to
very attentively and altogether approved. Later, however, she had to
be held back by main force, and when she cried out: "Do let me in to
Gregor, he is my unfortunate son! Can't you understand that I must go
to him?" Gregor thought that it might be well to have her come in, not
every day, of course, but perhaps once a week; she understood things,
after all, much better than his sister, who was only a child despite the
efforts she was making and had perhaps taken on so difficult a task
merely out of childish thoughtlessness.

Gregor's desire to see his mother was soon fulfilled. During the
daytime he did not want to show himself at the window, out of consideration for his parents, but he could not crawl very far around the
few square yards of floor space he had, nor could he bear lying quietly
at rest all during the night, while he was fast losing any interest he had
ever taken in food, so that for mere recreation he had formed the habit
of crawling crisscross over the walls and ceiling. He especially enjoyed
hanging suspended from the ceiling; it was much better than lying on
the floor; one could breathe more freely; one's body swung and rocked
lightly; and in the almost blissful absorption induced by this suspension
it could happen to his own surprise that he let go and fell plump on the
floor. Yet he now had his body much better under control than formerly,
and even such a big fall did him no harm. His sister at once remarked
the new distraction Gregor had found for himself—he left traces behind
him of the sticky stuff on his soles wherever he crawled—and she got
the idea in her head of giving him as wide a field as possible to crawl
in and of removing the pieces of furniture that hindered him, above all
the chest of drawers and the writing desk. But that was more than she
could manage all by herself; she did not dare ask her father to help her;
and as for the servant girl, a young creature of sixteen who had had
the courage to stay on after the cook's departure, she could not be asked
to help, for she had begged as an especial favor that she might keep the
kitchen door locked and open it only on a definite summons; so there
was nothing left but to apply to her mother at an hour when her father
was out. And the old lady did come, with exclamations of joyful eagerness, which, however, died away at the door of Gregor's room. Gregor's
sister, of course, went in first, to see that everything was in order before
letting his mother enter. In great haste Gregor pulled the sheet lower
and rucked it more in folds so that it really looked as if it had been
thrown accidentally over the sofa. And this time he did not peer out

from under it; he renounced the pleasure of seeing his mother on this occasion and was only glad that she had come at all. "Come in, he's out of sight," said his sister, obviously leading her mother in by the hand. Gregor could now hear the two women struggling to shift the heavy old chest from its place, and his sister claiming the greater part of the labor for herself, without listening to the admonitions of her mother who feared she might overstrain herself. It took a long time. After at least a quarter of an hour's tugging his mother objected that the chest had better be left where it was, for in the first place it was too heavy and could never be got out before his father came home, and standing in the middle of the room like that it would only hamper Gregor's movements, while in the second place it was not at all certain that removing the furniture would be doing a service to Gregor. She was inclined to think to the contrary; the sight of the naked walls made her own heart heavy, and why shouldn't Gregor have the same feeling, considering that he had been used to his furniture for so long and might feel forlorn without it. "And doesn't it look," she concluded in a low voice—in fact she had been almost whispering all the time as if to avoid letting Gregor, whose exact whereabouts she did not know, hear even the tones of her voice, for she was convinced that he could not understand her words— "doesn't it look as if we were showing him, by taking away his furniture, that we have given up hope of his ever getting better and are just leaving him coldly to himself? I think it would be best to keep his room exactly as it has always been, so that when he comes back to us he will find everything unchanged and be able all the more easily to forget what has happened in between."

On hearing these words from his mother Gregor realized that the lack of all direct human speech for the past two months together with the monotony of family life must have confused his mind, otherwise he could not account for the fact that he had quite earnestly looked forward to having his room emptied of furnishing. Did he really want his warm room, so comfortably fitted with old family furniture, to be turned into a naked den in which he would certainly be able to crawl unhampered in all directions but at the price of shedding simultaneously all recollections of his human background? He had indeed been so near the brink of forgetfulness that only the voice of his mother, which he had not heard for so long, had drawn him back from it. Nothing should be taken out of his room; everything must stay as it was; he could not dispense with the good influence of the furniture on his state of mind; and even if the furniture did hamper him in his senseless crawling round and round, that was no drawback but a great advantage.

Unfortunately his sister was of the contrary opinion; she had grown accustomed, and not without reason, to consider herself an expert in Gregor's affairs as against her parents, and so her mother's advice was now enough to make her determined on the removal not only of the chest and the writing desk, which had been her first intention, but of all the furniture except indispensable sofa. This determination was not, of course, merely the outcome of childish recalcitrance and of the self-confidence she had recently developed so unexpectedly and at such cost; she had in fact perceived that Gregor needed a lot of space to crawl about in, while on the other hand he never used the furniture at all, so far as could be seen. Another factor might have been also the enthusiastic temperament of an adolescent girl, which seeks to indulge itself on every opportunity and which now tempted Grete to exaggerate the horror of her brother's circumstances in order that she might do all the more for him. In a room where Gregor lorded it all alone over empty walls no one save herself was likely ever to set foot.

And so she was not to be moved from her resolve by her mother, who seemed moreover to be ill at ease in Gregor's room and therefore unsure of herself, was soon reduced to silence and helped her daughter as best she could to push the chest outside. Now, Gregor could do without the chest, if need be, but the writing desk he must retain. As soon as the two women had got the chest out of his room, groaning as they pushed it, Gregor stuck his head out from under the sofa to see how he might intervene as kindly and cautiously as possible. But as bad luck would have it, his mother was the first to return, leaving Grete clasping the chest in the room next door where she was trying to shift it all by herself, without of course moving it from the spot. His mother however was not accustomed to the sight of him, it might sicken her and so in alarm Gregor backed quickly to the other end of the sofa, yet could not prevent the sheet from swaying a little in front. That was enough to put her on the alert. She paused, stood still for a moment and then went back to Grete.

Although Gregor kept reassuring himself that nothing out of the way was happening, but only a few bits of furniture were being changed round, he soon had to admit that all this trotting to and fro of the two women, their little ejaculations and the scraping of furniture along the floor affected him like a vast disturbance coming from all sides at once, and however much he tucked in his head and legs and cowered to the very floor he was bound to confess that he would not be able to stand it for long. They were clearing his room out; taking away everything he loved; the chest in which he kept his fret saw and other tools was already dragged off; they were now loosening the writing desk which had almost sunk into the floor, the desk at which he had done all his homework when he was at the commercial academy, at the grammar school before that, and, yes, even at the primary school—he had no more time to waste in weighing the good intentions of the two women, whose existence he had by now almost forgotten, for they were so exhausted that they were laboring in silence and nothing could be heard but the heavy scuffling of their feet.

And so he rushed out—the women were just leaning against the writing desk in the next room to give themselves a breather—and four times changed his direction, since he really did not know what to rescue first, then on the wall opposite, which was already otherwise cleared, he was struck by the picture of the lady muffled in so much fur and quickly crawled up to it and pressed himself to the glass, which was a good surface to hold on to and comforted his hot belly. This picture at least, which was entirely hidden beneath him, was going to be removed by nobody. He turned his head towards the door of the living room so as to observe the women when they came back.

They had not allowed themselves much of a rest and were already coming; Grete had twined her arm round her mother and was almost supporting her. "Well, what shall we take now?" said Grete, looking round. Her eyes met Gregor's from the wall. She kept her composure, presumably because of her mother, bent her head down to her mother, to keep her from looking up, and said, although in a fluttering, unpremeditated voice: "Come, hadn't we better go back to the living room for a moment?" Her intentions were clear enough to Gregor, she wanted to bestow her mother in safety and then chase him down from the wall. Well, just let her try it! He clung to his picture and would not give it up. He would rather fly in Grete's face.

But Grete's words had succeeded in disquieting her mother, who took a step to one side, caught sight of the huge brown mass on the flowered wallpaper, and before she was really conscious that what she saw was Gregor screamed in a loud, hoarse voice: "Oh God, oh God!" fell with outspread arms over the sofa as if giving up and did not move. "Gregor!" cried his sister, shaking her fist and glaring at him. This was the first time she had directly addressed him since his metamorphosis. She ran into the next room for some aromatic essence with which to rouse her mother from her fainting fit. Gregor wanted to help too— there was still time to rescue the picture—but he was stuck fast to the glass and had to tear himself loose; he then ran after his sister into the next room as if he could advise her, as he used to do; but then had to stand helplessly behind her; she meanwhile searched among various small bottles and when she turned round started in alarm at the sight of him; one bottle fell on the floor and broke; a splinter of glass cut Gregor's face with some kind of corrosive medicine splashed him; without pausing a moment longer Grete gathered up all the bottles she could carry and ran to her mother with them; she banged the door shut with her foot. Gregor was now cut off from his mother, who was perhaps nearly dying because of him; he dared not open the door for fear of frightening away his sister, who had to stay with her mother; there was nothing he could do but wait; and harassed by self-reproach and worry he began now to crawl to and fro, over everything, walls, furniture and ceiling, and finally in his despair, when the whole room seemed to be reeling round him, fell down on to the middle of the big table.

A little while elapsed, Gregor was still lying there feebly and all around was quiet, perhaps that was a good omen. Then the doorbell rang. The servant girl was of course locked in her kitchen, and Grete would have to open the door. It was his father. "What's been happening?" were his first words; Grete's face must have told him everything. Grete an-

swered in a muffled voice, apparently hiding her head on his breast:
"Mother has been fainting, but she's better now. Gregor's broken loose."
"Just what I expected," said his father, "just what I've been telling you,
but you women would never listen." It was clear to Gregor that his father
had taken the worst interpretation of Grete's all too brief statement and
was assuming that Gregor had been guilty of some violent act. Therefore
Gregor must now try to propitiate his father, since he had neither time
nor means for an explanation. And so he fled to the door of his own room
and crouched against it, to let his father see as soon as he came in from
the hall that his son had the good intention of getting back into his room
immediately and that it was not necessary to drive him there, but that if
only the door were open he would disappear at once.

Yet his father was not in the mood to perceive such fine distinctions.
"Ah!" he cried as soon as he appeared, in a tone which sounded at once
angry and exultant. Gregor drew his head back from the door and lifted
it to look at his father. Truly, this was not the father he had imagined to
himself; admittedly he had been too absorbed of late in his new recreation of crawling over the ceiling to take the same interest as before in
what was happening elsewhere in the flat, and he ought really to be prepared for some changes. And yet, and yet, could that be his father? The
man who used to lie wearily sunk in bed whenever Gregor set out on a
business journey; who welcomed him back of an evening lying in a long
chair in a dressing gown; who could not really rise to his feet but only
lifted his arms in greeting, and on the rare occasions when he did go out
with his family, on one or two Sundays a year and on high holidays,
walked between Gregor and his mother, who were slow walkers anyhow,
even more slowly than they did, muffled in his old greatcoat, shuffling
laboriously forward with the help of crook-handled stick which he set
down most cautiously at every step and, whenever he wanted to say anything, nearly always came to a full stop and gathered his escort around
him? Now he was standing there in fine shape; dressed in a smart blue
uniform with gold buttons, such as bank messengers wear; his strong
double chin bulked over the stiff high collar of his jacket; from under his
bushy eyebrows his black eyes darted fresh and penetrating glances; his
onetime tangled white hair had been combed flat on either side of a shining and carefully exact parting. He pitched his cap, which bore a gold
monogram, probably the badge of some bank, in a wide sweep across the
whole room on to a sofa and with the tailends of his jacket thrown back,
his hands in his trouser pockets, advanced with a grim visage towards
Gregor. Likely enough he did not himself know what he meant to do; at
any rate he lifted his feet uncommonly high, and Gregor was dumb-
founded at the enormous size of his shoe soles. But Gregor could not risk
standing up to him, aware as he had been from the very first day of his
new life that his father believed only the severest measures suitable for
dealing with him. And so he ran before his father, stopping when he
stopped and scuttling foward again when his father made any kind of
move. In this way they circled the room several times without anything

decisive happening, indeed the whole operation did not even look like a pursuit because it was carried out so slowly. And so Gregor did not leave the floor, for he feared that his father might take as a piece of peculiar wickedness any excursion of his over the walls or the ceiling. All the same, he could not stay this course much longer, for while his father took one step he had to carry out a whole series of movements. He was already beginning to feel breathless, just as in his former life his lungs had not been very dependable. As he was staggering along, trying to concentrate his energy on running, hardly keeping his eyes open; in his dazed state never even thinking of any other escape than simply going forward; and having almost forgotten that the walls were free to him, which in this room were well provided with finely carved pieces of furniture full of knobs and crevices—suddenly something lightly flung landed close behind him and rolled before him. It was an apple; a second apple followed immediately; Gregor came to a stop in alarm; there was no point in running on, for his father was determined to bombard him. He had filled his pockets with fruit from the dish on the sideboard and was now shying apple after apple, without taking particularly good aim for the moment. The small red apples rolled about the floor as if magnetized and cannoned into each other. An apple thrown without much force grazed Gregor's back and glanced off harmlessly. But another following immediately landed right on his back and sank in; Gregor wanted to drag himself forward, as if this startling, incredible pain could be left behind him; but he felt as if nailed to the spot and flattened himself out in complete derangement of all his senses. With his last conscious look he saw the door of his room being torn open and his mother rushing out ahead of his screaming sister, in her underbodice, for her daughter had loosened her clothing to let her breathe more freely and recover from her swoon, he saw his mother rushing towards his father, leaving one after another behind her on the floor her loosened petticoats, stumbling over her petticoats straight to his father and embracing him, in complete union with him—but here Gregor's sight began to fail—with her hands clasped round his father's neck as she begged for her son's life.

III

The serious injury done to Gregor, which disabled him for more than a month—the apple went on sticking in his body as a visible reminder, since no one ventured to remove—seemed to have made even his father recollect that Gregor was a member of the family, despite his present unfortunate and repulsive shape, and ought not to be treated as an enemy, that, on the contrary, family duty required the suppression of disgust and the exercise of patience, nothing but patience.

And although his injury had impaired, probably for ever, his powers of movement, and for the time being it took him long, long minutes to creep across his room like an old invalid—there was no question now of crawling up the wall—yet in his own opinion he was sufficiently compensated for this worsening of his condition by the fact that towards evening the living-room door, which he used to watch intently for an hour or two beforehand, was always thrown open, so that lying in the darkness of his room, invisible to the family, he could seem them all at the lamp-lit table and listen to their talk, by general consent as it were, very different from his earlier eavesdropping.

True, their intercourse lacked the lively character of former times, which he had always called to mind with a certain wistfulness in the small hotel bedrooms where he had been wont to throw himself down, tired out, on damp bedding. They were now mostly very silent. Soon after supper his father would fall asleep in his armchair; his mother and sister would admonish each other to be silent; his mother, bending low over the lamp, stitched at fine sewing for an underwear firm; his sister, who had taken a job as a salesgirl, was learning shorthand and French in the evenings on the chance of bettering herself. Sometimes his father woke up, and as if quite unaware that he had been sleeping said to his mother: "What a lot of sewing you're doing today!" and at once fell asleep again, while the two women exchanged a tired smile.

With a kind of mulishness his father persisted in keeping his uniform on even in the house; his dressing gown hung uselessly on its peg and he slept fully dressed where he sat, as if he were ready for service at any moment and even here only at the beck and call of his superior. As a result, his uniform, which was not brand-new to start with, began to look dirty, despite all the loving care of the mother and sister to keep it clean, and Gregor often spent whole evenings gazing at the many greasy spots on the garment, gleaming with gold buttons always in a high state of polish, in which the old man sat sleeping in extreme discomfort and yet quite peacefully.

As soon as the clock struck ten his mother tried to rouse his father with gentle words and to persuade him after that to get into bed, for sitting there he could not have a proper sleep and that was what he needed most, since he had to go on duty at six. But with the mulishness that had obsessed him since he became a bank messenger he always insisted on staying longer at the table, although he regularly fell asleep again and in the end only with the greatest trouble could be got out of his armchair and into his bed. However insistently Gregor's mother and sister kept urging him with gentle reminders, he would go on slowly shaking his head for a quarter of an hour, keeping his eyes shut, and refuse to get to his feet. The mother plucked at his sleeve, whispering endearments in his ear, and the sister left her lessons to come to her mother's help, but Gregor's father was not to be caught. He would only sink down deeper in his chair. Not until the two women hoisted him up by the armpits did he open his eyes and look at them both, one after the other, usually with the remark: "This is a life. This is the peace and quiet of my old age." And leaning on the two of them he would heave himself up, with difficulty, as if he were a great burden to himself, suffer them to lead him as far as the door and then wave them off and go on alone, while the mother abandoned her needlework and the sister her pen in order to run after him and help him farther.

Who could find time, in this overworked and tired-out family, to bother about Gregor more than was absolutely needful? The household was reduced more and more; the servant girl was turned off; a gigantic bony charwoman with white hair flying round her head came in morning and evening to do the rough work; everything else was done by Gregor's mother, as well as great piles of sewing. Even various family ornaments, which his mother and sister used to wear with pride at parties and celebrations, had to be sold, as Gregor discovered of an evening from hearing them all discuss the prices obtained. But what they lamented most was the fact that they could not leave the flat which was much too big for their present circumstances, because they could not think of any way to shift Gregor. Yet Gregor saw well enough that consideration for him was not the main difficulty preventing the removal, for they could have easily shifted him in some suitable box with a few air holes in it; what really kept them from moving into another flat was rather their own complete hopelessness and the belief that they had been singled out for a misfortune such as had never happened to any of their relations or acquaintances. They fulfilled to the uttermost all that the world demands of poor people, the father fetched breakfast for the small clerks in the bank, the mother devoted her energy to making underwear for strangers, the sister trotted to and fro behind the counter at the behest of customers, but more than this they had not the strength to do. And the wound in Gregor's back began to nag at him afresh when his mother and sister, after getting his father into bed, came back again, left their work lying, drew close to each other and sat cheek by cheek; when his mother, pointing towards his room, said: "Shut that door now, Grete," and he was left again in darkness, while next door the women mingled their tears or perhaps sat dry-eyed staring at the table.

Gregor hardly slept at all by night or by day. He was often haunted by the idea that next time the door opened he would take the family's affairs in hand again just as he used to do; once more, after this long interval, there appeared in his thoughts the figures of the chief and the chief clerk, the commercial travelers and apprentices, the porter who was so dull-witted, two or three friends in other firms, a chambermaid in one of the rural hotels, a sweet and fleeting memory, a cashier in a milliner's shop, whom he had wooed earnestly but too slowly—they all appeared, together with strangers or people he had quite forgotten, but instead of helping him and his family they were one and all unapproachable and he was glad when they vanished. At other times he would not be in the mood to bother about his family, he was only filled with rage at the way they were neglecting him, and although he had no clear idea of what he might care to eat he would make plans for getting into the larder to take the food that was after all his due, even if he were not hungry. His sister no longer took thought to bring him what might especially please

him, but in the morning and at noon before she went to business hurriedly pushed into his room with her foot any food that was available,
and in the evening cleared it out again with one sweep of the broom,
heedless of whether it had been merely tasted, or—as most frequently
happened—left untouched. The cleaning of his room, which she now did
always in the evenings, could not have been more hastily done. Streaks
of dirt stretched along the walls, here and there lay balls of dust and filth.
At first Gregor used to station himself in some particularly filthy corner
when his sister arrived, in order to reproach her with it, so to speak. But
he could have sat there for weeks without getting her to make any improvement; she could see the dirt as well as he did, but she had simply
made up her mind to leave it alone. And yet, with a touchiness that was
new to her, which seemed anyhow to have infected the whole family, she
jealously guarded her claim to be the sole caretaker of Gregor's room. His
mother once subjected his room to a thorough cleaning, which was
achieved only by means of several buckets of water—all this dampness
of course upset Gregor too and he lay widespread, sulky and motionless
on the sofa—but she was well punished for it. Hardly had his sister noticed the changed aspect of his room that evening than she rushed in high
dudgeon into the living room and, despite the imploring raised hands of
her mother, burst into a storm of weeping, while her parents—her father
had of course been startled out of his chair—looked on at first in helpless
amazement; then they too began to go into action; the father reproached
the mother on his right for not having left the cleaning of Gregor's room
to his sister; shrieked at the sister on his left that never again was she to
be allowed to clean Gregor's room; while the mother tried to pull the
father into his bedroom, since he was beyond himself with agitation; the
sister, shaken with sobs, then beat upon the table with her small fists; and
Gregor hissed loudly with rage because not one of them thought of shutting the door to spare him such a spectacle and so much noise.

Still, even if the sister, exhausted by her daily work, had grown tired
of looking after Gregor as she did formerly, there was no need for his
mother's intervention or for Gregor's being neglected at all. The charwoman was there. The old widow, whose strong bony frame had enabled
her to survive the worst a long life could offer, by no means recoiled from
Gregor. Without being in the least curious she had once by chance opened
the door of his room and at the sight of Gregor, who, taken by surprise,
began to rush to and fro although no one was chasing him, merely stood
there with her arms folded. From that time she never failed to open his
door a little for a moment, morning and evening, to have a look at him.
At first she even used to call him to her, with words which apparently
she took to be friendly, such as: "Come along, then, you old dung beetle!"
or "Look at the old dung beetle, then!" To such allocutions Gregor made
no answer, but stayed motionless where he was, as if the door had never
been opened. Instead of being allowed to disturb him so senselessly whenever the whim took her, she should rather have been ordered to clean out
his room daily, that charwoman! Once, early in the morning—heavy rain

was lashing on the windowpanes, perhaps a sign that spring was on the way—Gregor was so exasperated when she began addressing him again that he ran at her, as if to attack her, although slowly and feebly enough. But the charwoman instead of showing fright merely lifted high a chair that happened to be beside the door, and as she stood there with her mouth wide open it was clear that she meant to shut it only when she brought the chair down on Gregor's back. "So you're not coming any nearer?" she asked, as Gregor turned away again, and quietly put the chair back into the corner.

Gregor was now eating hardly anything. Only when he happened to pass the food laid out for him did he take a bit of something in his mouth as a pastime, kept it there for an hour at a time and usually spat it out again. At first he thought it was chagrin over the state of his room that prevented him from eating, yet he soon got used to the various changes in his room. It had become a habit in the family to push into his room things there was no room for elsewhere, and there were plenty of these now, since one of the rooms had been let to three lodgers. These serious gentlemen—all three of them with full beards, as Gregor once observed through a crack in the door—had a passion for order, not only in their own room but, since they were now members of the household, in all its arrangements, especially in the kitchen. Superfluous, not to say dirty, objects they could not bear. Besides, they had brought with them most of the furnishings they needed. For this reason many things could be dispensed with that it was no use trying to sell but that should not be thrown away either. All of them found their way into Gregor's room. The ash can likewise and the kitchen garbage can. Anything that was not needed for the moment was simply flung into Gregor's room by the charwoman, who did everything in a hurry; fortunately Gregor usually saw only the object, whatever it was, and the hand that held it. Perhaps she intended to take the things away again as time and opportunity offered, or to collect them until she could throw them all out in a heap, but in fact they just lay wherever she happened to throw them, except when Gregor pushed his way through the junk heap and shifted it somewhat, at first out of necessity, because he had not room enough to crawl, but later with increasing enjoyment, although after such excursions, being sad and weary to death, he would lie motionless for hours. And since the lodgers often ate their supper at home in the common living room, the living-room door stayed shut many an evening, yet Gregor reconciled himself quite easily to the shutting of the door, for often enough on evenings when it was opened he had disregarded it entirely and lain in the darkest corner of his room, quite unnoticed by the family. But on one occasion the charwoman left the door open a little and it stayed ajar even when the lodgers came in for supper and the lamp was lit. They set themselves at the top end of the table where formerly Gregor and his father and mother had eaten their meals, unfolded their napkins and took knife and fork in hand. At once his mother appeared in the other doorway with a dish of meat and close behind her his sister with a dish of potatoes piled high. The food steamed with a thick vapor. The lodgers bent over the food set before them as if to scrutinize it before eating, in fact the man in the middle, who seemed to pass for an authority with the other two, cut a piece of meat as it lay on the dish, obviously to discover if it were tender or should be sent back to the kitchen. He showed satisfaction, and Gregor's mother and sister, who had been watching anxiously, breathed freely and began to smile.

The family itself took its meals in the kitchen. None the less, Gregor's father came into the living room before going into the kitchen and with one prolonged bow, cap in hand, made a round of the table. The lodgers all stood up and murmured something in their beards. When they were alone again they ate their food in almost complete silence. It seemed remarkable to Gregor that among the various noises coming from the table he could always distinguish the sound of their masticating teeth, as if this were a sign to Gregor that one needed teeth in order to eat, and that with toothless jaws even of the finest make one could do nothing. "I'm hungry enough," said Gregor sadly to himself, "but not for that kind of food. How these lodgers are stuffing themselves, and here am I dying of starvation!"

On that very evening—during the whole of his time there Gregor could not remember ever having heard the violin—the sound of violin-playing came from the kitchen. The lodgers had already finished their supper, the one in the middle had brought out a newspaper and given the other two a page apiece, and now they were leaning back at ease reading and smoking. When the violin began to play they pricked up their ears, got to their feet, and went on tiptoe to the hall door where they stood huddled together. Their movements must have been heard in the kitchen, for Gregor's father called out: "Is the violin-playing disturbing you, gentlemen? It can be stopped at once." "On the contrary," said the middle lodger, "could not Fräulein Samsa come and play in this room, beside us, where it is much more convenient and comfortable?" "Oh certainly," cried Gregor's father, as if he were the violin-player. The lodgers came back into the living room and waited. Presently Gregor's father arrived with the music stand, his mother carrying the music and his sister with the violin. His sister quietly made everything ready to start playing; his parents, who had never let rooms before and so had an exaggerated idea of the courtesy due to lodgers, did not venture to sit down on their own chairs; his father leaned against the door, the right hand thrust between two buttons of his livery coat, which was formally buttoned up; but his mother was offered a chair by one of the lodgers and, since she left the chair just where he had happened to put it, sat down in a corner to one side.

Gregor's sister began to play; the father and mother, from either side, intently watched the movements of her hands. Gregor, attracted by the playing, ventured to move forward a little until his head was actually inside the living room. He felt hardly any surprise at his growing lack of consideration for the others; there had been a time when he prided himself on being considerate. And yet just on this occasion he had more reason than ever to hide himself, since owing to the amount of dust which lay thick in his room and rose into the air at the slightest movement, he too was covered with dust; fluff and hair and remnants of food trailed with him, caught on his back and along his sides; his indifference to everything was much too great for him to turn on his back and scrape himself clean on the carpet, as once he had done several times a day. And in spite of his condition, no shame deterred him from advancing a little over the spotless floor of the living room.

To be sure, no one was aware of him. The family was entirely absorbed in the violin-playing; the lodgers, however, who first of all had stationed themselves, hands in pockets, much too close behind the music stand so that they could all have read the music, which must have bothered his sister, had soon retreated to the window, half-whispering with downbent heads, and stayed there while his father turned an anxious eye on them. Indeed, they were making it more than obvious that they had been disappointed in their expectation of hearing good or enjoyable violin-playing, that they had had more than enough of the performance and only out of courtesy suffered a continued disturbance of their peace. From the way they all kept blowing the smoke of their cigars high in the air through nose and mouth one could divine their irritation. And yet Gregor's sister was playing so beautifully. Her face leaned sideways, intently and sadly her eyes followed the notes of music. Gregor crawled a little farther forward and lowered his head to the ground so that it might be possible for his eyes to meet hers. Was he an animal, that music had such an effect upon him? He felt as if the way were opening before him to the unknown nourishment he craved. He was determined to push forward till he reached his sister, to pull at her skirt and so let her know that she was to come into his room with her violin, for no one here appreciated her playing as he would appreciate it. He would never let her out of his room, at least, not so long as he lived; his frightful appearance would become, for the first time, useful to him; he would watch all the doors of his room at once and spit at intruders; but his sister should need no constraint, she should stay with him of her own free will; she should sit beside him on the sofa, bend down her ear to him and hear him confide that he had had the firm intention of sending her to the Conservatorium, and that, but for his mishap, last Christmas—surely Christmas was long past?—he would have announced it to everybody without allowing a single objection. After this confession his sister would be so touched that she would burst into tears, and Gregor would then raise himself to her shoulder and kiss her on the neck, which, now that she went to business, she kept free of any ribbon or collar.

"Mr. Samsa!" cried the middle lodger, to Gregor's father, and pointed, without wasting any more words, at Gregor, now working him-

self slowly forwards. The violin fell silent, the middle lodger first smiled
to his friends with a shake of the head and then looked at Gregor again.
Instead of driving Gregor out, his father seemed to think it more needful
to begin by soothing down the lodgers, although they were not at all agitated and apparently found Gregor more entertaining than the violin-
playing. He hurried towards them and, spreading out his arms, tried to
urge them back into their own room and at the same time to block their
view of Gregor. They now began to be really a little angry, one could not
tell whether because of the old man's behavior or because it had just
dawned on them that all unwittingly they had such a neighbor as Gregor
next door. They demanded explanations of his father, they waved their
arms like him, tugged uneasily at their beards, and only with reluctance
backed towards their room. Meanwhile Gregor's sister, who stood there
as if lost when her playing was so abruptly broken off, came to life again,
pulled herself together all at once after standing for a while holding
violin and bow in nervelessly hanging hands and staring at her music,
pushed her violin into the lap of her mother, who was still sitting in her
chair fighting asthmatically for breath, and ran into the lodgers' room
to which they were now being shepherded by her father rather more
quickly than before. One could see the pillows and blankets on the beds
flying under her accustomed fingers and being laid in order. Before the
lodgers had actually reached their room she had finished making the
beds and slipped out.

The old man seemed once more to be so possessed by his mulish
self-assertiveness that he was forgetting all the respect he should show
to his lodgers. He kept driving them on and driving them on until in the
very door of the bedroom the middle lodger stamped his foot loudly on
the floor and so brought him to a halt. "I beg to announce," said the
lodger, lifting one hand and looking also at Gregor's mother and sister,
"that because of the disgusting conditions prevailing in this household
and family"—here he spat on the floor with emphatic brevity—"I give
you notice on the spot. Naturally I won't pay you a penny for the days I
have lived here, on the contrary I shall consider bringing an action for
damages against you, based on claims—believe me—that will be easily
susceptible of proof." He ceased and stared straight in front of him, as
if he expected something. In fact his two friends at once rushed into the
breach with these words: "And we too give notice on the spot." On that
he seized the door-handle and shut the door with a slam.

Gregor's father, groping with his hands, staggered forward and fell
into his chair; it looked as if he were stretching himself there for his
ordinary evening nap, but the marked jerkings of his head, which was
as if uncontrollable, showed that he was far from asleep. Gregor had
simply stayed quietly all the time on the spot where the lodgers had
espied him. Disappointment at the failure of his plan, perhaps also the
weakness arising from extreme hunger, made it impossible for him to
move. He feared, with a fair degree of certainty, that at any moment
the general tension would discharge itself in a combined attack upon

him, and he lay waiting. He did not react even to the noise made by
the violin as it fell off his mother's lap from under her trembling fingers
and gave out a resonant note.

"My dear parents," said his sister, slapping her hand on the table
by way of introduction, "things can't go on like this. Perhaps you don't
realize that, but I do. I won't utter my brother's name in the presence
of this creature, and so all I say is: we must try to get rid of it. We've
tried to look after it and to put up with it as far as is humanly possible,
and I don't think anyone could reproach us in the slightest."

"She is more than right," said Gregor's father to himself. His mother,
who was still choking for lack of breath, began to cough hollowly into
her hand with a wild look in her eyes.

His sister rushed over to her and held her forehead. His father's
thoughts seemed to have lost their vagueness at Grete's words, he sat
more upright, fingering his service cap that lay among the plates still
lying on the table from the lodgers' supper, and from time to time looked
at the still form of Gregor.

"We must try to get rid of it," his sister now said explicitly to her
father, since her mother was coughing too much to hear a word, "it will
be the death of both of you, I can see that coming. When one has to
work as hard as we do, all of us, one can't stand this continual torment
at home on top of it. At least I can't stand it any longer." And she burst
into such a passion of sobbing that her tears dropped on her mother's
face, where she wiped them off mechanically.

"My dear," said the old man sympathetically, and with evident
understanding, "but what can we do?"

Gregor's sister merely shrugged her shoulders to indicate the feeling
of helplessness that had now overmastered her during her weeping fit,
in contrast to her former confidence.

"If he could understand us," said her father, half questioningly;
Grete, still sobbing, vehemently waved a hand to show how unthinkable
that was.

"If he could understand us," repeated the old man, shutting his
eyes to consider his daughter's conviction that understanding was impossible, "then perhaps we might come to some agreement with him.
But as it is—"

"He must go," cried Gregor's sister, "that's the only solution, Father.
You must just try to get rid of the idea that this is Gregor. The fact that
we've believed it for so long is the root of all our trouble. But how can it
be Gregor? If this were Gregor, he would have realized long ago that
human beings can't live with such a creature, and he'd have gone away
on his own accord. Then we wouldn't have any brother, but we'd be able
to go on living and keep his memory in honor. As it is, this creature
persecutes us, drives away our lodgers, obviously wants the whole apartment to himself and would have us all sleep in the gutter. Just look,
Father," she shrieked all at once, "he's at it again!" And in an access
of panic that was quite incomprehensible to Gregor she even quitted her

mother, literally thrusting the chair from her as if she would rather sacrifice her mother than stay so near to Gregor, and rushed behind her
father, who also rose up, being simply upset by her agitation, and half-
spread his arms out as if to protect her.

Yet Gregor had not the slightest intention of frightening anyone, far
less his sister. He had only begun to turn round in order to crawl back
to his room, but it was certainly a startling operation to watch, since because of his disabled condition he could not execute the difficult turning
movements except by lifting his head and then bracing it against the
floor over and over again. He paused and looked round. His good intentions seemed to have been recognized; the alarm had only been momentary. Now they were all watching him in melancholy silence. His mother
lay in her chair, her legs stiffly outstretched and pressed together, her
eyes almost closing for sheer weariness; his father and his sister were
sitting beside each other, his sister's arm around the old man's neck.

Perhaps I can go on turning round now, thought Gregor, and began
his labors again. He could not stop himself from panting with the effort,
and had to pause now and then to take breath. Nor did anyone harass
him, he was left entirely to himself. When he had completed the turn-
round he began at once to crawl straight back. He was amazed at the
distance separating him from his room and could not understand how in
his weak state he had managed to accomplish the same journey so recently, almost without remarking it. Intent on crawling as fast as possible, he barely noticed that not a single word, not an ejaculation from
his family, interfered with his progress. Only when he was already in
the doorway did he turn his head round, not completely, for his neck
muscles were getting stiff, but enough to see that nothing had changed
behind him except that his sister had risen to her feet. His last glance
fell on his mother, who was not quite overcome by sleep.

Hardly was he well inside his room when the door was hastily
pushed shut, bolted and locked. The sudden noise in his rear startled
him so much that his little legs gave beneath him. It was his sister who
had shown such haste. She had been standing ready waiting and had
made a light spring forward, Gregor had not even heard her coming, and
she cried "At last!" to her parents as she turned the key in the lock.

"And what now?" said Gregor to himself, looking round in the darkness. Soon he made the discovery that he was now unable to stir a limb.
This did not surprise him, rather it seemed unnatural that he should
ever actually have been able to move on these feeble little legs. Otherwise he felt relatively comfortable. True, his whole body was aching, but
it seemed that the pain was gradually growing less and would finally
pass away. The rotting apple in his back and the inflamed area around
it, all covered with soft dust, already hardly troubled him. He thought
of his family with tenderness and love. The decision that he must disappear was one that he held to even more strongly than his sister, if
that were possible. In this state of vacant and peaceful meditation he
remained until the tower clock struck three in the morning. The first

broadening of light in the world outside the window entered his consciousness once more. Then his head sank to the floor of its own accord and from his nostrils came the last faint flicker of his breath.

When the charwoman arrived early in the morning—what between her strength and her impatience she slammed all the doors so loudly, never mind how often she had been begged not to do so, that no one in the whole apartment could enjoy any quiet sleep after her arrival—she noticed nothing unusual as she took her customary peep into Gregor's room. She thought he was lying motionless on purpose, pretending to be in the sulks; she credited him with every kind of intelligence. Since she happened to have the long-handled broom in her hand she tried to tickle him up with it from the doorway. When that too produced no reaction she felt provoked and poked at him a little harder, and only when she had pushed him along the floor without meeting any resistance was her attention aroused. It did not take her long to establish the truth of the matter, and her eyes widened, she let out a whistle, yet did not waste much time over it but tore open the door of the Samsas' bedroom and yelled into the darkness at the top of her voice: "Just look at this, it's dead; it's lying here dead and done for!"

Mr. and Mrs. Samsa started up in their double bed and before they realized the nature of the charwoman's announcement had some difficulty in overcoming the shock of it. But then they got out of bed quickly, one on either side, Mr. Samsa throwing a blanket over his shoulders, Mrs. Samsa in nothing but her nightgown; in this array they entered Gregor's room. Meanwhile the door of the living room opened, too, where Grete had been sleeping since the advent of the lodgers; she was completely dressed as if she had not been to bed, which seemed to be confirmed also by the paleness of her face. "Dead?" said Mrs. Samsa, looking questioningly at the charwoman, although she could have investigated for herself, and the fact was obvious enough without investigation. "I should say so," said the charwoman, proving her words by pushing Gregor's corpse a long way to one side with her broomstick. Mrs. Samsa made a movement as if to stop her, but checked it. "Well," said Mr. Samsa, "now thanks be to God." He crossed himself, and the three women followed his example. Grete, whose eyes never left the corpse, said: "Just see how thin he was. It's such a long time since he's eaten anything. The food came out again just as it went in." Indeed, Gregor's body was completely flat and dry, as could only now be seen when it was no longer supported by the legs and nothing prevented one from looking closely at it.

"Come in beside us, Grete, for a little while," said Mrs. Samsa with a tremulous smile, and Grete, not without looking back at the corpse, followed her parents into their bedroom. The charwoman shut the door and opened the window wide. Although it was so early in the morning a certain softness was perceptible in the fresh air. After all, it was already the end of March.

The three lodgers emerged from their room and were surprised to see no breakfast; they had been forgotten. "Where's our breakfast?" said the middle lodger peevishly to the charwoman. But she put her finger to her lips and hastily, without a word, indicated by gestures that they should go into Gregor's room. They did so and stood, their hands in the pockets of their somewhat shabby coats, around Gregor's corpse in the room where it was now fully light.

At that the door of the Samsas' bedroom opened and Mr. Samsa appeared in his uniform, his wife on one arm, his daughter on the other. They all looked a little as if they had been crying; from time to time Grete hid her face on her father's arm.

"Leave my house at once!" said Mr. Samsa, and pointed to the door without disengaging himself from the women. "What do you mean by that?" said the middle lodger, taken somewhat aback, with a feeble smile. The two others put their hands behind them and kept rubbing them together, as if in gleeful expectation of a fine set-to in which they were bound to come off the winners. "I mean just what I say," answered Mr. Samsa, and advanced in a straight line with his two companions towards the lodger. He stood his ground at first quietly, looking at the floor as if his thoughts were taking a new pattern in his head. "Then let us go, by all means," he said, and looked up at Mr. Samsa as if in a sudden access of humility he were expecting some renewed sanction for this decision. Mr. Samsa merely nodded briefly once or twice with meaning eyes. Upon that the lodger really did go with long strides into the hall, his two friends had been listening and had quite stopped rubbing their hands for some moments and now went scuttling after him as if afraid that Mr. Samsa might get into the hall before them and cut them off from their leader. In the hall they all three took their hats from the rack, their sticks from the umbrella stand, bowed in silence and quitted the apartment. With a suspiciousness which proved quite unfounded Mr. Samsa and the two women followed them out to the landing; leaning over the banister they watched the three figures slowly but surely going down the long stairs, vanishing from sight at a certain turn of the staircase on every floor and coming into view again after a moment or so; the more they dwindled, the more the Samsa family's interest in them dwindled, and when a butcher's boy met them and passed them on the stairs coming up proudly with a tray on his head, Mr. Samsa and the two women soon left the landing and as if a burden had been lifted from them went back into their apartment.

They decided to spend this day in resting and going for a stroll; they had not only deserved such a respite from work, but absolutely needed it. And so they sat down at the table and wrote three notes of excuse, Mr. Samsa to his board of management, Mrs. Samsa to her employer and Grete to the head of her firm. While they were writing, the charwoman came in to say that she was going now, since her morning's work was finished. At first they only nodded without looking up, but as she kept hovering there they eyed her irritably. "Well?" said Mr. Samsa. The charwoman stood grinning in the doorway as if she had good news to impart to the family but meant not to say a word unless properly questioned. The small ostrich feather standing upright on her hat, which had annoyed Mr. Samsa ever since she was engaged, was waving gaily in all directions. "Well, what is it then?" asked Mrs. Samsa, who obtained more respect from the charwoman than the others. "Oh," said the charwoman, giggling so amiably that she could not at once continue, "just this, you don't need to bother about how to get rid of the thing next door. It's been seen to already." Mrs. Samsa and Grete bent over their letters again, as if preoccupied; Mr. Samsa, who perceived that she was eager to begin describing it all in detail, stopped her with a decisive hand. But since she was not allowed to tell her story, she remembered the great hurry she was in, being obviously deeply huffed: "Bye, everybody," she said, whirling off violently, and departed with a frightful slamming of doors.

"She'll be given notice tonight," said Mr. Samsa, but neither from his wife nor his daughter did he get any answer, for the charwoman seemed to have shattered again the composure they had barely achieved. They rose, went to the window and stayed there, clasping each other tight. Mr. Samsa turned in his chair to look at them and quietly observed them for a little. Then he called out: "Come along, now, do. Let bygones be bygones. And you might have some consideration for me." The two of them complied at once, hastened to him, caressed him and quickly finished their letters.

Then they all three left the apartment together, which was more than they had done for months, and went by tram into the open country outside the town. The tram, in which they were the only passengers, was filled with warm sunshine. Leaning comfortably back in their seats they canvassed their prospects for the future, and it appeared on closer inspection that these were not at all bad, for the jobs they had got, which so far they had never really discussed with each other, were all three admirable and likely to lead to better things later on. The greatest immediate improvement in their condition would of course arise from moving to another house; they wanted to take a smaller and cheaper but also better situated and more easily run apartment than the one they had, which Gregor had selected. While they were thus conversing, it struck both Mr. and Mrs. Samsa, almost at the same moment, as they became aware of their daughter's increasing vivacity, that in spite of all the sorrow of recent times, which had made her cheeks pale, she had bloomed into a pretty girl with a good figure. They grew quieter and half unconsciously exchanged glances of complete agreement, having come to the conclusion that it would soon be time to find a good husband for her. And it was like a confirmation of their new dreams and excellent intentions that at the end of their journey their daughter sprang to her feet first and stretched her young body.

# CHAPTER SIX

# Suicide:
# An End to Alienation

Sociology has traditionally held that the personal circumstances of a victim will do little to explain either suicide or suicide rates.

> ... The circumstances are almost infinite in number which are supposed to cause suicide. . . . This suggests that none of them is the specific cause. Could we perhaps at least describe causality to those qualities known to be common to all? But are there any such? We see some men resist horrible misfortune, while others kill themselves after slight troubles. Moreover, we have shown that those who suffer most are not those who kill themselves most. Rather it is too great comfort which turns a man against himself. Life is most readily renounced at the time and among the classes where it is least harsh. At least, if it really sometimes occurs that the victim's personal situation is the effective cause of his resolve, such cases are very rare indeed and accordingly cannot explain the social suicide-rate.[1]

The above contention served as the cornerstone of Emile Durkheim's argument that we should abandon the search for the "essential characteristics" of suicide through the thorough study of numerous case histories, and seek instead the "causes" of suicide through an interpretation of official statistical rates. (For a fuller critique of the latter recommendation the reader

[1] Emile Durkheim, *Suicide: A Study in Sociology* (New York: Free Press, 1951), pp. 297–298.

185

is referred to works of Jacobs and Douglas.[2] Let it suffice to say at this juncture that, if Durkheim's suggestion were taken literally, sociologists pursuing the interactionist perspective would be wasting their time and, of course, not be doing sociology. Although some sociologists still hold to this point of view, a growing number of them, especially in the area of deviant behavior, are adopting the interactionist perspective.

Better understanding can be reached through a study of the personal circumstances of suicides and attempted suicides, as related by them in notes, letters, diaries, personal interviews, and by way of interviews with survivors—especially "significant others." A great deal of useful information has already accrued through such studies,[3] especially given sociology's late interest in these methods and sources of data.

The richness of the following reading stems from the fact that it includes such considerations and offers the reader, who is attuned to their importance, the possibility of acquiring greater insight into the question of suicide than can be had from many more, sociologically speaking, "formal" and/or "scientific" studies.

Since the personal circumstances of the potential suicide are frequently (if not always) responsible for his suicide, a better understanding of suicide can be had through a study of the suicides' and suicide attempters' personal situations, and a common denominator to the personal circumstances of suicides can be found when viewed as a formal process. Suicides are subject to two sets of processes: the first (the sequential ordering of the social-structural events in their lives and how they were experienced) leads them to contemplate suicide; the second (the moral justification for their prohibited act)

[2] Jerry Jacobs, *Adolescent Suicide* (New York: John Wiley and Sons, 1971) and "A Phenomenological Study of Suicide Notes," *Social Problems* 15, no. 1 (Summer 1967): 60–71; "The Use of Religion in Constructing the Moral Justification of Suicide," *Deviance and Respectability: The Social Construction of Moral Meanings*, ed. Jack Douglas (New York: Basic Books, 1970), pp. 229–251; and Jack Douglas, *The Social Meanings of Suicide* (Princeton, New Jersey: Princeton University Press, 1967).

[3] See, for example, footnote 2 and Jerry Jacobs and Joseph D. Teicher, "Broken Homes and Social Isolation in Attempted Suicides of Adolescents," *International Journal of Social Psychiatry* 13, no. 2 (1967): 139–149; Jerry Jacobs, "Harry Haller's Private Sky Hook: The Role of Suicidal Ideation in the Prolongation of Life," *Existential Psychiatry* (in press); James M. Henslin, "Guilt and Guilt Neutralization: Response and Adjustment in Suicide," in *Deviance and Respectability: The Social Construction of Moral Meanings*, ed. Douglas, pp. 192–228; and Arthur L. Kobler and Ezra Stotland, *The End of Hope* (New York: Free Press, 1964).

allows for them to actually attempt suicide. The formal features of the first sequence are outlined below:

1. A longstanding history of problems.
2. A more recent escalation of problems, i.e., the inability to resolve old problems at the same time that many new ones have been added.
3. The progressive failure of available adaptive techniques for coping with old and increasing problems, leading the individual to feel a progressive isolation from meaningful social relationships.
4. The final stage—the days and weeks immediately preceding the suicide—at which time the individual feels he has experienced an abrupt and unanticipated dissolution of any remaining meaningful relationships and the prospects of ever establishing them in the future. He experiences, in short, "the end of hope."[4]

Having reached the point of contemplating suicide (as many do), one must successfully initiate and fulfill the conditions of the second sequence if he is to be able to undertake and/or realize his suicidal intent. The second set of conditions is outlined below. In order to overcome the social norms against suicides the potential suicide must:

1. Be faced with an unexpected, intolerable, and unsolvable problem;
2. View this not as an isolated unpleasant incident, but within the context of a long biography of such troubled situations, and the expectation of future ones;
3. Believe that death is the only absolute answer to this apparent absolute dilemma of life;
4. Come to this point of view (a) by way of an increasing social isolation whereby he is unable to share his problem with the person or persons who must share it if it is to be resolved, or (b) being isolated from the cure of some incurable illness, that in turn isolates him from health and the community, thereby doubly ensuring the insolubility of the problem;
5. Overcome the social constraints, i.e., the social norms he had internalized whereby he views suicide as irrational and/or immoral;

[4] Jacobs, "The Use of Religion in Constructing the Moral Justification of Suicide," p. 234.

6. Succeed in this because he feels himself less an integral part of the society than the others and therefore is held less firmly by its bonds;
7. Succeed in accomplishing step six by applying to his intended suicide a verbalization that enables him to adjust his conception of himself as a trusted person with his intended act of trust violation (he is about to violate the sacred trust of life);
8. Succeed in doing this by defining the situation such that the problem is (a) not of his own making, (b) unresolved, but not from any lack of personal effort, and (c) not given to any resolution known to him except death (he doesn't want it this way, but . . . it's "the only way out");
9. Define death as necessary by the above process and in so doing remove all choice and with it sin and immorality; and finally,
10. Make some provision for ensuring against the recurrence of these problems in the afterlife.[5]

The reader is asked to keep the above formulation in mind when reading the following selection. It will help him to understand at least one empirically based explanation of suicide as viewed from an interactionist perspective.

## HERMANN HESSE

## Steppenwolf

The day had gone by just as days go by. I had killed it in accordance with my primitive and retiring way of life. I had worked for an hour or two and perused the pages of old books. I had had pains for two hours, as elderly people do. I had taken a powder and been very glad when the pains consented to disappear. I had lain in a hot bath and absorbed its kindly warmth. Three times the mail had come with undesired letters and

---

[5] Jacobs, "Phenomenological Study of Suicide Notes," p. 67.

circulars to look through. I had done my breathing exercises, but found
it convenient today to omit the thought exercises. I had been for an
hour's walk and seen the loveliest feathery cloud patterns penciled
against the sky. That was very delightful. So was the reading of the old
books. So was the lying in the warm bath. But, taken all in all, it had not
been exactly a day of rapture. No, it had not even been a day brightened
with happiness and joy. Rather, it had been just one of those days which
for a long while now had fallen to my lot; the moderately pleasant, the
wholly bearable and tolerable, lukewarm days of a discontented middle-
aged man; days without special pains, without special cares, without particular worry, without despair; days when I calmly wonder, objective and
fearless, whether it isn't time to follow the example of Adalbert Stifter
and have an accident while shaving.

He who has known the other days, the angry ones of gout attacks,
or those with that wicked headache rooted behind the eyeballs that casts
a spell on every nerve of eye and ear with a fiendish delight in torture,
or soul-destroying, evil days of inward vacancy and despair, when, on
this distracted earth, sucked dry by the vampires of finance, the world
of men and of so-called culture grins back at us with the lying, vulgar,
brazen glamor of a Fair and dogs us with the persistence of an emetic,
and when all is concentrated and focused to the last pitch of the intolerable upon your own sick self—he who has known these days of hell
may be content indeed with normal half-and-half days like today. Thankfully you sit by the warm stove, thankfully you assure yourself as you
read your morning paper that another day has come and no war broken
out, no new dictatorship has been set up, no particularly disgusting
scandal been unveiled in the worlds of politics or finance. Thankfully you
tune the strings of your moldering lyre to a moderated, to a passably joyful, nay, to an even delighted psalm of thanksgiving and with it bore your
quiet, flabby and slightly stupefied half-and-half god of contentment; and
in the thick warm air of a contented boredom and very welcome painlessness the nodding mandarin of a half-and-half god and the nodding
middle-aged gentleman who sings his muffled psalm look as like each
other as two peas.

There is much to be said for contentment and painlessness, for
these bearable and submissive days, on which neither pain nor pleasure
is audible, but pass by whispering and on tip-toe. But the worst of it is
that it is just this contentment that I cannot endure. After a short time
it fills me with irrepressible hatred and nausea. In desperation I have to
escape and throw myself on the road to pleasure, or, if that cannot be,
on the road to pain. When I have neither pleasure nor pain and have
been breathing for a while the lukewarm insipid air of these so-called
good and tolerable days, I feel so bad in my childish soul that I smash
my moldering lyre of thanksgiving in the face of the slumbering god
of contentment and would rather feel the very devil burn in me than
this warmth of a well-heated room. A wild longing for strong emotions

and sensations seethes in me, a rage against this toneless, flat, normal and sterile life. I have a mad impulse to smash something, a warehouse, perhaps, or a cathedral, or myself, to commit outrages, to pull off the wigs of a few revered idols, to provide a few rebellious schoolboys with the longed-for ticket to Hamburg, or to stand one or two representatives of the established order on their heads. For what I always hated and detested and cursed above all things was this contentment, this healthiness and comfort, this carefully preserved optimism of the middle classes, this fat and prosperous brood of mediocrity.

It was in such a mood then that I finished this not intolerable and very ordinary day as dusk set in. I did not end it in a manner becoming a rather ailing man and go to bed tempted by a hot water bottle. Instead I put on my shoes ill-humoredly, discontended and disgusted with the little work I had done, and went out into the dark and foggy streets to drink what men according to an old convention call "a glass of wine," at the sign of the Steel Helmet.

So I went down the stairs from my room in the attic, those difficult stairs of this alien world, those thoroughly bourgeois, well-swept and scoured stairs of a very respectable three-family apartment house under whose roof I have my refuge. I don't know how it comes about, but I, the homeless Steppenwolf, the solitary, the hater of life's petty conventions, always take up my quarters in just such houses as this. It is an old weakness of mine. I live neither in palatial houses nor in those of the humble poor, but instead and deliberately in these respectable and wearisome and spotless middle-class homes, which smell of turpentine and soap and where there is a panic if you bang the door or come in with dirty shoes. The love of this atmosphere comes, no doubt, from the days of my childhood, and a secret yearning I have for something homelike drives me, though with little hope, to follow the same old stupid road. Then again, I like the contrast between my lonely, loveless, hunted, and thoroughly disorderly existence and this middle-class family life. I like to breathe in on the stairs this odor of quiet and order, of cleanliness and respectable domesticity. There is something in it that touches me in spite of my hatred for all it stands for. I like to step across the threshold of my room where all this suddenly stops; where, instead, cigar ash and wine bottles lie among the heaped-up books and there is nothing but disorder and neglect; and where everything—books, manuscripts, thoughts—is marked and saturated with the plight of lonely men, with the problem of existence and with the yearning after a new orientation for an age that has lost its bearings.

And now I came to the araucaria. I must tell you that on the first floor of this house the stairs pass by a little vestibule at the entrance to a flat which, I am convinced, is even more spotlessly swept and garnished than the others; for this little vestibule shines with a superhuman housewifery. It is a little temple of order. On the parquet floor, where it seems desecration to tread, are two elegant stands and on each a large

pot. In the one grows an azalea. In the other a stately araucaria, a
thriving, straight-grown baby tree, a perfect specimen, which to the last
needle of the topmost twig reflects the pride of frequent ablutions. Sometimes, when I know that I am unobserved, I use this place as a temple. I
take my seat on a step of the stairs above the araucaria and, resting
awhile with folded hands, I contemplate this little garden of order and
let the touching air it has and its somewhat ridiculous loneliness move
me to the depths of my soul. I imagine behind this vestibule, in the
sacred shadow, one may say, of the araucaria, a home full of shining
mahogany, and a life full of sound respectability—early rising, attention
to duty, restrained but cheerful family gatherings, Sunday church going,
early to bed.

Affecting lightheartedness, I trod the moist pavements of the narrow streets. As though in tears and veiled, the lamps glimmered through
the chill gloom and sucked their reflections slowly from the wet ground.
The foregotten years of my youth came back to me. How I used to love
the dark, sad evenings of late autumn and winter, how eagerly I imbibed
their moods of loneliness and melancholy when wrapped in my cloak
I strode for half the night through rain and storm, through the leafless
winter landscape, lonely enough then too, but full of deep joy, and full
of poetry which later I wrote down by candlelight sitting on the edge of
my bed! All that was past now. The cup was emptied and would never
be filled again. Was that a matter for regret? No, I did not regret the
past. My regret was for the present day, for all the countless hours and
days that I lost in mere passivity and that brought me nothing, not even
the shocks of awakening. But, thank God, there were exceptions. There
were now and then, though rarely, the hours that brought the welcome
shock, pulled down the walls and brought me back again from my wan-
derings to the living heart of the world. Sadly and yet deeply moved, I
set myself to recall the last of these experiences. It was at a concert of
lovely old music. After two or three notes of the piano the door was
opened of a sudden to the other world. I sped through heaven and saw
God at work. I suffered holy pains. I dropped all my defences and was
afraid of nothing in the world. I accepted all things and to all things I
gave up my heart. It did not last very long, a quarter of an hour perhaps;
but it returned to me in a dream at night, and since, through all the
barren days, I caught a glimpse of it now and then. Sometimes for a
minute or two I saw it clearly, threading my life like a divine and golden
track. But nearly always it was blurred in dirt and dust. Then again it
gleamed out in golden sparks as though never to be lost again and yet
was soon quite lost once more. Once it happened, as I lay awake at night,
that I suddenly spoke in verses, in verses so beautiful and strange that
I did not venture to think of writing them down, and then in the morning
they vanished; and yet they lay hidden within me like the hard kernel
within an old brittle husk. Once it came to me while reading a poet, while
pondering a thought of Descartes, of Pascal; again it shone out and drove

its gold track far into the sky while I was in the presence of my beloved. Ah, but it is hard to find this track of the divine in the midst of this life we lead, in this besotted humdrum age of spiritual blindness, with its architecture, its business, its politics, its men! How could I fail to be a lone wolf, and an uncouth hermit, as I did not share one of its aims nor understand one of its pleasures? I cannot remain for long in either theater or picture-house. I can scarcely read a paper, seldom a modern book. I cannot understand what pleasures and joys they are that drive people to the overcrowded railways and hotels, into the packed cafés with the suffocating and oppressive music, to the Bars and variety entertainments, to World Exhibitions, to the Corsos. I cannot understand nor share these joys, though they are within my reach, for which thousands of others strive. On the other hand, what happens to me in my rare hours of joy, what for me is bliss and life and ecstasy and exaltation, the world in general seeks at most in imagination; in life it finds it absurd. And in fact, if the world is right, if this music of the cafés, these mass enjoyments and these Americanised men who are pleased with so little are right, then I am wrong, I am crazy. I am in truth the Steppenwolf that I often call myself; that beast astray who finds neither home nor joy nor nourishment in a world that is strange and incomprehensible to him.

With these familiar thoughts I went along the wet street through one of the quietest and oldest quarters of the town. On the opposite side there stood in the darkness an old stone wall which I always noticed with pleasure. Old and serene, it stood between a little church and an old hospital and often during the day I let my eyes rest on its rough surface. There were few such quiet and peaceful spaces in the center of the town where from every square foot some lawyer, or quack, or doctor, or barber, or chiropodist shouted his name at you. This time, too, the wall was peaceful and serene and yet something was altered in it. I was amazed to see a small and pretty doorway with a Gothic arch in the middle of the wall, for I could not make up my mind whether this doorway had always been there or whether it had just been made. It looked old without a doubt, very old; apparently this closed portal with its door of blackened wood had opened hundreds of years ago onto a sleepy convent yard, and did so still, even though the convent was no longer there. Probably I had seen it a hundred times and simply not noticed it. Perhaps it had been painted afresh and caught my eye for that reason. I paused to examine it from where I stood without crossing over, as the street between was so deep in mud and water. From the sidewalk where I stood and looked across, it seemed to me in the dim light that a garland, or something gaily colored, was festooned round the doorway, and now that I looked more closely I saw over the portal a bright shield, on which, it seemed to me, there was something written. I strained my eyes and at last, in spite of the mud and puddles, went across, and there over the door I saw a stain showing up faintly on the grey-green of the wall, and over the stain bright letters dancing and then disappearing, returning and vanishing once more. So that's it, thought I. They've disfigured this good old wall with an electric sign. Meanwhile I deciphered one or two of the letters as they appeared again for an instant; but they were hard to read even by guess work, for they came with very irregular spaces between them and very faintly, and then abruptly vanished. Whoever hoped for any result from a display like that was not very smart. He was a Steppenwolf, poor fellow. Why have his letters playing on this old wall in the darkest alley of the Old Town on a wet night with not a soul passing by, and why were they so fleeting, so fitful and illegible? But wait, at last I succeeded in catching several words on end. They were:

MAGIC THEATER
ENTRANCE NOT FOR EVERYBODY

I tried to open the door, but the heavy old latch would not stir. The display too was over. It had suddenly ceased, sadly convinced of its uselessness. I took a few steps back, landing deep into the mud, but no more letters came. The display was over. For a long time I stood waiting in the mud, but in vain.

Then, when I had given up and gone back to the alley, a few colored letters were dropped here and there, reflected on the asphalt in front of me. I read:

FOR MADMEN ONLY!

My feet were wet and I was chilled to the bone. Nevertheless, I stood waiting. Nothing more. But while I waited, thinking how prettily the letters had danced in their ghostly fashion over the damp wall and the black sheen of the asphalt, a fragment of my former thoughts came suddenly to my mind; the similarity to the track of shining gold which suddenly vanishes and cannot be found.

I was freezing and walked on following that track in my dreams, longing too for that doorway to an enchanted theater, which was for madmen only. Meanwhile I had reached the market place, where there is never a lack of evening entertainments. At every other step were placards and posters with their various attractions, Ladies' Orchestra, Variété, Cinema, Ball. But none of these was for me. They were for "everybody," for those normal persons whom I saw crowding every entrance. In spite of that my sadness was a little lightened. I had had a greeting from another world, and a few dancing, colored letters had played upon my soul and sounded its secret strings. A glimmer of the golden track had been visible once again.

I sought out the little ancient tavern where nothing had altered since my first visit to this town a good twenty-five years before. Even the landlady was the same as then and many of the patrons who sat there in those days sat there still at the same places before the same glasses. There I took refuge. True, it was only a refuge, something like the one on the stairs opposite the araucaria. Here, too, I found neither home nor company, nothing but a seat from which to view a stage where strange people played strange parts. Nonetheless, the quiet of the place was worth something; no crowds, no music; only a few peaceful townsfolk at bare wooden tables (no marble, no enamel, no plush, no brass) and before each his evening glass of good old wine. Perhaps this company of habitués, all of whom I knew by sight, were all regular Philistines and had in their Philistine dwellings their altars of the home dedicated to sheepish idols of contentment; perhaps, too, they were solitary fellows who had been sidetracked, quiet, thoughtful topers of bankrupt ideals, lone wolves and poor devils like me. I could not say. Either homesickness or disappointment, or need of change drew them there, the married to recover the atmosphere of his bachelor days, the old official to recall his student years. All of them were silent, and all were drinkers who would rather, like me, sit before a pint of Elsasser than listen to a Ladies' Orchestra. Here I cast anchor, for an hour, or it might be two. With the first sip of Elsasser I realised that I had eaten nothing that day since my morning roll.

It is remarkable, all that men can swallow. For a good ten minutes I read a newspaper. I allowed the spirit of an irresponsible man who chews and munches another's words in his mouth, and gives them out again undigested, to enter into me through my eyes. I absorbed a whole column of it. And then I devoured a large piece cut from the liver of a slaughtered calf. Odd indeed! The best was the Elsasser. I am not fond, for everyday at least, of racy, heady wines that diffuse a potent charm and have their own particular flavor. What I like the best is a clean, light, modest country vintage of no special name. One can carry plenty of it and it has the good and homely flavor of the land, and of earth and sky and woods. A pint of Elsasser and a piece of good bread is the best of all meals. By this time, however, I had already eaten my portion of liver, an unusual indulgence for me, as I seldom eat meat, and the second pint had been set before me. And this too was odd: that somewhere in a green valley vines were tended by good, strong fellows and the wine pressed so that here and there in the world, far away, a few disappointed, quietly drinking townsfolk and dispirited Steppenwolves could sip a little heart and courage from their glasses.

I didn't really care whether all this was odd or not. It was good, it helped, it raised my spirits. As I thought again of that newspaper article and its jumble of words, a refreshing laughter rose in me, and suddenly the forgotten melody of those notes of the piano came back to me again. It soared aloft like a soap bubble, reflecting the whole world in miniature on its rainbow surface, and then softly burst. Could I be altogether lost when that heavenly little melody had been secretly rooted within me and now put forth its lovely bloom with all its tender hues? I might be a beast astray, with no sense of its environment, yet there was some meaning in my foolish life, something in me gave an answer and was the receiver of those distant calls from worlds far above. In my brain were stored a thousand pictures:

Giotto's flock of angels from the blue vaulting of a little church in Padua, and near them walked Hamlet and the garlanded Ophelia, fair similitudes of all sadness and misunderstanding in the world, and there stood Gianozzo, the aeronaut, in his burning balloon and blew a blast on his horn, Attila carrying his new headgear in his hand, and the Borobudur reared its soaring sculpture in the air. And though all these figures lived in a thousand other hearts as well, there were ten thousand more unknown pictures and tunes there which had no dwelling place but in me, no eyes to see, no ears to hear them but mine. The old hospital wall with its grey-green weathering, its cracks and stains in which a thousand frescoes could be fancied, who responded to it, who looked into its soul, who loved it, who found the charm of its colors ever delicately dying away? The old books of the monks, softly illumined with their miniatures, and the books of the German poets of two hundred and a hundred years ago whom their own folk have forgotten, all the thumbed and damp-stained volumes, and the works in print and manuscripts of the old composers, the stout and yellowing music sheets dreaming their music through a winter sleep—who heard their spirited, their roguish and yearning tones, who carried through a world estranged from them a heart full of their spirit and their charm? Who still remembered that slender cypress on a hill over Gubbio, that though split and riven by a fall of stone yet held fast to life and put forth with its last resources a new sparse tuft at top? Who read by night above the Rhine the cloudscript of the drifting mists? It was the Steppenwolf. And who over the ruins of his life pursued its fleeting, fluttering significance, while he suffered its seeming meaninglessness and lived its seeming madness, and who hoped in secret at the last turn of the labyrinth of Chaos for revelation and God's presence?

I held my hand over my glass when the landlady wanted to fill it once more, and got up. I needed no more wine. The golden trail was blazed and I was reminded of the eternal, and of Mozart, and the stars. For an hour I could breathe once more and live and face existence, without the need to suffer torment, fear, or shame.

A cold wind was sifting the fine rain as I went out into the deserted street. It drove the drops with a patter against the streetlamps where they glimmered with a glassy sparkle. And now, whither? If I had had a magic wand at this moment I should have conjured up a small and charming Louis Seize music room where a few musicians would have played me two or three pieces of Handel and Mozart. I was in the very mood for it, and would have sipped the cool and noble music as gods sip nectar. Oh, if I had had a friend at this moment, a friend in an attic room, dreaming by candlelight and with a violin lying ready at his hand!

How I should have slipped up to him in his quiet hour, noiselessly climbing the winding stair to take him by surprise, and then with talk and music we should have held heavenly festival throughout the night! Once, in years gone by, I had often known such happiness, but this too time had taken away. Withered years lay between those days and now.

I loitered as I wended my way homeward; turned up my collar and struck my stick on the wet pavement. However long I lingered outside I should find myself all too soon in my top-floor room, my makeshift home, which I could neither love nor do without; for the time had gone by when I could spend a wet winter's night in the open. And now my prayer was not to let the good mood the evening had given me be spoiled, neither by the rain, nor by gout, nor by the araucaria; and though there was no chamber music to be had nor a lonely friend with his violin, still that lovely melody was in my head and I could play it through to myself after a fashion, humming the rhythm of it as I drew my breath. Reflecting thus, I walked on and on. Yes, even without the chamber music and the friend. How foolish to wear oneself out in vain longing for warmth! Solitude is independence. It had been my wish and with the years I had attained it. It was cold. Oh, cold enough! But it was also still, wonderfully still and vast like the cold stillness of space in which the stars revolve.

From a dance hall there met me as I passed by the strains of lively jazz music, hot and raw as the steam of raw flesh. I stopped a moment. This kind of music, much as I detested it, had always had a secret charm for me. It was repugnant to me, and yet ten times preferable to all the academic music of the day. For me too, its raw and savage gaiety reached an underworld of instinct and breathed a simple honest sensuality.

I stood for a moment on the scent, smelling this shrill and blood-raw music, sniffing the atmosphere of the hall angrily, and hankering after it a little too. One half of this music, the melody, was all pomade and sugar and sentimentality. The other half was savage, temperamental and vigorous. Yet the two went artlessly well together and made a whole. It was the music of decline. There must have been such music in Rome under the later emperors. Compared with Bach and Mozart and real music it was, naturally, a miserable affair; but so was all our art, all our thought, all our makeshift culture in comparison with real culture. This music was at least sincere, unashamedly primitive and childishly happy. There was something of the Negro in it, and something of the American, who with all his strength seems so boyishly fresh and childlike to us Europeans. Was Europe to become the same? Was it on the way already? Were we, the old connoisseurs, the reverers of Europe as it used to be, of genuine music and poetry as once they were, nothing but a pig-headed minority suffering from a complex neurosis, whom tomorrow would forget or deride? Was all that we called culture, spirit, soul, all that we called beautiful and sacred, nothing but a ghost long dead, which only a few fools like us took for true and living? Had it perhaps indeed never been true and living? Had all that we poor fools bothered our heads about never been anything but a phantom?

I was now in the old quarter of the town. The little church stood up dim and grey and unreal. At once the experience of that evening came back to me, mysterious Gothic doorway, the mysterious tablet above it and the illuminated letters dancing in mockery. How did the writing run? "Entrance not for Everybody." And: "For madmen only." I scrutinised the old wall opposite in the secret hope that the magic night might begin again; the writing invite me, the madman; the little doorway give me admittance. There perhaps lay my desire, and there perhaps would my music be played.

The dark stone wall looked back at me with composure, shut off in a deep twilight, sunk in a dream of its own. And there was no gateway anywhere and no pointed arch; only the dark unbroken masonry. With a smile I went on, giving it a friendly nod. "Sleep well. I will not awake you. The time will come when you will be pulled down or plastered with covetous advertisements. But for the present, there you stand, beautiful and quiet as ever, and I love you for it."

From the black mouth of an alley a man appeared with startling suddeness at my elbow, a lone man going his homeward way with weary step. He wore a cap and a blue blouse, and above his shoulders he carried a signboard fixed on a pole, and in front of him an open tray suspended by straps such as pedlars carry at fairs. He walked on wearily in front of me without looking round. Otherwise I should have bidden him a good evening and given him a cigar. I tried to read the device on his standard —a red signboard on a pole—in the light of the next lamp; but it swayed to and fro and I could decipher nothing. Then I called out and asked him to let me read his placard. He stopped and held his pole a little steadier. Then I could read the dancing reeling letters:

ANARCHIST EVENING ENTERTAINMENT

MAGIC THEATER

ENTRANCE NOT FOR EVERYBODY

"I've been looking for you," I shouted with delight. "What is this Evening Entertainment? Where is it? When?"

He was already walking on.

"Not for everybody," he said dully with a sleepy voice. He had had enough. He was for home, and on he went.

"Stop," I cried, and ran after him. "What have you got there in your box? I want to buy something from you."

Without stopping, the man felt mechanically in his box, pulled out a little book and held it out to me. I took it quickly and put it in my pocket. While I felt for the buttons of my coat to get out some money, he turned in at a doorway, shut the door behind him and disappeared. His heavy steps rang on a flagged yard, then on wooden stairs; and then I heard no more. And suddenly I too felt very tired. It came over me that it must be very late—and high time to go home. I walked on faster and, following the road to the suburb, I was soon in my own neighborhood among the well-kept gardens, where in clean little apartment houses behind lawn and ivy are the dwellings of officialdom and people of modest means. Passing the ivy and the grass and the little fir tree I reached the door of the house, found the keyhole and the switch, slipped past the glazed doors, and the polished cupboards and the potted plants and unlocked the door of my room, my little pretence of a home, where the armchair and the stove, the ink-pot and the paint-box, Novalis and Dostoievski, awaited me just as do the mother, or the wife, the children, maids, dogs and cats in the case of more sensible people.

As I threw off my wet coat I came upon the little book, and took it out. It was one of those little books wretchedly printed on wretched paper that are sold at fairs, "Were you born in January?" or "How to be twenty years younger in a week."

However, when I settled myself in my armchair and put on my glasses, it was with great astonishment and a sudden sense of impending fate that I read the title on the cover of this companion volume to fortune-telling booklets. *"Treatise on the Steppenwolf. Not for Everybody."*

I read the contents at a sitting with an engrossing interest that deepened page by page.


## TREATISE ON THE STEPPENWOLF

There was once a man, Harry, called the Steppenwolf. He went on two legs, wore clothes and was a human being, but nevertheless he was in reality a wolf of the Steppes. He had learned a good deal of all that people of good intelligence can, and was a fairly clever fellow. What he had not learned, however, was this: to find contentment in himself and his own life. The cause of this apparently was that at the bottom of his heart he knew all the time (or thought he knew) that he was in reality not a man, but a wolf of the Steppes. Clever men might argue the point whether he truly was a wolf, whether, that is, he had been changed, before birth perhaps, from a wolf into a human being, or had been given the soul of a wolf, though born as a human being; or whether, on the other hand, this belief that he was a wolf was no more than a fancy or a disease of his. It might, for example, be possible that in his childhood he was a little wild and disobedient and disorderly, and that those who brought him up had declared a war of extinction against the beast in him; and precisely this had given him the idea and the belief that he was in fact actually a beast with only a thin covering of the human. On this point one could speak at length and entertainingly, and indeed write a book about it. The Steppenwolf, however, would be none the better for it, since for him it was all one whether the wolf had been bewitched or beaten into him, or whether it was merely an idea of his own. What others chose to think about it or what he chose to think himself was no good to him at all. It left the wolf inside him just the same.

And so the Steppenwolf had two natures, a human and a wolfish one. This was his fate, and it may well be that it was not a very exceptional one. There must have been many men who have had a good deal of the dog or the fox, of the fish or the serpent in them without experiencing any extraordinary difficulties on that account. In such cases, the man and the fish lived on together and neither did the other any harm. The one even helped the other. Many a man indeed has carried this condition to such enviable lengths that he has owed his happiness more to the fox or the ape in him than to the man. So much for common knowledge. In the case of Harry, however, it was just the opposite. In him the man and the wolf did not go the same way together, but were in continual and deadly enmity. One existed simply and soley to harm the other, and when there are two in one blood and in one soul who are at deadly enmity, then life fares ill. Well, to each his lot, and none is light.

Now with our Steppenwolf it was so that in his conscious life he lived now as a wolf, now as a man, as indeed the case is with all mixed beings. But, when he was a wolf, the man in him lay in ambush, ever on the watch to interfere and condemn, while at those times that he was man the wolf did just the same. For example, if Harry, as man, had a beautiful thought, felt a fine and noble emotion, or performed a so-called good act, then the wolf bared his teeth at him and laughed and showed him with bitter scorn how laughable this whole pantomime was in the eyes of a beast, of a wolf who knew well enough in his heart what suited him, namely, to trot alone over the Steppes and now and then to gorge himself with blood or to pursue a female wolf. Then, wolfishly seen, all human activities became horribly absurd and misplaced, stupid and vain. But it was exactly the same when Harry felt and behaved as a wolf and showed others his teeth and felt hatred and enmity against all human beings and their living and degenerate manners and customs. For then the human part of him lay in ambush and watched the wolf, called him brute and beast, and spoiled and embittered for him all pleasure in his simple and healthy and wild wolf's being.

Thus it was then with the Steppenwolf, and one may well imagine that Harry did not have an exactly pleasant and happy life of it. This does not mean, however, that he was unhappy in any extraordinary degree (although it may have seemed so to himself all the same, inasmuch as every man takes the sufferings that fall to his share as the greatest). That cannot be said of any man. Even he who has no wolf in him, may be none the happier for that. And even the unhappiest life has its sunny moments and its little flowers of happiness between sand and stone. So it was, then, with the Steppenwolf too. It cannot be denied that he was generally very unhappy; and he could make others unhappy also, that is, when he loved them or they him. For all who got to love him, saw always the one side in him. Many loved him as a refined and clever and interesting man, and were horrified and disappointed when they had come upon the wolf in him. And they had to because Harry wished, as every sentient being does, to be loved as a whole and therefore it was just with those whose love he most valued that he could least of all conceal and belie the wolf. There were those, however, who loved precisely the wolf in him, the free, the savage, the untamable, the dangerous and the strong, and these found it peculiarly disappointing and deplorable when suddenly the wild and wicked wolf was also a man, and had hankerings after goodness and refinement, and wanted to hear Mozart, to read poetry and to cherish human ideals. Usually these were the most disappointed and angry of all; and so it was that the Steppenwolf brought his own dual and divided nature into the destinies of others besides himself whenever he came into contact with them.

Now, whoever thinks that he knows the Steppenwolf and that he can imagine to himself his lamentably divided life is nevertheless in error. He does not know all by a long way. He does not know that, as there is no rule without an exception and as one sinner may under certain circumstances be dearer to God than ninety and nine righteous persons, with Harry too there were now and then exceptions and strokes of good luck, and that he could breathe and think and feel sometimes as the wolf, sometimes as the man, clearly and without confusion of the two; and even on very rare occasions, they made peace and lived for one another in such fashion that not merely did one keep watch whilst the other slept but each strengthened and confirmed the other. In the life of this man, too, as well as in all things else in the world, daily use and the accepted and common knowledge seemed sometimes to have no other aim than to be arrested now and again for an instant, and broken through, in order to yield the place of honor to the exceptional and miraculous. Now whether these short and occasional hours of happiness balanced and alleviated the lot of the Steppenwolf in such a fashion that in the upshot happiness and suffering held the scales even, or whether perhaps the short but intense happiness of those few hours outweighed all suffering and left a balance over is again a question over which idle persons may meditate to their hearts' content. Even the wolf brooded often over this, and those were his idle and unprofitable days.

In this connection one thing more must be said. There are a good many people of the same kind as Harry. Many artists are of his kind. These persons all have two souls, two beings within them. There is God and the devil in them; the mother's blood and the father's; the capacity for happiness and the capacity for suffering; and in just a state of enmity and entanglement towards and within each other as were the wolf and man in Harry. And these men, for whom life has no repose, live at times in their rare moments of happiness with such strength and indescribable

beauty, the spray of their moment's happiness is flung so high and daz-
zlingly over the wide sea of suffering, that the light of it, spreading its
radiance, touches others too with its enchantment. Thus, like a precious
fleeting foam over the sea of suffering arise all those works of art, in
which a single individual lifts himself for an hour so high above his
personal destiny that his happiness shines like a star and appears to all
who see it as something eternal and as a happiness of their own. All
these men, whatever their deeds and works may be, have really no life;
that is to say, their lives are not their own and have no form. They are
not heroes, artists or thinkers in the same way that other men are judges,
doctors, shoemakers, or schoolmasters. Their life consists of a per-
petual tide, unhapy and torn with pain, terrible and meaningless, unless
one is ready to see its meaning in just those rare experiences, acts,
thoughts and works that shine out above the chaos of such a life. To
such men the desperate and horrible thought has come that perhaps
the whole of human life is but a bad joke, a violent and ill-fated abortion
of the primal mother, a savage and dismal catastrophe of nature. To
them, too, however, the other thought has come that man is perhaps not
merely a half-rational animal but a child of the gods and destined to
immortality.

Men of every kind have their characteristics, their features, their
virtues and vices and deadly sins. Prowling about at night was one of
the Steppenwolf's favorite tendencies. The morning was a wretched
time of day for him. He feared it and it never brought him any good.
On no morning of his life had he ever been in good spirits nor done
any good before midday, nor ever had a happy idea, nor devised any
pleasure for himself or others. By degrees during the afternoon he
warmed and became alive, and only towards evening, on his good days,
was he productive, active and, sometimes, aglow with joy. With this
was bound up his need for loneliness and independence. There was
never a man with deeper and more passionate craving for independence
than he. In his youth when he was poor and had difficulty in earning
his bread, he preferred to go hungry and in torn clothes rather than
endanger his narrow limit of independence. He never sold himself
for money or an easy life or to women or those in power; and had
thrown away a hundred times what in the world's eyes was his advantage and happiness in order to safeguard his liberty. No prospect was
more hateful and distasteful to him than that he should have to go
to an office and conform to daily and yearly routine and obey others.
He hated all kinds of offices, governmental or commercial, as he hated
death, and his worst nightmare was confinement in barracks. He contrived, often at great sacrifice, to avoid all such predicaments. It was
here that his strength and his virtue rested. On this point he could
neither be bent nor bribed. Here his character was firm and indeflectable.
Only, through this virtue, he was bound the closer to his destiny of suffering. It happened to him as it does to all; what he strove for with the

deepest and most stubborn instinct of his being fell to his lot, but more than is good for men. In the beginning his dream and his happiness, in the end it was his bitter fate. The man of power is ruined by power, the man of money by money, the submissive man by subservience, the pleasure seeker by pleasure. He achieved his aim. He was ever more independent. He took orders from no man and ordered his ways to suit no man. Independently and alone, he decided what to do and to leave undone. For every strong man attains to that which a genuine impulse bids him seek. But in the midst of the freedom he had attained Harry suddenly became aware that his freedom was a death and that he stood alone. The world in an uncanny fashion left him in peace. Other men concerned him no longer. He was not even concerned about himself. He began to suffocate slowly in the more and more rarefied atmosphere of remoteness and solitude. For now it was his wish no longer, nor his aim, to be alone and independent, but rather his lot and his sentence. The magic wish had been fulfilled and could not be cancelled, and it was no good now to open his arms with longing and good will to welcome the bonds of society. People left him alone now. It was not, however, that he was an object of hatred and repugnance. On the contrary, he had many friends. A great many people liked him. But it was no more than sympathy and friendliness. He received invitations, presents, pleasant letters; but no more. No one came near to him. There was no link left, and no one could have had any part in his life even had anyone wished it. For the air of lonely men surrounded him now, a still atmosphere in which the world around him slipped away, leaving him incapable of relationship, an atmosphere against which neither will nor longing availed. This was one of the significant earmarks of his life.

Another was that he was numbered among the suicides. And here it must be said that to call suicides only those who actually destroy themselves is false. Among these, indeed, there are many who in a sense are suicides only by accident and in whose being suicide has no necessary place. Among the common run of men there are many of little personality and stamped with no deep impress of fate, who find their end in suicide without belonging on that account to type of the suicide by inclination; while on the other hand, of those who are to be counted as suicides by the very nature of their beings are many, perhaps a majority, who never in fact lay hands on themselves. The "suicide," and Harry was one, need not necessarily live in a peculiarly close relationship to death. One may do this without being a suicide. What is peculiar to the suicide is that his ego, rightly or wrongly, is felt to be an extremely dangerous, dubious, and doomed germ of nature; that he is always in his own eyes exposed to an extraordinary risk, as though he stood with the slightest foothold on the peak of a crag whence a slight push from without or an instant's weakness from within suffices to precipitate him into the void. The line of fate in the case of these men is marked by the belief they have that suicide is their most probable manner of death. It might be presumed that such temperaments, which usually manifest themselves in early youth and persist through life, show a singular defect of vital force. On the contrary, among the "suicides" are to be found unusually tenacious and eager and also hardy natures. But just as there are those who at the least indisposition develop a fever, so do those whom we call suicides, and who are always very emotional and sensitive, develop at the least shock the notion of suicide. Had we a science with the courage and authority to concern itself with mankind, instead of with the mechanism merely of vital phenomena, had we something of the nature of an anthropology, or a psychology, these matters of fact would be familiar to everyone.

What was said above on the subject of suicides touches obviously nothing but the surface. It is psychology, and, therefore partly physics. Metaphysically considered, the matter has a different and much clearer aspect. In this aspect suicides present themselves as those who are overtaken by the sense of guilt inherent in individuals, those souls that find the aim of life not in the perfecting and molding of the self, but in liberating themselves by going back to the mother, back to God, back to the all. Many of these natures are wholly incapable of ever having recourse to real suicide, because they have a profound consciouness of the sin of doing so. For us they are suicides nonetheless; for they see death and not life as the releaser. They are ready to cast themselves away in surrender, to be extinguished and to go back to the beginning.

As every strength may become a weakness (and under some circumstances must) so, on the contrary, may the typical suicide find a strength and a support in his apparent weakness. Indeed, he does so more often than not. The case of Harry, the Steppenwolf, is one of these. As thousands of his like do, he found consolation and support, and not merely the melancholy play of youthful fancy, in the idea that the way to death was open to him at any moment. It is true that with him, as with all men of his kind, every shock, every pain, every untoward predicament at once called forth the wish to find an escape in death. By degrees, however, he fashioned for himself out of this tendency a philosophy that was actually serviceable to life. He gained strength through familiarity with the thought that the emergency exit stood always open, and became curious, too, to taste his suffering to the dregs. If it went too badly with him he could feel sometimes with a grim malicious pleasure: "I am curious to see all the same just how much a man can endure. If the limit of what is bearable is reached, I have only to open the door to escape." There are a great many suicides to whom this thought imparts an uncommon strength.

On the other hand, all suicides have the responsibility of fighting against the temptation of suicide. Every one of them knows very well in some corner of his soul that suicide, though a way out, is rather a mean and shabby one, and that it is nobler and finer to be conquered by life than to fall by one's own hand. Knowing this, with a morbid conscience whose source is much the same as that of the militant conscience of so-called self-contented persons, the majority of suicides are left to a protracted struggle against their temptation. They struggle as the kleptomaniac against his own vice. The Steppenwolf was not unfamiliar with this struggle. He had engaged in it with many a change of weapons. Finally, at the age of forty-seven or thereabouts, a happy and not unhumorous idea came to him from which he often derived some amusement. He appointed his fiftieth birthday as the day on which he might allow himself to take his own life. On this day, according to his mood, so he agreed with himself, it should be open to him to employ the emergency exit or not. Let happen to him what might, illness, poverty, suffering and bitterness, there was a time-limit. It could not extend beyond these few years, months, days whose number daily diminished. And in fact he bore much adversity, which previously would have cost him severer and longer tortures and shaken him perhaps to the roots of his being, very much more easily. When for any reason it went particularly badly with him, when peculiar pains and penalties were added to the desolateness and loneliness and savagery of his life, he could say to his tormentors: "Only wait, two years and I am your master." And with this he cherished the thought of the morning of his fiftieth birthday. Letters of congratulation would arrive, while he, relying on his razor, took leave of all his pains and closed the door behind him. Then gout in the joints, depression of spirits, and all pains of head and body could look for another victim.

It still remains to elucidate the Steppenwolf as an isolated phenomenon, in his relation, for example, to the bourgeois world, so that his symptoms may be traced to their source. Let us take as a starting point, since it offers itself, his relation to the bourgeoisie.

To take his own view of the matter, the Steppenwolf stood entirely outside the world of convention, since he had neither family life nor social ambitions. He felt himself to be single and alone, whether as a queer fellow and a hermit in poor health, or as a person removed from the common run of men by the prerogative of talents that had something of genius in them. Deliberately, he looked down upon the ordinary man and was proud that he was not one. Nevertheless his life in many aspects was thoroughly ordinary. He had money in the bank and supported poor relations. He was dressed respectably and inconspicuously, even though without particular care. He was glad to live on good terms with the police and the tax collectors and other such powers. Besides this, he was secretly and persistently attracted to the little bourgeois world, to those quiet and respectable homes with tidy gardens, irreproachable stair-cases and their whole modest air of order and comfort. It pleased him to set himself outside it, with his little vices and extravagances, as a queer fellow or a genius, but he never had his domicile in those provinces of life where the bourgeoisie had ceased to exist. He was not at ease with violent and exceptional persons or with criminals and outlaws, and he took up his abode always among the middle classes, with whose habits and standards and atmosphere he stood in a constant relation, even though it might be one of contrast and revolt. Moreover, he had been brought up in a provincial and conventional home and many of the notions and much of the examples of those days had never left him. In theory he had nothing whatever against the servant class, yet in practice it would have been beyond him to take a servant quite seriously as his equal. He was capable of loving the political criminal, the revolutionary or intellectual seducer, the outlaw of state and society, as his brother, but as for theft and robbery, murder and rape, he would not have known how to deplore them otherwise than in a thoroughly bourgeois manner.

In this way he was always recognising and affirming with one half of himself, in thought and act, what with the other half he fought against and denied. Brought up, as he was, in a cultivated home in the approved manner, he never tore part of his soul loose from its conventionalities even after he had long since individualised himself to a degree beyond its scope and freed himself from the substance of its ideals and beliefs.

Now what we call "bourgeois," when regarded as an element always to be found in human life, is nothing else than the search for a balance. It is the striving after a mean between the countless extremes and opposites that arise in human conduct. If we take any one of these coupled opposites, such as piety and profligacy, the analogy is immediately comprehensible. It is open to a man to give himself up wholly to spiritual views, to seeking after God, to the ideal of saintliness. On the other hand, he can equally give himself up entirely to the life of instinct, to the lusts of the flesh, and so direct all his efforts to the attainment of momentary pleasures. The one path leads to the saint, to the martyrdom of the spirit and surrender to God. The other path leads to the profligate, to the martyrdom of the flesh, the surrender to corruption. Now it is between the two, in the middle of the road, that the bourgeois seeks to walk. He will never surrender himself either to lust or to asceticism. He will never be a martyr or agree to his own destruction. On the contrary, his ideal is not to give up but to maintain his own identity. He strives neither for the saintly nor its opposite. The absolute is his abhorrence. He may be ready to serve God, but not by giving up the fleshpots. He is ready to be virtuous, but likes to be easy and comfortable in this world as well. In short, his aim is to make a home for himself between two extremes in a temperate zone without violent storms and tempests; and in this he succeeds though it be at the cost of that intensity of life and feeling which an extreme life affords. A man cannot live intensely except at the cost of the self. Now the bourgeois treasures nothing more highly than the self (rudimentary as his may be). And so at the cost of intensity he achieves his own preservation and security. His harvest is a quiet mind which he prefers to being possessed by God, as he does comfort to pleasure, convenience to liberty, and a pleasant temperature to that deathly inner consuming fire. The bourgeois is consequently by nature a creature of weak impulses, anxious, fearful of giving himself away and easy to rule. Therefore, he has substituted majority for power, law for force, and the polling booth for responsibility.

It is clear that this weak and anxious being, in whatever numbers he exists, cannot maintain himself, and that qualities such as his can play no other rôle in the world than that of a herd of sheep among free roving wolves. Yet we see that, though in times when commanding natures are uppermost, the bourgeois goes at once to the wall, he never goes under; indeed at times he even appears to rule the world. How is this possible? Neither the great numbers of the herd, nor virtue, nor common sense, nor organization could avail to save it from destruction. No medicine in the world can keep a pulse beating that from the outset was so weak. Nevertheless the bourgeoisie prospers. Why?

The answer runs: Because of the Steppenwolves. In fact, the vital force of the bourgeoisie resides by no means in the qualities of its normal members, but in those of its extremely numerous "outsiders" who by virtue of the extensiveness and elasticity of its ideals it can embrace. There is always a large number of strong and wild natures who share the life of the fold. Our Steppenwolf, Harry, is a characteristic example. He who is developed far beyond the level possible to the bourgeois, he who knows the bliss of meditation no less than the gloomy joys of hatred and self-hatred, he who despises law, virtue and common sense, is nevertheless captive to the bourgeoisie and cannot escape it. And so all through the mass of the real bourgeoisie are interposed numerous layers of humanity, many thousands of lives and minds, every one of whom, it is true, would have outgrown it and have obeyed the call to unconditioned life, were they not fastened to it by sentiments of their childhood and infected for the most part with its less intense life; and so they are kept lingering, obedient and bound by obligation and service. For with the bourgeoisie the opposite of the formula for the great is true: He who is not against me is with me.

If we now pause to test the soul of the Steppenwolf, we find him distinct from the bourgeois in the higher development of his individuality—for all extreme individuation turns against itself, intent upon its own destruction. We see that he had in him strong impulses both to be a saint and a profligate; and yet he could not, owing to some weakness or inertia, make the plunge into the untrammelled realms of space. The parent constellation of the bourgeoisie binds him with its spell. This is his place in the universe and this his bondage. Most intellectuals and most artists belong to the same type. Only the strongest of them force their way through the atmosphere of the bourgeois earth and attain to the cosmic. The others all resign themselves or make compromises. Despising the bourgeoisie, and yet belonging to it, they add to its strength and glory; for in the last resort they have to share their beliefs in order to live. The lives of these infinitely numerous persons make no claim to

the tragic; but they live under an evil star in a quite considerable affliction; and in this hell their talents ripen and bear fruit. The few who
break free seek their reward in the unconditioned and go down in splen-
dor. They wear the thorn crown and their number is small. The others,
however, who remain in the fold and from whose talents the bourgeoisie
reaps much gain, have a third kingdom left open to them, an imaginary
and yet a sovereign world, humor. The lone wolves who know no peace,
these victims of unceasing pain to whom the urge for tragedy has been
denied and who can never break through the starry space, who feel
themselves summoned thither and yet cannot survive in its atmosphere
—for them is reserved, provided suffering has made their spirits tough
and elastic enough, a way of reconcilement and an escape into humor.
Humor has always something bourgeois in it, although the true bourgeois
is incapable of understanding it. In its imaginary realm the intricate
and many-faceted ideal of all Steppenwolves finds its realisation. Here
it is possible not only to extol the saint and the profligate in one breath
and to make the poles meet, but to include the bourgeois, too, in the
same affirmation. Now it is possible to be possessed by God and to
affirm the sinner, and vice versa, but it is not possible for either saint
or sinner (or for any other of the unconditioned) to affirm as well that
lukewarm mean, the bourgeois. Humor alone, that magnificent discovery
of those who are cut short in their calling to highest endeavor, those who
falling short of tragedy are yet as rich in gifts as in affliction, humor
alone (perhaps the most inborn and brilliant achievement of the spirit)
attains to the impossible and brings every aspect of human existence
within the rays of its prism. To live in the world as though it were not the
world, to respect the law and yet to stand above it, to have possessions as
though "one possessed nothing," to renounce as though it were no renunciation, all these favorite and often formulated propositions of an exalted world wisdom, it is in the power of humor alone to make efficacious.

    And supposing the Steppenwolf were to succeed, and he has gifts
and resources in plenty, in decocting this magic draught in the sultry
mazes of his hell, his rescue would be assured. Yet there is much lacking.
The possibility, the hope only are there. Whoever loves him and takes
his part may wish him this rescue. It would, it is true, keep him forever
tied to the bourgeois world, but his suffering would be bearable and productive. His relation to the bourgeois world would lose its sentimentality
both in its love and in its hatred, and his bondage to it would cease to
cause him the continual torture of shame.

    To attain to this, or, perhaps it may be, to be able at last to dare the
leap into the unknown, a Steppenwolf must once have a good look at
himself. He must look deeply into the chaos of his own soul and plumb
its depths. The riddle of his existence would then be revealed to him at
once in all its changelessness, and it would be impossible for him ever
after to escape first from the hell of the flesh to the comforts of a sentimental philosophy and then back to the blind orgy of his wolfishness.

Man and wolf would then be compelled to recognise one another without the masks of false feeling and to look one another straight in the eye. Then they would either explode and separate forever, and there would be no more Steppenwolf, or else they would come to terms in the dawning light of humor.

It is possible that Harry will one day be led to this latter alternative. It is possible that he will learn one day to know himself. He may get hold of one of our little mirrors. He may encounter the Immortals. He may find in one of our magic theaters the very thing that is needed to free his neglected soul. A thousand such possibilities await him. His fate brings them on, leaving him no choice; for those outside of the bourgeoisie live in the atmosphere of these magic possibilities. A mere nothing suffices—and the lightning strikes.

And all this is very well known to the Steppenwolf, even though his eye may never fall on this fragment of his inner biography. He has a suspicion of his allotted place in the world, a suspicion of the Immortals, a suspicion that he may meet himself face to face; and he is aware of the existence of that mirror in which he has such bitter need to look and from which he shrinks in such deathly fear.

For the close of our study there is left one last fiction, a fundamental delusion to make clear. All interpretation, all psychology, all attempts to make things comprehensible, require the medium of theories, mythologies and lies; and a self-respecting author should not omit, at the close of an exposition, to dissipate these lies so far as may be in his power. If I say "above" or "below," that is already a statement that requires explanation, since an above and a below exist only in thought, only as abstractions. The world itself knows nothing of above or below.

So too, to come to the point, is the Steppenwolf a fiction. When Harry feels himself to be a were-wolf, and chooses to consist of two hostile and opposed beings, he is merely availing himself of a mythological simplification. He is no were-wolf at all, and if we appeared to accept without scrutiny this lie which he invented for himself and believes in, and tried to regard him literally as a two-fold being and a Steppenwolf, and so designated him, it was merely in the hope of being more easily understood with the assistance of a delusion, which we must now endeavor to put in its true light.

The division into wolf and man, flesh and spirit, by means of which Harry tries to make his destiny more comprehensible to himself is a very great simplification. It is a forcing of the truth to suit a plausible, but erroneous, explanation of that contradiction which this man discovers in himself and which appears to himself to be the source of his by no means negligible sufferings. Harry finds in himself a human being, that is to say, a world of thoughts and feelings, of culture and tamed or sublimated nature, and besides this he finds within himself also a wolf, that is to say, a dark world of instinct, of savagery and cruelty, of unsublimated or raw nature. In spite of this apparently clear division of his being between two spheres, hostile to one another, he has known happy moments now and then when the man and the wolf for a short while were reconciled with one another. Suppose that Harry tried to ascertain in any single moment of his life, any single act, what part the man had in it and what part the wolf, he would find himself at once in a dilemma, and his whole beautiful wolf-theory would go to pieces. For there is not a single human being, not even the primitive Negro, not even the idiot, who is so conveniently simple that his being can be explained as the sum of two or three principal elements; and to explain so complex a man as Harry by the artless division into wolf and man is a hopelessly childish attempt. Harry consists of a hundred or a thousand selves, not of two. His life oscillates, as everyone's does, not merely between two poles, such as the body and the spirit, the saint and the sinner, but between thousand and thousands.

We need not be surprised that even so intelligent and educated a man as Harry should take himself for a Steppenwolf and reduce the rich and complex organism of his life to a formula so simple, so rudimentary and primitive. Man is not capable of thought in any high degree, and even the most spiritual and highly cultivated of men habitually sees the world and himself through the lenses of delusive formulas and artless simplifications—and most of all himself. For it appears to be an inborn and imperative need of all men to regard the self as a unit. However often and however grievously this illusion is shattered, it always mends again. The judge who sits over the murderer and looks into his face, and at one moment recognizes all the emotions and potentialities and possibilities of the murderer in his own soul and hears the murderer's voice as his own, is at the next moment one and indivisible as the judge, and scuttles back into the shell of his cultivated self and does his duty and condemns the murderer to death. And if ever the suspicion of their manifold being dawns upon men of unusual powers and of unusually delicate perceptions, so that, as all genius must, they break through the illusion of the unity of the personality and perceive that the self is made up of a bundle of selves, they have only to say so and at once the majority puts them under lock and key, calls science to aid, establishes schizomania and protects humanity from the necessity of hearing the cry of truth from the lips of these unfortunate persons. Why then waste words, why utter a thing that every thinking man accepts as self-evident, when the mere utterance of it is a breach of taste? A man, therefore, who gets so far as making the supposed unity of the self two-fold is already almost a genius, in any case a most exceptional and interesting person. In reality, however, every ego, so far from being a unity is in the highest degree, a manifold world, a constellated heaven, a chaos of forms, of states and stages, of inheritances and potentialities. It appears to be a necessity as imperative as eating and breathing for everyone to be forced to regard this chaos as a unity and to speak of his ego as though it were a one-fold and clearly detached and fixed phenomenon. Even the best of us shares the delusion.

The delusion rests simply upon a false analogy. As a body everyone

is single, as a soul never. In literature, too, even in its ultimate achievement, we find this customary concern with apparently whole and single
personalities. Of all literature up to our days the drama has been the
most highly prized by writers and critics, and rightly, since it offers (or
might offer) the greatest possibilities of representing the ego as a manifold entity, but for the optical illusion which makes us believe that the
characters of the play are one-fold entities by lodging each one in an
undeniable body, singly, separately and once and for all. An artless
esthetic criticism, then, keeps its highest praise for this so-called charac-
ter-drama in which each character makes his appearance unmistakably
as a separate and single entity. Only from afar and by degrees the
suspicion dawns here and there that all this is perhaps a cheap and super-
ficial esthetic philosophy, and that we make a mistake in attributing to
our great dramatists those magnificent conceptions of beauty that come
to us from antiquity. These conceptions are not native to us, but are
merely picked up at second hand, and it is in them, with their common
source in the visible body, that the origin of the fiction of an ego, an individual, is really to be found. There is no trace of such a notion in the
poems of ancient India. The heroes of the epics of India are not individuals, but whole reels of individualities in a series incarnations. And
in modern times there are poems, in which, behind the veil of a concern
with individuality and character that is scarcely, indeed, in the author's
mind, the motive is to present a manifold activity of soul. Whoever wishes
to recognize this must resolve once and for all not to regard the characters of such a poem as separate beings, but as the various facets and
aspects of a higher unity, in my opinion, of the poet's soul. If "Faust" is
treated in this way, Faust, Mephistopheles, Wagner and the rest form a
unity and a supreme individuality; and it is in this higher unity alone,
not in the several characters, that something of the true nature of the
soul is revealed. When Faust, in a line immortalized among schoolmasters and greeted with a shudder of astonishment by the Philistine, says:
"Two souls, alas, do dwell within my breast!" he has forgotten Mephisto
and a whole crowd of other souls that he has in his breast likewise. The
Steppenwolf, too, believes that he bears two souls (wolf and man) in his
breast and even so finds his breast disagreeably cramped because of them.
The breast and the body are indeed one, but the souls that dwell in it
are not two, nor five, but countless in number. Man is an onion made
up of a hundred integuments, a texture made up of many threads. The
ancient Asiatics knew this well enough, and in the Buddhist Yoga an
exact technique was devised for unmasking the illusion of the personality. The human merry-go-round sees many changes: the illusion that
cost India the efforts of thousands of years to unmask is the same illusion
that the West has labored just as hard to maintain and strengthen.

If we consider the Steppenwolf from this standpoint it will be clear
to us why he suffered so much under his ludicrous dual personality. He
believes, like Faust, that two souls are far too many for a single breast

and must tear the breast asunder. They are on the contrary far too few, and Harry does shocking violence to his poor soul when he endeavors to apprehend it by means of so primitive an image. Although he is a most cultivated person, he proceeds like a savage that cannot count further than two. He calls himself part wolf, part man, and with that he thinks he has come to an end and exhausted the matter. With the "man" he packs in everything spiritual and sublimated or even cultivated to be found in himself, and with the wolf all that is instinctive, savage and chaotic. But things are not so simple in life as in our thoughts, nor so rough and ready as in our poor idiotic language; and Harry lies about himself twice over when he employs this niggardly wolf-theory. He assigns, we fear, whole provinces of his soul to the "man" which are a long way from being human, and parts of his being to the wolf that long ago have left the wolf behind.

Like all men Harry believes that he knows very well what man is and yet does not know at all, although in dreams and other states not subject to control he often has his suspicions. If only he might not forget them, but keep them, as far as possible at least, for his own. Man is not by any means of fixed and enduring form (this, in spite of suspicions to the contrary on the part of their wise men, was the ideal of the ancients). He is much more an experiment and a transition. He is nothing else than the narrow and perilous bridge between nature and spirit. His innermost destiny drives him on to the spirit and to God. His innermost longing draws him back to nature, the mother. Between the two forces his life hangs tremulous and irresolute. "Man," whatever people think of him, is never anything more than a temporary bourgeois compromise. Convention rejects and bans certain of the more naked instincts, a little consciousness, morality and debestialization is called for, and a modicum of spirit is not only permitted but even thought necessary. The "man" of this concordat, like every other bourgeois ideal, is a compromise, a timid and artlessly sly experiment, with the aim of cheating both the angry primal mother Nature and the troublesome primal father Spirit of their pressing claims, and of living in a temperate zone between the two of them. For this reason the bourgeois today burns as heretics and hangs as criminals those to whom he erects monuments tomorrow.

That man is not yet a finished creation but rather a challenge of the spirit; a distant possibility dreaded as much as it is desired; that the way towards it has only been covered for a very short distance and with terrible agonies and ecstasies even by those few for whom it is the scaffold today and the monument tomorrow—all this the Steppenwolf, too, suspected. What, however, he calls the "man" in himself, as opposed to the wolf, is to a great extent nothing else than this very same average man of the bourgeois convention.

As for the way to true manhood, the way to the immortals, he has, it is true, an inkling of it and starts upon it now and then for a few hesitating steps and pays for them with much suffering and many pangs of loneliness. But as for striving with assurance, in response to that supreme demand, towards the genuine manhood of the spirit, and going the one narrow way to immortality, he is deeply afraid of it. He knows too well that it leads to still greater sufferings, to proscription, to the last renunciation, perhaps to the scaffold, and even though the enticement of immortality lies at the journey's end, he is still unwilling to suffer all these sufferings and to die all these deaths. Though the goal of manhood is better known to him than to the bourgeois, still he shuts his eyes. He is resolved to forget that the desperate clinging to the self and the desperate clinging to life are the surest way to eternal death, while the power to die, to strip one's self naked, and the eternal surrender of the self bring immortality with them. When he worships his favorites among the immortals, Mozart, perchance, he always looks at him in the long run through bourgeois eyes. His tendency is to explain Mozart's perfected being, just as a schoolmaster would, as a supreme and special gift rather than as the outcome of his immense powers of surrender and suffering, of his indifference to the ideals of the bourgeois, and of his patience under that last extremity of loneliness which rarefies the atmosphere of the bourgeois world to an ice-cold ether, around those who suffer to become men, that loneliness of the Garden of Gethsemane.

This Steppenwolf of ours has always been aware of at least the Faustian two-fold nature within him. He has discovered that the one-fold of the body is not inhabited by a one-fold of the soul, and that at best he is only at the beginning of a long pilgrimage towards this ideal harmony. He would like either to overcome the wolf and become wholly man or to renounce mankind and at last to live wholly a wolf's life. It may be presumed that he has never carefully watched a real wolf. Had he done so he would have seen, perhaps, that even animals are not undivided in spirit. With them, too, the well-knit beauty of the body hides a being of manifold states and strivings. The wolf, too, has his abysses. The wolf, too, suffers. No, back to nature is a false track that leads nowhere but to suffering and despair. Harry can never turn back again and become wholly wolf, and could he do so he would find that even the wolf is not of primeval simplicity, but already a creature of manifold complexity. Even the wolf has two, and more than two, souls in his wolf's breast, and he who desires to be a wolf falls into the same forgetfulness as the man who sings: "If I could be a child once more!" He who sentimentally sings of blessed childhood is thinking of the return to nature and innocence and the origin of things, and has quite forgotten that these blessed children are beset with conflict and complexities and capable of all suffering.

There is, in fact, no way back either to the wolf or to the child. From the very start there is no innocence and no singleness. Every created thing, even the simplest, is already guilty, already multiple. It has been thrown into the muddy stream of being and may never more swim back again to its source. The way to innocence, to the uncreated and to God leads on, not back, not back to the wolf or to the child, but ever further into sin, ever deeper into human life. Nor will suicide really solve your problem, unhappy Steppenwolf. You will, instead, embark on the longer and wearier and harder road of life. You will have to multiply many times your two-fold being and complicate your complexities still further. Instead of narrowing your world and simplifying your soul, you will have to absorb more and more of the world and at last take all of it up in your painfully expanded soul, if you are ever to find peace. This is the road that Buddha and every great man has gone, whether consciously or not, insofar as fortune favored his quest. All births mean separation from the All, the confinement within limitation, the separation from God, the pangs of being born ever anew. The return into the All, the dissolution of painful individuation, the reunion with God means the expansion of the soul until it is able once more to embrace the All.

We are not dealing here with man as he is known to economics and statistics, as he is seen thronging the streets by the million, and of whom no more account can be made than of the sand of the sea or the spray of its waves. We are not concerned with the few millions less or more. They are a stock-in-trade, nothing else. No, we are speaking of man in the highest sense, of the end of the long road to true manhood, of kingly men, of the immortals. Genius is not so rare as we sometimes think; nor, certainly, so frequent as may appear from history books or, indeed, from the newspapers. Harry has, we should say, genius enough to attempt the quest of true manhood instead of discoursing pitifully about his stupid Steppenwolf at every difficulty encountered.

It is as much a matter for surprise and sorrow that men of such possibilities should fall back on Steppenwolves and "Two souls, alas!" as that they reveal so often that pitiful love for the bourgeoisie. A man who can understand Buddha and has an intuition of the heaven and hell of humanity ought not to live in a world ruled by "common sense" and democracy and bourgeois standards. It is only from cowardice that he lives in it; and when its dimensions are too cramping for him and the bourgeois parlor too confining, he lays it at the wolf's door, and refuses to see that the wolf is as often as not the best part of him. All that is wild in himself he calls wolf and considers it wicked and dangerous and the bugbear of all decent life. He cannot see, even though he thinks himself an artist and possessed of delicate perceptions, that a great deal else exists in him besides and behind the wolf. He cannot see that not all that bites is wolf and that fox, dragon, tiger, ape and bird of paradise are there also. And he cannot see that this whole world, this Eden and its manifestations of beauty and terror, of greatness and meanness, of strength and tenderness is crushed and imprisoned by the wolf legend just as the real man in him is crushed and imprisoned by that sham existence, the bourgeois.

Man designs for himself a garden with a hundred kinds of trees, a thousand kinds of flowers, a hundred kinds of fruit and vegetables. Suppose, then, that the gardener of this garden knew no other distinction than between edible and inedible, nine-tenths of this garden would be useless to him. He would pull up the most enchanting flowers and hew down the noblest trees and even regard them with a loathing and envious eye. This is what the Steppenwolf does with the thousand flowers of his soul. What does not stand classified as either man or wolf he does not see at all. And consider all that he imputes to "man"! All that is cowardly and apish, stupid and mean—while to the wolf, only because he has not succeeded in making himself its master, is set down all that is strong and noble.

Now we bid Harry good-bye and leave him to go on his way alone. Were he already among the immortals—were he already there at the goal to which his difficult path seems to be taking him, with what amazement he would look back to all this coming and going, all this in-decision and wild zig-zag trail. With what a mixture of encouragement and blame, pity and joy, he would smile at this Steppenwolf.

When I had read to the end it came to my mind that some weeks before I had written one night a rather peculiar poem, likewise about the Steppenwolf. I looked for it in the pile of papers on my cluttered writing table, found it, and read:

The Wolf trots to and fro,
The world lies deep in snow,
The raven from the birch tree flies,
But nowhere a hare, nowhere a roe.
The roe—she is so dear, so sweet—
If such a thing I might surprise
In my embrace, my-teeth would meet,
What else is there beneath the skies?
The lovely creature I would so treasure,
And feast myself deep on her tender thigh,
I would drink of her red blood full measure,
Then howl till the night went by.
Even a hare I would not despise;
Sweet enough its warm flesh in the night.
Is everything to be denied
That could make life a little bright?
The hair on my brush is getting grey.
The sight is failing from my eyes.
Years ago my dear mate died.
And now I trot and dream of a roe.
I trot and dream of a hare.
I hear the wind of midnight howl.
I cool with the snow my burning jowl,
And on to the devil my wretched soul I bear.

So now I had two portraits of myself before me, one a self-portrait in doggerel verse, as sad and sorry as myself; the other painted with the air of a lofty impartiality by one who stood outside and who knew more and yet less of me than I did myself. And both these pictures of myself, my dispirited and halting poem and the clever study by an unknown hand, equally afflicted me. Both were right. Both gave the unvarnished truth about my shiftless existence. Both showed clearly how unbearable and untenable my situation was. Death was decreed for this Steppenwolf. He must with his own hand make an end of his detested existence—unless, molten in the fire of a renewed self-knowledge, he underwent a change and passed over to a self, new and undisguised. Alas! this transition was not unknown to me. I had already experienced it several times, and always in periods of utmost despair. On each occasion of this terribly uprooting experience, my self, as it then was, was shattered to fragments. Each time deep-seated powers had shaken and destroyed it; each time there had followed the loss of a cherished and particularly beloved part of my life that was true to me no more. Once, I had lost my profession and livelihood. I had had to forfeit the esteem of those who before had touched their caps to me. Next, my family life fell in ruins over night, when my wife, whose mind was disordered, drove me from house and home. Love and confidence had changed of a sudden to hate and deadly enmity and the neighbors saw me go with pitying scorn. It was then that my solitude had its beginning. Years of hardship and bitterness went by. I had built up the ideal of a new life, inspired by the asceticism of the intellect. I had attained a certain serenity and elevation of life once more, submitting myself to the practice of abstract thought and to a rule of austere meditation. But this mold, too, was broken and lost at one blow all its exalted and noble intent. A whirl of travel drove me afresh over the earth; fresh sufferings were heaped up, and fresh guilt. And every occasion when a mask was torn off, an ideal broken, was preceded by this hateful vacancy and stillness, this deathly constriction and loneliness and unrelatedness, this waste and empty hell of lovelessness and despair, such as I had now to pass through once more.

It is true that every time my life was shattered in this way I had in the end gained something, some increase in liberty and in spiritual growth and depth, but with it went an increased loneliness, an increasing chill of severance and estrangement. Looked at with the bourgeois eye, my life had been a continuous descent from one shattering to the next that left me more remote at every step from all that was normal, permissible and healthful. The passing years had stripped me of my calling, my family, my home. I stood outside all social circles, alone, beloved by none, mistrusted by many, in unceasing and bitter conflict with public opinion and morality; and though I lived in a bourgeois setting, I was all the same an utter stranger to this world in all I thought and felt. Religion, country, family, state, all lost their value and meant nothing to me any more. The pomposity of the sciences, societies, and arts disgusted me. My views and tastes and all that I thought, once the shining adornments of a gifted and sought-after person, had run to seed in neglect and were looked at askance. Granting that I had in the course of all my painful transmutations made some invisible and unaccountable gain, I had to pay dearly for it; and at every turn my life was harsher, more difficult, lonely and perilous. In truth, I had little cause to wish to continue in that way which led on into ever thinner air, like the smoke in Nietzsche's harvest song.

Oh, yes, I had experienced all these changes and transmutations that fate reserves for her difficult children, her ticklish customers. I knew them only too well. I knew them as well as a zealous but unsuccessful sportsman knows the stands at a shoot; as an old gambler on the Exchange knows each stage of speculation, the scoop, the weakening market, the break and bankruptcy. Was I really to live through all this again? All this torture, all this pressing need, all these glimpses into the paltriness and worthlessness of my own self, the frightful dread lest I succumb, and the fear of death. Wasn't it better and simpler to prevent a repetition of so many sufferings and to quit the stage? Certainly, it was simpler and better. Whatever the truth of all that was said in the little book on the Steppenwolf about "suicides," no one could forbid me the satisfaction of invoking the aid of coal gas or a razor or revolver, and so sparing myself this repetition of a process whose bitter agony I had had to drink often enough, surely, and to the dregs. No, in all conscience, there was no power in the world that could prevail with me to go through the mortal terror of another encounter with myself, to face another reorganisation, a new incarnation, when at the end of the road there was no peace or quiet—but forever destroying the self, in order to renew the self. Let suicide be as stupid, cowardly, shabby as you please, call it an infamous and ignominious escape; still, any escape, even the most ignominious, from this treadmill of suffering was the only thing to wish for. No stage was left for the noble and heroic heart. Nothing was left but the simple choice between a slight and swift pang and an unthinkable, a devouring and endless suffering. I had played Don Quixote often enough in my difficult, crazed life, had put honor before comfort, and heroism before reason. There was an end of it!

Daylight was dawning through the window panes, the leaden, infernal daylight of a rainy winter's day, when at last I got to bed. I took my resolution to bed with me. At the very last, however, on the last verge of consciousness in the moment of falling asleep, the remarkable passage in the Steppenwolf pamphlet which deals with the immortals flashed through me. With it came the enchanting recollection that several times, the last quite recently, I had felt near enough to the immortals to share in one measure of old music their cool, bright, austere and yet smiling wisdom. The memory of it soared, shone out, then died away; and heavy as a mountain, sleep descended on my brain.

I woke about midday, and at once the situation, as I had disen-
tangled it, came back to me. There lay the little book on my night stand,
and my poem. My resolution, too, was there. After the night's sleep it had
taken shape and looked at me out of the confusion of my youth with a
calm and friendly greeting. Haste makes no speed. My resolve to die
was not the whim of an hour. It was the ripe, sound fruit that had grown
slowly to full size, lightly rocked by the winds of fate whose next breath
would bring it to the ground.

I had in my medicine chest an excellent means of stilling pain—
an unusually strong tincture of laudanum. I indulged very rarely in it
and often refrained from using it for months at a time. I had recourse
to the drug only when physical pain plagued me beyond endurance. Unfortunately, it was of no use in putting an end to myself. I had proved
this some years before. Once when despair had again got the better of
me I had swallowed a big dose of it—enough to kill six men, and yet it
had not killed me. I fell asleep, it is true, and lay for several hours completely stupefied; but then to my frightful disappointment I was half
awakened by violent convulsions of the stomach and fell asleep once
more. It was the middle of the next day when I woke up in earnest in a
state of dismal sobriety. My empty brain was burning and I had almost
lost my memory. Apart from a spell of insomnia and severe pains in the
stomach no trace of the poison was left.

This expedient, then, was no good. But I put my resolution in this
way: the next time I felt that I must have recourse to the opium, I might
allow myself to use big means instead of small, that is, a death of absolute certainty with a bullet or a razor. Then I could be sure. As for waiting till my fiftieth birthday, as the little book wittily prescribed—this
seemed to me much too long a delay. There were still two years till then.
Whether it were a year hence or a month, were it even the following
day, the door stood open.

I cannot say that the resolution altered my life very profoundly. It
made me a little more indifferent to my afflictions, a little freer in the use
of opium and wine, a little more inquisitive to know the limits of endurance, but that was all. The other experiences of that evening had a
stronger after-effect. I read the Steppenwolf treatise through again many
times, now submitting gratefully to an invisible magician because of his
wise conduct of my destiny, now with scorn and contempt for its futility,
and the little understanding it showed of my actual disposition and predicament. All that was written there of Steppenwolves and suicides was
very good, no doubt, and very clever. It might do for the species, the type;
but it was too wide a mesh to catch my own individual soul, my unique
and unexampled destiny.

What, however, occupied my thoughts more than all else was the
hallucination, or vision, of the church wall. The announcement made by
the dancing illuminated letters promised much that was hinted at in the
treatise, and the voices of that strange world had powerfully aroused my

curiosity. For hours I pondered deeply over them. On these occasions I was more and more impressed by the warning of that inscription—"Not for everybody!" and "For madmen only!" Madman, then, I must certainly be and far from the mold of "everybody" if those voices reached me and that world spoke to me. In heaven's name, had I not long ago been remote from the life of everybody and from normal thinking and normal existence? Had I not long ago given ample margin to isolation and madness? All the same, I understood the summons well enough in my innermost heart. Yes, I understood the invitation to madness and the jettison of reason and the escape from the clogs of convention in surrender to the unbridled surge of spirit and fantasy.

One day after I had made one more vain search through streets and squares for the man with the signboard and prowled several times past the wall of the invisible door with watchful eye, I met a funeral procession in St. Martin's. While I was contemplating the faces of the mourners who followed the hearse with halting step, I thought to myself, "Where in this town or in the whole world is the man whose death would be a loss to me? And where is the man to whom my death would mean anything?" There was Erica, it is true, but for a long while we had lived apart. We rarely saw one another without quarreling and at the moment I did not even know her address. She came to see me now and then, or I made the journey to her, and since both of us were lonely, difficult people related somehow to one another in soul, and sickness of soul, there was a link between us that held in spite of all. But would she not perhaps breathe more freely if she heard of my death? I did not know. I did not know either how far my own feeling for her was to be relied upon. To know anything of such matters one needs to live in a world of practical possibilities.

Meanwhile, obeying my fancy, I had fallen in at the rear of the funeral procession and jogged along behind the mourners to the cemetery, an up-to-date set-up all of concrete, complete with crematorium and what not. The deceased in question was not however to be cremated. His coffin was set down before a simple hole in the ground, and I saw the clergyman and the other vultures and functionaries of a burial establishment going through their performances, to which they endeavored to give all the appearance of great ceremony and sorrow and with such effect that they outdid themselves and from pure acting they got caught in their own lies and ended by being comic. I saw how their black professional robes fell in folds, and what pains they took to work up the company of mourners and to force them to bend the knee before the majesty of death. It was labor in vain. Nobody wept. The deceased did not appear to have been indispensable. Nor could anyone be talked into a pious frame of mind; and when the clergyman addressed the company repeatedly as "dear fellow-Christians," all the silent faces of these shop people and master bakers and their wives were turned down in embarrassment and expressed nothing but the wish that this uncomfortable function might soon be over. When the end came, the two fore-most of the fellow-Christians shook the clergyman's hand, scraped the moist clay in which the dead had been laid from their shoes at the next scraper and without hesitation their faces again showed their natural expression; and then it was that one of them seemed suddenly familiar. It was, so it seemed to me, the man who had carried the signboard and thrust the little book into my hands.

At the moment when I thought I recognized him he stopped and, stooping down, carefully turned up his black trousers, and then walked away at a smart pace with his umbrella clipped under his arm. I walked after him, but when I overtook him and gave him a nod, he did not appear to recognize me.

"Is there no show tonight?" I asked with an attempt at a wink such as two conspirators give each other. But it was long ago that such panto-mime was familiar to me. Indeed, living as I did, I had almost lost the habit of speech, and I felt myself that I only made a silly grimace.

"Show tonight?" he growled, and looked at me as though he had never set eyes on me before. "Go to the Black Eagle, man, if that's what you want."

And, in fact, I was no longer certain it was he. I was disappointed and feeling the disappointment I walked on aimlessly. I had no motives, no incentives to exert myself, no duties. Life tasted horribly bitter. I felt that the long-standing disgust was coming to a crisis and that life pushed me out and cast me aside. I walked through the grey streets in a rage and everything smelt of moist earth and burial. I swore that none of these death-vultures should stand at my grave, with cassock and sentimental Christian murmurings. Ah, look where I might and think what I might, there was no cause for rejoicing and nothing beckoned me. There was nothing to charm me or tempt me. Everything was old, with-ered, grey, limp and spent, and stank of staleness and decay. Dear God, how was it possible? How had I, with the wings of youth and poetry, come to this! Art and travel and the glow of ideals—and now this! How had this paralysis crept over me so slowly and furtively, this hatred against myself and everybody, this deep-seated anger and ob-struction of all feelings, this filthy hell of emptiness and despair.

Passing by the Library I met a young professor of whom in earlier years I used occasionally to see a good deal. When I last stayed in the town, some years before, I had even been several times to his house to talk Oriental mythology, a study in which I was then very much inter-ested. He came in my direction walking stiffly and with a short-sighted air and only recognized me at the last moment as I was passing by. In my lamentable state I was half-thankful for the cordiality with which he threw himself on me. His pleasure in seeing me became quite lively as he recalled the talks we had had together and assured me that he owed a great deal to the stimulus they had given him and that he often thought of me. He had rarely had such stimulating and productive discussions with any colleague since. He asked how long I had been in the town (I lied and said "a few days") and why I had not looked him up. The learned man held me with his friendly eye and, though I really found it all ridiculous, I could not help enjoying these crumbs of warmth and kindliness, and was lapping them up like a starved dog. Harry, the Steppenwolf, was moved to a grin. Saliva collected in his parched throat and against his will he bowed down to sentiment. Yes, zealously piling lie upon lie, I said that I was only here in passing, for the purpose of research, and should of course have paid him a visit but that I had not been feeling very fit. And when he went on to invite me very heartily to spend the evening with him, I accepted with thanks and sent my greetings to his wife, until my cheeks fairly ached with the unaccustomed efforts of all these forced smiles and speeches. And while I, Harry Haller, stood there in the street, flattered and surprised and studiously polite and smiling into the good fellow's kindly, short-sighted face, there stood the other Harry, too, at my elbow and grinned likewise. He stood there and grinned as he thought what a funny, crazy, dishonest fellow I was to show my teeth in rage and curse the whole world one moment and, the next, to be falling all over myself in the eagerness of my response to the first amiable greeting of the first good honest fellow who came my way, to be wallowing like a suckling-pig in the luxury of a little pleasant feeling and friendly esteem. Thus stood the two Harrys, neither playing a very pretty part, over against the worthy professor, mocking one another, watching one another, and spitting at one another, while as always in such predicaments, the eternal question presented itself whether all this was simple stupidity and human frailty, a common depravity, or whether this sentimental egoism and perversity, this slovenliness and two-facedness of feeling was merely a personal idiosyncrasy of the Steppenwolves. And if this nastiness was common to men in general, I could rebound from it with renewed energy into hatred of all the world, but if it was a personal frailty, it was good occasion for an orgy of hatred of myself.

While my two selves were thus locked in conflict, the professor was almost forgotten; and when the oppressiveness of his presence came suddenly back to me, I made haste to be relieved of it. I looked after him for a long while as he disappeared into the distance along the leafless avenue with the good-natured and slightly comic gait of an ingenuous idealist. Within me, the battle raged furiously. Mechanically I bent and unbent my stiffened fingers as though to fight the ravages of a secret poison, and at the same time had to realize that I had been nicely framed. Round my neck was the invitation for 8:30, with all its obligations of politeness, of talking shop and of contemplating another's domestic bliss. And so home—in wrath. Once there, I poured myself out some brandy and water, swallowed some of my gout pills with it, and, lying on the sofa, tried to read. No sooner had I succeeded in losing myself for a moment in *Sophia's Journey from Memel to Saxony*, a delightful old book of the eighteenth century, than the invitation came over me of a sudden and reminded me that I was neither shaved nor dressed. Why, in heaven's name, had I brought all this on myself? Well, get up, so I told myself, lather yourself, scrape your chin till it bleeds, dress and show an amiable disposition towards your fellow-men. And while I lathered my face, I thought of that sordid hole in the clay of the cemetery into which some unknown person had been lowered that day. I thought of the pinched faces of the bored fellow-Christians and I could not even laugh. There in that sordid hole in the clay, I thought, to the accompaniment of stupid and insincere ministrations and the no less stupid and insincere demeanor of the group of mourners, in the discomforting sight of all the metal crosses and marble slabs and artificial flowers of wire and glass, ended not only that unknown man, and, tomorrow or the day after, myself as well, buried in the soil with a hypocritical show of sorrow—no, there and so ended everything; all our striving, all our culture, all our beliefs, all our joy and pleasure in life—already sick and soon to be buried there too. Our whole civilization was a cemetery where Jesus Christ and Socrates, Mozart and Haydn, Dante and Goethe were but the indecipherable names on moldering stones; and the mourners who stood round affecting a pretence of sorrow would give much to believe in these inscriptions which once were holy, or at least to utter one heart-felt word of grief and despair about this world that is no more. And nothing was left them but the embarrassed grimaces of a company round a grave. As I raged on like this I cut my chin in the usual place and had to apply a caustic to the wound; and even so there was my clean collar, scarce put on, to change again, and all this for an invitation that did not give me the slightest pleasure. And yet a part of me began play-acting again, calling the professor a sympathetic fellow, yearning after a little talk and intercourse with my fellow men, reminding me of the professor's pretty wife, prompting me to believe that an evening spent with my pleasant host and hostess would be in reality positively cheering, helping me to clap some court plaster to my chin, to put on my clothes and tie my tie well, and gently putting me, in fact, far from my genuine desire of staying at home. Whereupon it occurred to me—so it is with every one. Just as I dress and go out to visit the professor and exchange a few more or less insincere compliments with him, without really wanting to at all, so it is with the majority of men day by day and hour by hour in their daily lives and affairs. Without really wanting to at all, they pay calls and carry on conversations, sit out their hours at desks and on office chairs; and it is all compulsory, mechanical and against the grain, and it could all be done or left undone just as well by machines; and indeed it is this never-ceasing machinery that prevents their being, like me, the critics of their own lives and recognizing the stupidity and shallowness, the hopeless tragedy and waste of the lives they lead, and the awful ambiguity grinning over it all. And they are right, right a thousand times to live as they do, playing their games and pursuing their business, instead of resisting the dreary machine and staring into the void as I do, who have left the track. Let no one think that I blame other men, though now and then in these pages I scorn and even deride them, or that I accuse them of the responsibility of my personal misery. But now that I have come so far, and standing as I do on the extreme verge of life where the ground falls away before me into bottomless darkness, I should do wrong and I should lie if I pretended to myself or to others that that machine still revolved for me and that I was still obedient to the eternal child's play of that charming world.

On all this the evening before me afforded a remarkable commentary. I paused a moment in front of the house and looked up at the windows. There he lives, I thought, and carries on his labors year by year, reads and annotates texts, seeks for analogies between western Asiatic and Indian mythologies, and it satisfies him, because he believes in the value of it all. He believes in the studies whose servant he is; he believes in the value of mere knowledge and its acquisition, because he believes in progress and evolution. He has not been through the war, nor is he acquainted with the shattering of the foundations of thought by Einstein (that, thinks he, only concerns the mathematicians). He sees nothing of the preparations for the next war that are going on all round him. He hates Jews and Communists. He is a good, unthinking, happy child, who takes himself seriously; and, in fact, he is much to be envied. And so, pulling myself together, I entered the house. A maid in cap and apron opened the door. Warned by some premonition, I noticed with care where she laid my hat and coat, and was then shown into a warm and well-lighted room and requested to wait. Instead of saying a prayer or taking a nap, I followed a wayward impulse and picked up the first thing I saw. It chanced to be a small picture in a frame that stood on the round table leaning back on its paste-board support. It was an engraving and it represented the poet Goethe as an old man full of character, with a finely chiseled face and a genius' mane. Neither the renowned fire of his eyes nor the lonely and tragic expression beneath the courtly whitewash was lacking. To this the artist had given special care, and he had succeeded in combining the elemental force of the old man with a somewhat professional make-up of self-discipline and righteousness, without prejudice to his profundity; and had made of him, all in all, a really charming old gentleman, fit to adorn any drawing room. No doubt this portrait was no worse than others of its description. It was much the same as all those representations by careful craftsmen of saviors, apostles, heroes, thinkers and statesmen. Perhaps I found it exasperating only because of a certain pretentious virtuosity. In any case, and whatever the cause, this empty and self-satisfied presentation of the aged Goethe shrieked at me at once as a fatal discord, exasperated and oppressed as I was already. It told me that I ought never to have come. Here fine Old Masters and the Nation's Great Ones were at home, not Steppenwolves.

If only the master of the house had come in now, I might have had the luck to find some favorable opportunity for finding my way out. As it was, his wife came in, and I surrendered to fate though I scented danger. We shook hands and to the first discord there succeeded nothing but new ones. The lady complimented me on my looks, though I knew only too well how sadly the years had aged me since our last meeting. The clasp of her hand on my gouty fingers had reminded me of it already. Then she went on to ask after my dear wife, and I had to say that my wife had left me and that we were divorced. We were glad enough when the professor came in. He too gave me a hearty welcome and the awkward comedy came to a beautiful climax. He was holding a newspaper to which he subscribed, an organ of the militarist and jingoist party, and after shaking hands he pointed to it and commented on a paragraph about a namesake of mine—a publicist called Haller, a bad fellow and a rotten patriot—who had been making fun of the Kaiser and expressing the view that his own country was no less responsible for the outbreak of war than the enemy nations. There was a man for you! The editor had given him his deserts and put him in the pillory. However, when the professor saw that I was not interested, we passed to other topics, and the possibility that this horrid fellow might be sitting in front of them did not even remotely occur to either of them. Yet so it was, I myself was that horrid fellow. Well, why make a fuss and upset people? I laughed to myself, but gave up all hope now of a pleasant evening.

I have a clear recollection of the moment when the professor spoke of Haller as a traitor to his country. It was then that the horrid feeling of depression and despair which had been mounting in me and growing stronger and stronger ever since the burial scene condensed to a dreary dejection. It rose to the pitch of a bodily anguish, arousing within me a dread and suffocating foreboding. I had the feeling that something lay in wait for me, that a danger stalked me from behind. Fortunately the announcement that dinner was on the table supervened. We went into the dining room, and while I racked my brains again and again for something harmless to say, I ate more than I was accustomed to do and felt myself growing more wretched with every moment. Good heavens, I thought all the while, why do we put ourselves to such exertions? I felt distinctly that my hosts were not at their ease either and that their liveliness was forced, whether it was that I had a paralyzing effect on them or because of some other and domestic embarrassment. There was not a question they put to me that I could answer frankly, and I was soon fairly entangled in my lies and wrestling with my nausea at every word. At last, for the sake of changing the subject, I began to tell them of the funeral which I had witnessed earlier in the day. But I could not hit the right note. My efforts at humor fell entirely flat and we were more than ever at odds. Within me the Steppenwolf bared his teeth in a grin. By the time we had reached dessert, silence had descended on all three of us.

We went back to the room we had come from to invoke the aid of coffee and cognac. There, however, my eye fell once more on the magnate of poetry, although he had been put on a chest of drawers at one side of the room. Unable to get away from him, I took him once more in my hands, though warning voices were plainly audible, and proceeded to attack him. I was as though obsessed by the feeling that the situation was intolerable and that the time had come either to warm my hosts up, to carry them off their feet and put them in tune with myself, or else to bring about a final explosion.

"Let us hope," said I, "that Goethe did not really look like this. This conceited air of nobility, the great man ogling the distinguished company, and beneath the manly exterior what a world of charming sentimentality! Certainly, there is much to be said against him. I have a good deal against his venerable pomposity myself. But to represent him like this—no, that is going too far."

The lady of the house finished pouring out the coffee with a deeply wounded expression and then hurriedly left the room; and her husband explained to me with mingled embarrassment and reproach that the picture of Goethe belonged to his wife and was one of her dearest possessions. "And even if, objectively speaking, you are right, though I don't agree with you, you need not have been so outspoken."

"There you are right," I admitted. "Unfortunately it is a habit, a vice of mine, always to speak my mind as much as possible, as indeed Goethe did, too, in his better moments. In this chaste drawing-room Goethe would certainly never have allowed himself to use an outrageous, a genuine and unqualified expression. I sincerely beg your wife's pardon and your own. Tell her, please, that I am a schizomaniac. And now, if you will allow me, I will take my leave."

To this he made objections in spite of his perplexity. He even went back to the subject of our former discussions and said once more how interesting and stimulating they had been and how deep an impression my theories about Mithras and Krishna had made on him at the time. He had hoped that the present occasion would have been an opportunity to renew these discussions. I thanked him for speaking as he did. Unfortunately, my interest in Krishna had vanished and also my pleasure in learned discussions. Further, I had told him several lies that day. For example, I had been many months in the town, and not a few days, as I had said. I lived, however, quite by myself, and was no longer fit for decent society; for in the first place, I was nearly always in a bad temper and afflicted with the gout, and in the second place, usually drunk. Lastly, to make a clean slate, and not to go away, at least, as a liar, it was my duty to inform him that he had grievously insulted me that evening. He had endorsed the attitude taken up by a reactionary paper towards Haller's opinions; a stupid bull-necked paper, fit for an officer on half-pay, not for a man of learning. This bad fellow and rotten patriot, Haller, however, and myself were one and the same person, and it would be better for our country and the world in general, if at least the few people who were capable of thought stood for reason and the love of peace instead of heading wildly with a blind obsession for a new war. And so I would bid him good-bye.

With that I got up and took leave of Goethe and of the professor. I seized my hat and coat from the rack outside and left the house. The wolf in me howled in gleeful triumph, and a dramatic struggle between my two selves followed. For it was at once clear to me that this disagreeable evening had much more significance for me than for the indignant professor. For him, it was a disillusionment and a petty outrage. For me, it was a final failure and flight. It was my leave-taking from the respectable, moral and learned world, and a complete triumph for the Steppenwolf. I was sent flying and beaten from the field, bankrupt in my own eyes, dismissed without a shred of credit or a ray of humor to comfort me. I had taken leave of the world in which I had once found a home, the world of convention and culture, in the manner of the man with a weak stomach who has given up pork. In a rage I went on my way beneath the street lamps, in a rage and sick unto death. What a hideous day of shame and wretchedness it had been from morning to night, from the cemetery to the scene with the professor. For what? And why? Was there any sense in taking up the burden of more such days as this or of sitting out any more such suppers? There was not. This very night I would make an end of the comedy, go home and cut my throat. No more tarrying.

I paced the streets in all directions, driven on by wretchedness. Naturally it was stupid of me to bespatter the drawing-room ornaments of the worthy folk, stupid and ill-mannered, but I could not help it; and even now I could not help it. I could not bear this tame, lying, well-mannered life any longer. And since it appeared that I could not bear my loneliness any longer either, since my own company had become so unspeakably hateful and nauseous, since I struggled for breath in a vacuum and suffocated in hell, what way out was left me? There was none. I thought of my father and mother, of the sacred flame of my youth long extinct, of the thousand joys and labors and aims of my life. Nothing of them all was left me, not even repentance, nothing but agony and nausea. Never had the clinging to mere life seemed so grievous as now. . . .